Anonymous

Temporal Prosperity and Spiritual Decline

Or, Free Thoughts on Some Aspects of Modern Methodism

Anonymous

Temporal Prosperity and Spiritual Decline
Or, Free Thoughts on Some Aspects of Modern Methodism

ISBN/EAN: 9783337091156

Printed in Europe, USA, Canada, Australia, Japan

Cover: Foto ©Thomas Meinert / pixelio.de

More available books at **www.hansebooks.com**

CONTENTS.

INTRODUCTION.

CHAPTER VII.

TIME TO MOURN—CORRUPTIONS—THE SENSUOUS.

CHAPTER VIII.

THE PIOUS POOR.

CHAPTER IX.

LACK OF LEADERS.

CHAPTER X.

SUSTENTATION FUND.

CHAPTER XI.

CHAPTER XII.

CHAPTER XIII.

LAY AGENCY.

CHAPTER XIV.

OUR MINISTRY.

CHAPTER XV.

" RESUSCITATION OF DISCIPLINE."

TEMPORAL PROSPERITY

SPIRITUAL DECLINE.

INTRODUCTION.

THE creature is subject to change. Whatever is merely of man, is mutable and mortal. Human *systems* perish. Some of these may have long lives, and last too long a time; but the seeds of decline are sown within them. Although they may live to be as old as Methuselah, they are but mortal still. They may linger,—they may cling with great tenacity to life,—but they must decay and die. The dying day of old Mohammedanism, and of the ancient "mystery of iniquity, the mother of harlots,"—that long-lived and many-headed monster,—like the dying day of Methuselah, may slowly, but must surely, come. "And HE died,"—less slowly, yet not less surely, than the martyrs died.

Human *laws*, although, when first enacted, they

B

assume the changeless character of the laws of the Medes and Persians, are soon modified or reversed, or become obsolete.

The most glorious human *institutions* of which men vainly boast have often a glory as transient as that of the grass, or the still frailer flower of the grass, which fadeth and falleth away.

The mightiest *monarchies*, and the envied *empires* of antiquity,—as that of ancient Rome,—have had, besides their dim dawn, and their dazzling meridian, their " decline and fall." And not a few of them have died because they became unfit to live.

Churches cannot claim exemption from constantly revolving changes. The Churches of Asia arose, flourished, and faded away. All the *true* Churches of Christ must have in them essential elements of undecaying life. Whatever may be the mould those Churches take, or the material fabrics in which they live, yet in the houses of their earthly sojourn, in the temples terrestrial, there is lodged a celestial life,—

" A life that pain and death defies."

The fabrics fade and fall ; they are of the earth, and tend thitherward ; but there are unearthly elements strangely allied with them, which are " eternal, immortal," as " the King invisible."

There must be vital and vitalizing principles in every true Church, which, like the Inspirer and

Implanter of them, can never die. There is a stream that beautifies, refreshes, and gladdens the garden of God, which to the end of time can never stagnate. In its sparkling vitality and spirituality, it springs up to everlasting life. It is the " water of life."

The stony structures in which Churches congregate, though lovely, are not lively. They may be beautiful, but at best they are but dead stones, inert, lifeless material. The Churches contained in them are " *lively* stones," they are *God's* building. Those lifeless though lovely temples must, ere the end of time, crumble into decay; or else, when time shall end, must, as " the gorgeous palaces," pass away and perish.

But long before the end of time, this union between the living, the spiritual, the immaterial, the immortal principle, and the lifeless and material fabric, may be dissolved. The " vital spark of heavenly flame " may quit the material tenement. There may be so much clogging earth, so much cumbrous clay, so much cleaving to the dust, that the celestial dove may flutter, and then flee away, and find its rest amid more congenial, because more sacred and celestial, elements. The lifeless body, the body bereft of the immaterial and deathless spirit, gravitates more closely to the material and earthy, and sees corruption. " Earth to earth, dust to dust." The sanctuaries of the living, spiritual God may become utterly bereft of spiritual life; they may be God-forsaken. Temples may be as the tomb which the Lord had left. "Ichabod" may be written upon them; the glory may depart. All their architectural splendours, their sensuous externalism, their imposing forms, and gorgeous ceremonials, may be but as the beauteous flowers that decorate the chilled corpse, and mock the ghastly countenance of the lifeless clay; they may be but the dismal drapery of death; a sort of spiritual lying in state,—only far worse than the material mockery of the mortal remains.

The more, therefore, any Church has of the spiritual, the more it has of that which abideth; the more it has of the imperishable and incorruptible. With the spiritual is the kingdom which, while all else is as the shifting sand, cannot be moved. There is that which, among all the fluctuations and revolutions of time, remains as the Rock of Ages, and must remain "when rolling years shall cease to move."

Changes often take place slowly, stealthily, gradually, and, like the moving hand of time, almost imperceptibly. The petrifying process must in many cases be very slow. The writer has held in his hand what was said to be, and seemed to be, a petrified sponge; also petrified moss from the well of King Alfred. How long a time was required for this strange process, how long it was before such soft substances could become so stone-like, we cannot tell.

But we thought that, in like manner, on the brink of the living wells of salvation it is possible that the petrifying process may be going on. The earth, which has drunk in the same rains, may bring forth not only useful herbs, but briers and thorns, whose end is to be burned. So the same Gospel may prove the savour of life unto life, and of death unto death. Whilst living streams flow fresh from the well, there may be the surroundings of spiritual death. Stone, —stone,—hard, dead stone, is a fit symbol of those who are dead in sin !

Lot's wife lingered and looked back, and became instantly a pillar of salt. God can in a moment, by His gracious power, by a look, the "stone to flesh convert." Converted souls, Christian Churches, sometimes look back to the beggarly elements of the world, and are converted back again to stone. Any tendency towards this petrifying process should be vigilantly guarded against. None should cherish a morbid eagerness to predict such changes in Churches; none should be too ready dogmatically to deny them. It would be better to be too cautious in this matter than to be careless. Better be too sensitive than not sensitive enough. If not sensitive enough, a Church may safely conclude that it has something of the petrifying process going on within it.

The most flourishing Churches have faded and fallen away. The lessons to the living, from the tombs of the dead, and from the blanched bones of those who perished in the wilderness, is, " Be not high-minded, but fear."

Prudent caution may sometimes be peevishly termed " croaking." Yet most will admit that it is better to have at times needless alarm, than to have no alarm when it is needed. Fear is closely allied with the instinct of self-preservation, which is so deeply implanted in our nature. And a jealous godly fear may be as a " guardian angel " of the soul. It is better for the steam-whistle of the engine to send forth its shrill and ominous scream long before it rushes into the dismal tunnel, than to run the risk of one disastrous collision ; a collision which will cause that tunnel to echo with the shrieks of the wounded, the groans of the dying, and strew it with the man-gled flesh and broken bones of the hapless victims of criminal carelessness and fatal neglect. Better for the sentinel to sound the clarion note, and startle the encamped army from their midnight slumbers, when there is no real danger at hand, than to wait, in order to be quite sure, till the enemy is at the gates, and an irreparable breach is made. Better for the trum-pet blast of the watchman to be blown when he sees the sword *coming,* than to wait till the sword *is come* before the warning be given. The warning cannot harm, the warning cannot slay ; the sword may. Better for Churches to watch long and wait for their

Lord's coming, than for the Bridegroom's voice to summon the servants when they are all sleeping, with no lamp trimmed, no oil obtained, no loins girt. Better for Christians and Churches to think soberly than to think too highly of themselves. Better to condemn ourselves than to be condemned by a righteous Judge.

Searching self-scrutiny has, from the first, been a striking feature of Methodism, and one of its most salutary elements. It has been far more prone, in the past, to probe into than to paint over any of those errors and evils which have arisen in the body. It has not been wont to daub over its own defects and deformities with untempered mortar. It may be said that year after year they have been "examined one by one." "Examine yourselves," is one of its great and godly mottoes. It has, therefore, needed no awkward and alien hand to intermeddle in the times of its troubles, rudely to touch its rankling sores, or to pull the "mote out of its eye;" none of that sort of aid which has sometimes been so gratuitously "lent for the occasion." Let the officious and the intermeddling first cast the beam out of their own eye. These have sought to kill rather than to cure. But "faithful are the wounds of a friend."

"There is a fit season to look closely, and chiefly, into evils and their causes, not forgetting the good." And this seems to be such a season. It was very far

from the purpose of the writer, when he first took up
his pen, to write a book. A few lines only, addressed
to one of the papers of the day, was all that he
intended. But whilst passing in review the various
reasons which have been assigned for the apparent
decline of Methodism, many thoughts crowded upon
and oppressed the mind of the writer; involving a
weight of responsibility from which he has found
some relief in penning the following pages,—a task
to which he has been "led or driven" by an almost
irresistible impulse. He hardly need say that this
book has been written in much haste,—a fact which
will appear obvious to the critical eye. It has been
written in the midst of many cares, toils, and conflicts; and nothing but a deep sense of the importance
of the subjects treated upon would have led him to
persevere in his task, and to publish this book.
Several ministers and friends, in whose judgment he
could confide, thought that such a book was much
needed, and must do good. At their suggestion some
parts have been omitted, and others modified. Some
have thought it would be better to print the author's
name : but mere *names* are of little moment, and of less
still if they are looked at in the light of eternity :
things, and especially those touching the kingdom of
God, are of vast and eternal concern. Let the latter,
rather than the former,—the things written, rather
than the writer, — be pondered by the courteous

reader. " Measures, not men," should be a guiding motto. Should the book find favour and do good, its authorship will be of little consequence. Should any frowns gather over it, these can only be as a fleeting cloud to shadow for a moment the fair fame of any author. Should they be so surcharged as to break, the same head which occasioned will doubtless attract them.

If, with the increase of external splendour, the spiritual vitality of Methodism is, as some think, in danger of a decline, then, as one of her many lovers, the writer would wish, before she reaches the second and third stages, that the causes of such decline, however flattering and insidious, should be checked, and the " plague stayed." He would not like to see her with wasted strength, with a feeble pulse, fading away from the earth; but, on the contrary, renewing her youth as the eagle. Nay, all who love her would rather that all prudent means, even if involving some pain, should be promptly used, to check any consumptive tendency,—to check it when possibly it only can be checked,—in its earliest stages, and whilst some seriously doubt, and others somewhat boldly deny, that there are any symptoms at all of decline in the body.

If, in the midst of increasing external splendour in the places where the God of her Founder is wor-shipped, there be less of spiritual soundness, less of moral might, less of robust religious vigour; if there be a spiritual languishing and wasting away; then let the serious and searching inquiry resound; let it echo and re-echo through all her splendid sanctuaries,—" Why, then, is not the health of the daughter of My people recovered?"

Let us well mind the Master's monition: " What I say unto you I say unto all, Watch."

Let us watch and pray, that, amid the enchantments of wealth, and the world's seducing smiles, we enter not into temptation. And let us remember, too, that these are not the less fraught with danger because unsuspected. Then the Bicentenary of Methodism may show that she has not even then reached the meridian of her might. Meanwhile we hope to remain quiet for a short season, cherishing the " graver thoughts of a country parson," commending in prayer the results of those thoughts to the God of all wisdom and grace, looking at the signs of the times, and listening to what has, in solemn tones, been long and loudly sounding in our ears, " Watchman, what of the night?"

CHAPTER I.

WHO can look at the vast and wondrous machinery of Methodism, and its mighty spiritual achievements in the past, and not exclaim with grateful heart, " What hath God wrought ! " Dr. Candlish speaks of Methodism as " the grandest development of Christianity since the Apostles' days." And Dr. Chalmers said, " Methodism is Christianity in earnest." Methodism was doubtless in earnest when, at the early dawn of " the great revival," she arose to bless the wide world, as the populous but neglected parish which her great-souled founder claimed as his own. Methodism was in earnest when " the sect " was " everywhere spoken against." Methodism was in earnest when her classic collegians and princely plebeians, her first publishers, were pelted with pitiless fury from place to place. Methodism was in earnest when, driven from churches, cathedrals, and consecrated ground, she set up her glorious banners where Satan had his seat, and had long swayed an undisputed sceptre, but where now the Spirit's sword spread dismay among those to whom few would dare to deny the title of " the devil's own." Methodism was in earnest when, on Kennington Common and in Moorfields, in the eager ear of thousands she spake "the words of this life," and began her mighty mission. Methodism was in earnest when her first memorial-stones were not laid with silver trowels, in stately ceremony, but were hurled with strong hand and sinewy arm at the noble men who proclaimed words of peace, who feared no frowns, courted no smiles, and counted " not their lives dear unto themselves." Methodism was in earnest when from rough horse-blocks and noisy market-stands; behind crazy chairs, and on the top of tottering tubs; in rude barns; in lanes and in fields, in the highways and hedges; with the wide canopy of heaven as the roof of her grand cathedral, with the harsh blasts of rams' horns as well as with the sweet notes of silver trumpets, her glorious and imperishable doctrines were proclaimed with resistless power, and " with signs following."

And who will eagerly jump to the conclusion that Methodism is not in earnest now? Who shall venture dogmatically to assert that in these times of Gothic structures, and in this age of " golden days," Methodism has lost its " first love," its primitive power, its intense and wonted earnestness? Who is so simply spiritual as to sigh for former days,—the days of barns, of rounds, of saddlebags? Who will presume to maintain that in the "mountain" of material barbarism only, men can worship God in spirit and in truth? What is there necessarily fragrant and acceptable in worship arising from buildings whose lack of decency and order disgusts ordinary mortals? What can there be in such structures so peculiarly pleasing to the God of Sabaoth, and the world's great Architect; whose glory the heavens declare; whose handiwork the firmament showeth forth; whose wisdom shines in every star, and who gave so grand a pattern of the ancient tabernacle and temple? What was there in some of these superannuated structures so attractive as to lead us to seek a similar style? They, indeed, served their generation well. Properly, we think, were these called "*places* of worship." They were the shelter and sanctuary of many now sainted ones, who serve God day and night in His glorious temple above, whose lives adorned the doctrine of God their Saviour, whose death was precious in His sight; counted as the "offscouring of all things," "of whom the world was not worthy."

> "In a milder clime they dwell,
> Region of eternal day."

Yet what, after all, was there in these places so peculiarly pleasing, either to the senses or to the soul, either to God or man? These "places," with their crazy walls, and creaking timbers; their cobweb curtains, and candle drippings; their comically carved columns, cornice, copings, corbels, and crocketted gables; their open roofs above, and "well-dripped water tablings" below; their fretted floors; their filthy forms, with no "*gentle* inclination to the back;" their odd flights of steps, and stained glass windows;—to say nothing of the wondrous ways leading to these places of worship; the awkward avenues and alleys, the straitened paths, the suspicious streets, the crooked corners "leading straight" to the chapel, the pestiferous puddles, and miasmatic mud-pools, calling so loudly for Macadam and for sanitary reform, the heaps of building, behind which the conventicle was so carefully concealed from public gaze as to bewilder a stranger, rather than lead him up to the house of the Lord :—what, we ask, could there be in all these things,—so offensive to the senses, the inlets and portals of the soul,—to fan the flame of devotion?

But what a marvellous change is now passing upon Methodism,—at least in these mundane and material matters! Surely we have now entered, in many respects, upon a new and grand era. Many "old things," with "the old men" of Methodism, are now swiftly passing away. It was the sentiment of an old French philosopher, that he would not like to see an old post removed on which he had been accustomed long to look in bygone years ; and though we may not belong to the Antiquarian Society, and do not care much for old coin and old costumes, yet we like to look on old faces, and to meet old friends. Lord Bacon somewhere says, " Old wood is the best to burn ; old wine is the best to drink ; and old friends the best to trust." One long before Lord Bacon said, " The old wine is better."

We do not much prize sentimental devotions, paid either to old wood or stone, however curiously carved, or "graven by art and man's device." Old Method- ism we do much love, and highly esteem for her work's sake. And old Methodism was so established in her essential elements, her scriptural doctrines, and her salutary discipline, by what was more than man's wisdom in her far-seeing founder, that in these respects it would seem she hardly can change, while her chapel trusts continue: and this, we hope, will be till the full course of time is past. Yet her coun- tenance, her contour, and her general garb may so change ; and, casting aside her old chrysalis covering, she may appear clad in so altered and gay a costume that her old companions and friends may hardly know her again. And well may they be perplexed to recognise her, should she, or her people, ever become more akin to the bespangled butterfly, fluttering about in sunbeams, than to the busy bee, diligently working in the hive. Then she will need a little

more discipline; and it may be said to her, as is
often said to young recruits, " As you were."

Let her, as soon as she can, cast away "childish
things." But let her not lose the hard lessons which
she learnt when she was a child, lest she herself
should "become a castaway;" lest, at least, God
take her from the summit and sunshine of her prosperity into the wilderness, and give her the troublous
valley, the Valley of Achor, for a door of hope.
Let her not forget the hole of the pit whence she was
digged, nor the desert waste in which she was found.
No, nor forget how, "as an eagle stirreth up her
nest, fluttereth over her young, taketh them, beareth
them on her wings; so the Lord alone did lead her."

The Methodists as a body are no longer proverbially poor, but are gaining the repute of being rich.
Even Members of Parliament, who have read of their
princely givings, have said that the Methodists could
devise a plan to pay off the National Debt. What a host
of the noble lay members of Methodism have proved
that "godliness is profitable to all things," and that "to
live well is to have two lives!" So fully have they
proved it to have "the promise of the life that now
is," that they could as well now pay their pound as
they could once pay their penny per week. And
some, to their honour be it spoken, do pay more than
their pound per week, to sustain the benevolent institutions, the Ministry, and the Missions of Methodism.

How many among the Methodist people have risen to be merchant princes; risen from poverty to great prosperity, from penury to plenty of this world's good things! What a series of "Successful Merchants" might be written, if time and will would but permit! And surely, if things still go on and prosper, of making such books there would be "no end."

We think of one of these of whom we have heard, who at the commencement of his successful course had promised a pound towards a new chapel in his Circuit. The chapel collector came. But, alas! he came when the person who had promised the pound had but little in the world besides a pound which he had just received. He had lately taken to himself "a good thing" in the form of a "help-meet." Yet this did not lessen the difficulty, or his need of help. What was to be done? They wanted a little money to go on with during the next week. The pound, however, had been promised; and the person who came for it was not sent empty away, and awkwardly told to call again sometime in the course of a few weeks. No: the promised pound was punctually and promptly paid, and Providence was trusted to make provision for the future. And not in vain. The pound then paid was the only pound that person then had; but he has never lacked a pound since; nor has he lacked the grace to give, nor any good thing. That good and great man asked for wisdom, and with wisdom he has also had wealth and honour. These have been liberally superadded; and having freely received, he has also freely given. Few in the wide range of Methodism, for their consecrated wealth and sanctified talent, are likely to have a richer fragrance, a more blessed memory, and a more lasting memorial. Having faithfully performed the precepts of Sacred Wisdom, he has fully proved the truth of her promise: "Exalt her, and she shall promote thee."

We think of another, who, freely speaking to a Minister, said, "I knew a poor lad who lived at a time when bread was scarce and very dear in this land. That lad would go out in a morning, before he went to his work, in search of something to satisfy his hunger, and would eagerly seize even the parings of potatoes as food." He then, with rare candour and simplicity, added, "That poor lad is now speaking to thee." We may add, that lad is now on the bright side of seventy: he is about six feet in stature, of erect form, of dignified mien, of simple manners, and of gentlemanly bearing. He has an ample fortune, and withal enjoys "pure religion and undefiled." Still he retains the old Methodist stamp. Of about fifty years' standing, he is one of the honoured laity of Methodism, and among Heaven's true nobility. When, a short time ago, he heard of the loss in a moment of more than one thousand pounds, he not only did so without a murmur, but at once said, as did the stricken Job, "Shall we receive good at the hand of the Lord, and shall we not receive evil?"

We remember another, about the same age and stature, and of a strikingly similar style and type. Speaking to the same minister, he said, "Fifty years ago I used to walk with my tools on my back to such a town, then a poor man; and now, thank God, I am able to give, as I have done this last year, some hundreds of pounds to God's cause."

But what are these among so many similar specimens of those who, once poor, are now rich?—rich in this world, and rich too in faith and in good works; and who, whilst heirs of possessions that are perishing and passing away, are heirs, also, of an inheritance incorruptible and eternal. Yes, and we think of others, too,—and these are not few,—who, with ever-expanding substance, have had ever-contracting souls. As they have spread out their borders, in a corresponding ratio have they straitened their "systematic beneficence." With large capability for getting, they have cherished a lesser capacity for giving: more treasures laid up on earth, and less laid up in heaven: mansions rising, made with mortal hands, glittering "beneath the sun," for a moment's sojourn "on the earth," land well secured, title-deeds safely kept; whilst "the pilgrim's roll" is lost, faith falters, hope darkens, charity contracts, love lan-

guishes, zeal waxes cold, and there are missing titles
to those mansions above, whose Maker is God. The
sun of secular prosperity shines brightly; and the
sacred fires on the altar burn dimly, and then, like
"the lamps," they go out.. Gold comes in at one
door, and Grace is driven out at another. Wealth
wends its crooked way into the temple, and whips
Wisdom straightway out. The consecrated temple
of God changes hands, is consigned over to the idol
of covetousness, and becomes a place of carnal traffic.
Where there was the merchandise of wisdom, there
are now the money-changers and a market-place for
Mammon. The dedicated temple is now desecrated.
There is now the love of the world; and the love of
the Father is not in them. The dwelling of the
Triune God becomes a den of thieves, the resort of
the darkest demons, the shrine of Satan, the abode
of "seven other devils:" and "the last state of that
man is worse than the first."

Alas! how often have we thus seen temporal prosperity and spiritual decline; and with advanced
revenues, religious retrogression!—"minding the main
chance," as it is said, and missing the "mark for the
prize of the high calling;" gaining the world, and
losing the soul; pursuing pelf, and robbing God, and
pilfering the soul of the pearl of great price; perched
for "a point of time" on the pinnacle of prosperity,
and then drawn back and drawn down to "per-

berforce standing on a table and addressing his con-
stituents, the man so small in stature "seemed
but as a shrimp; but before he had finished, he grew
to a whale." But many, whatever there may be
whale-like in their material nature and physical proportions, in their worldly wealth, and possibly in
their own esteem, yet, under the contracting and
withering influence of covetousness, after which their
souls are gone, have become so stunted and shrivelled,
that the slender shrimp rather than the colossal whale
is the fit symbol of that soul which should make the
man. So compressed and contracted are they, that,
as a friend of Robert Hall, when speaking of one of
these miserly molecules, said, " His soul is so narrow
that it could live in a nutshell." " Yes," replied
Mr. Hall, with biting satire, "And then he would
creep out at the maggot-hole."

We think of a long and a sad series of such souls;
souls of whom it is indeed melancholy to think.
They have long sat under the sound of the Gospel:
what has been its savour to them? No fruits were
brought forth : no sure signs appeared, to prove that
it was to them " the savour of life unto life." Alas!
the good seed was choked by covetousness and the
cares of this life. How many, like Demas, have forsaken Christ because they loved this present world!
How many are there, whose parsimony in the cause
of God, and for the Church of Christ, has increased

in proportion to their worldly prosperity! The more freely they have received, the more grudgingly have they given.

We remember a very respectable farmer, living at the large —— Hall, under Lord ——. He presided at a public meeting, the object of which was to aid Christian Missions, and to send forth the message of mercy to the perishing heathen for whom Christ died. What did the respectable chairman give? Scarcely so much as it would cost to bait his horse. *One Shilling!* Small as this may seem, it seems smaller by contrast with the giving of a good and simple shepherd, his own humble servant, who sat at the feet of his master the chairman, and at the foot of the platform. This poor man smilingly put " double the money " (two shillings) on the plate.

Mr. A——, in the county of B——, at the beginning of his business, toiled hard and struggled much with straitened circumstances. Things went on well; business extended; money came in; and wealth began to loom in the distance. He rose from the pressure of poverty to the plenitude of prosperity. And there were soon some outward signs of steadily advancing wealth. Step by step and stage by stage, in safe progression, business branched out, and his borders were extended on every hand. Worldly success, like a sun, gradually rose higher and shone brighter upon him. Premises were pulled down, and others and greater soon put up to provide better accommodation for an extending business and an increasing family. At length he was said to be a wealthy man and worth many thousands of pounds. With all he was a very prudent and particular man ; and he liked to have everything very exact, and to make every penny go as far as it possibly could, especially in the Church of which he was a member. Still he could not keep his children, as one after another they grew up, from appearing in gay attire, and from doing very differently from what he had done when he began life. He thought children must not be curbed or restrained in religious matters too much. "Parents could not give their children grace." Nor did he scruple, in the midst of a wicked agitation, to allow ministers to be maligned at his table and in the presence of his children, and to be represented as anything but honest men and faithful Ministers of Christ. Under the preaching of these maligned Ministers, is it strange that these children were not converted to God? Is it strange that the sharp arrows of truth were blunted, when they came to the consciences of these children? Is it strange that the preachers' pulpit power in the poisoned minds of this " rising family " was paralysed? Is it strange that those doctrines which should have distilled as the dew were only as oil on polished marble? Is it strange that the daughters should have been

vain and volatile? or that the eldest son should have
been a source of shame and sorrow to that father,
a spendthrift, a ruinous and ruined prodigal? When
that father was a poor and plodding man of business,
he was punctual in his pew, and in his payment of
one penny per week "for the support of the
preachers." What more did this prosperous man do
for God's cause in his prosperity than in his penury?
His penurious spirit kept him close to the *letter*
of Wesley's rule,—one "penny per week!" When
he had his thousands, he as precisely paid his penny
as when he had not a hundred pence to spare. He
was as strict and as stereotyped in his subscription of
one penny per week "for the support of the
preachers," as though it had been "entered at Sta-
tioners' Hall;" and evinced as much care in keeping
this rule of the Methodists, as though it had been a
law of the Medes, which was not to be altered or
improved with the times. But what made the matter
more striking still was that one at least of his men
met in the same class with the master; and though
he had but small earnings, the servant would have
liked, but did not dare or presume, to give more than
his master. So the prosperous master and the poor
servant both gave their penny; master and man gave
each his mite; but the one mite came from a
"mickle,"—from much abundance; the other came
from very little. But that was not all. The poor

servant was a pious, plodding, earnest Local Preacher, and, besides his penny, gladly gave of time, of travel, and of toil, for the glory of that God to whom he felt that his more than all was due. But it did not appear to that man of wealth that either the poor man's penny was *too much* for him, or that the rich master's penny was *too little* for him. Yet, somehow or other, there was a secret, sly, stealthy influence about that secreted silver, that concealed cash, that eagerly-gotten and closely-grasped gold, that hoarded wealth, that would steal away, in spite of everybody, by night or by day, from even Chubb's safe, without Chubb's key. It was well known, without much being said or much being done, except " in the way of business," that Mr. A. was a man of money ; and if anything was to be done in any way connected with the chapel, the cause, the congregation, or the collections there, the first and chief inquiry would be, " What does Mr. A. think ? For, you know, it would be no use to try to do anything here without consulting him. Though it might be just the thing he would like to have done, yet he would be sure to oppose it ' to the teeth ' if he were not first asked about it." By some a willing, and by others a constrained, homage was paid to the resistless power of this temporal prince in our Israel. A prince ! although he only paid,—as the poor people paid,—*a penny !*

The pastors and the pious poor of their flock, in

that part of their wide fold, could not but painfully
feel that this rich man had far more than his lawful
pennyworth of privilege, of preeminence and power.
He had, alas! his greater power, not because he had
a greater soul, or more wisdom, or deeper spirituality,
but because he had greater wealth. He had influence
because he had affluence. He had power, not from
his piety, but from his pelf. Though he had little
grace, he had much gold. And though he had not
grace to give, yet the gold gave him, in the eyes of
others, " a little grace " and glory too.

You cannot see that subtle magnetic influence
which turns the trembling needle towards the pole :
you cannot tell why the needle turns, but it does
turn. Crystal and costly pearls may be near to the
point of the magnetic needle, but that needle turns
not towards the precious pearls, but towards the distant pole. This attractive power seems strange, but
is beyond doubt. And so there seems to be a strange,
secret, subtle, stealthy power about what we purposely
and properly call " pelf." For " pelf " means money
or " riches in an odious sense." Although, then, this
pelf may be always in its own private apartments, in
the patent safe,—lodged in the bank,—safe in a mine
or in railway shares ; and though, for all the public
good it does, it might be as far off as " thrice from
the centre to the farthest pole ; " still, if it were at
the farthest pole, it would not only attract the pos-

sessor, but would have a little luring power for a money-loving and money-worshipping people, though they could not " tell the reason why."

Judicious Methodist pastors of long standing know full well the pernicious power of pelf, when painful discipline has to be exercised. Pelf had, perhaps, placed the guilty party in some false position in the Church of Christ, and given him a power which nothing else he had could give him. The Achan in the camp is brought before the Church court. But what if Mr. A—— will not himself "give glory to God in the confession of sin?" which, alas! is too rarely the case. What can be done in some of our Church courts? Could not some of the judges in such courts solemnly declare that they have seen sure signs of the secret, subtle influence of the invisible gold, rather than of the sacred influence of a good conscience and of the invisible God? And there has been something very near akin to perjury, bribery, and corruption. Money had obtained a kind of magician's might, or a sort of mesmeric power, in that Church court, or "Leaders' Meeting," if that name be preferred. How often are souls thus held in servile subjection by the subtle power of money!

Often, when duty has to be done by the professed soldiers of Christ, and loss and danger have threatened them, criminal cowardice has taken the place of Christian courage. They have not quitted themselves like men. Their covetous and craven spirits have crouched low at the shrine of Mammon. And at that shrine the true riches, the wealth of grace, the merchandise of wisdom, the immortal interests of the soul, have all been strangely sacrificed and madly bartered away.

Such "fearful" spirits could never seal the truth with blood, or win a martyr's crown. Their way to the kingdom, to crowns of glory, to songs of triumph, to the glorious throne of the Great Captain who overcame the world, would not be by way of the Cross, or through much tribulation, not through the dungeon and the lions' den, not through the heated furnace and the martyrs' fires. Ah, no! They seek the smooth rather than the right path. The lion in the way, or his grim shadow, would be quite enough to lead them from beneath the Almighty's shield; enough to lead them from the side and the sure shelter of the Good Shepherd; enough to lead them from the good and the right way, which, though it may not always *seem* to be, yet always *is*, the way of safety.

Pilate, fearing Herod, willing to content the people and to do the Jews a pleasure, condemned the Just One; and "the same day Pilate and Herod were made friends." The boasting Peter, when life was in danger, followed his Lord afar off: and the rest of the fear-stricken disciples did not *follow*, but they all *forsook* Him and fled. The Shepherd was smitten, and the sheep were scattered.

The way, not of the cross, but of *carnal policy,*—the way, not of self-denial, but of self-seeking, of worldly profit and pleasure,—is the way which many of the professed followers of the Crucified choose to pursue. They need not be shown *all* the kingdoms of this world and the glories of them: a very small fraction is sufficient to seduce them from their allegiance to Christ, away to the shrine of Satan. The loss they feared was but a shadow compared with the loss which, from a lack of fidelity, they soon felt,—the loss of the testimony of a good conscience, which Arminius affirmed to be "a constant paradise."

They have not in the evil day had manliness and moral courage to do that which was right, and to leave results with God. There has been a cowardly and guilty compromise with their consciences. Indeed, sometimes it seems to require a soul "such as in the martyrs glowed," to enable a man to be independent, thoroughly upright and outspoken, and to sing with the spirit,—

> "What then is he whose scorn I dread,
> Whose wrath or hate makes me afraid?
> A man! an heir of death! a slave
> To sin! a bubble on the wave!"

We can scarcely refrain from saying, "Woe, woe

to the man of money who, though not a priest, presses with more than priestly power upon the consciences of his poorer brethren, who, being members of the Church of Christ, arc all "members one of another." And who will say that there are not many cases of this class in the churches of Christendom? Is not their name " legion ? " For they " are many."

Poor miserly souls, and miserable sinners, enslaved to wealth, enslaved to the world and sin, and who would enslave others! Shall these lovers of the world, ever grasping and never giving, except in little mites, with great grudging and much grumbling, shall these world-wedded souls be saved? If so, must it not be as by fire? Shall these, with their corrupted rather than consecrated riches, enter into the kingdom of heaven? " How hardly ! "

But leaving these for a little time, we are led, when we look at the Reports of our various funds, to exclaim, How vast are the material resources of modern Methodism ! How vast, compared with that time when saddles and stones were pillows, or rude boards, instead of soft beds, gave balmy sleep, and blackberries supplied dinners to the giants of those days, those mighty men of moral muscle who were " cradled in the storm ! " How vast the material resources, compared with the period when one sage and prudent layman said, that, at the rate they were going on in

their scale of expenditure for the foreign work, it
would require nine or ten thousand pounds per annum
for Missions alone! and when the apostolic Benson
spake to the Conference, with weakly voice, but in
telling tones, to the effect that the Lord had during
the past year poured out upon our people a spirit of
unprecedented liberality, and they had raised for the
Missions alone the astonishing sum of seven thousand
pounds! adding, that it must be economically expended, as they could hardly expect to see the
like again. A sum, singular to say, which is now
more than equalled by the little children of our
Churches, in their "Christmas Offerings." What
vast funds are now raised! On what a mighty scale
do many now cast their money into the treasury!
Three or four of such noble givers as we now have
would have made up nearly the entire sum which so
astonished good Joseph Benson, and which kindled
his soul into such an ecstasy of gratitude.

What a marvellous moral machinery Methodism
now has in perpetual motion! What an astonishing
apparatus of means and appliances in daily action
almost all over the world! We have a mighty and
an envied Ministry, our enemies themselves being
judges. We have men of high attainments and lofty
scholarship; men of clear perception, of calm and
cautious judgment, and comprehensive knowledge, at
the helm of our Connexional Church; men of great

prudence and profound wisdom; men of fervent zeal
and matchless eloquence. We have sons of thunder
and sons of consolation. We have men that can pull
down, and men that can build up; wise master-
builders; men that wound as they mightily wield the
Spirit's sword, and men that heal with Gilead's balm,
and "comfort the people." We have rough blasts
from rams' horns, and charming notes from silver
trumpets. We have a host of faithful publishers of
the Gospel of peace in the provinces; many of them
men of retiring habits and of superior genius; some
of them sound scholars; hard students; able Ministers of the New Testament; plodding Pastors; truly
Travelling Preachers, who travel, alas! too far, and
preach faithfully and fervently at the end of a long
journey, though it be to a handful of hearers. Workmen that need not to be ashamed! though ye may
seem "born to blush unseen," and to waste your
strength on rough and dreary roads. Many of you
we have known, and have loved and esteemed you
highly for your works' sake. And whilst we write
we weep, as we think of your great fight of afflictions,
your hard work, your hard fare, and your hard warfare, in the midst of abounding wealth and luxurious
repose; your daily care of and conflicts in the
Churches, your nightly journeys and midnight watch-
ings through wearisome hours, when well nigh "worn
out," by the bedside of loved little ones, or the faith-

ful but failing help-meet, the sympathetic sharer of your sufferings and sorrows. Yes, and soon too, in a few short weeks, you were watched by others, as you sweetly "fell asleep," and passed away to your eternal rest. "Lovely and pleasant in their lives, in their death they were not divided;" gone, in close companionship,

> " From a suffering Church beneath
> To a reigning Church above."

Your work is done, and your "warfare is accomplished."

Yet we have doubted much whether all of these were " immortal till their work was done." We think the law, "Thou shalt not kill," may be broken. And the shrewd and venerable Jay said that " whilst some of the Churches despised, some ruled, some starved, the Methodists *killed* their Preachers." We have seen some of these so balanced between life and death, that it did not require much either to kill or make alive. When the question has been asked, " Do we recommend that any Minister become a Supernumerary ? " we have seen them standing like silently speaking statuary with starting tears, seeming half petrified and struck dumb at the thought, that they must sit down in comparative silence and seclusion as Supernumeraries; " sit down," when they were able to go and stand and speak in the temple to the people all the words of this life ! " Sit down," because, though they could do well the work of a man and a minister, they could not do the work also of a horse; especially when they were "allowed," for both, little more than enough for the keep of the latter! "Sit down," when they could accept the tempting offer,—"To a Supernumerary who could preach twice or thrice, give tickets, take the charge of a country Society,"—the tempting offer of "a house to live in!" "A house to live in,"—whilst they were expected to give pretty full proof of their ministry, almost as full as some ministerial brethren who are in their "full work!" "A house to live *in;*" but what to live *upon?* Upon the house-top by faith and by fasting, to feed on the wind, on the fresh and fine country air? "O, but they have a little besides." And so have many others; "much every way."

Many, however, if they can, with their "little besides," accept such offers, may thereby make their last days, not, as Dr. Clarke said, "*super*miserable," but *super*happy, by wearing rather than rusting away; and by trusting the "Faithful Promiser," who has said, by His servant, "Therefore, my beloved brethren, be ye steadfast, unmovable, *always* abounding in the work of the Lord, forasmuch as ye know that your labour is not in vain in the Lord." *

· "We have now a ministerial force numbering

* 1 Cor. xv. 58.

nearly 1420 &ffective labourers;" compassing sea
and land, not to make proselytes to a creed and a
Church, as some are so officiously seeking to do,
but striving to win souls to Christ. And of these
Ministers we may say,—

> "There stands the messenger of truth! there stands
> The legate of the skies! his theme Divine,
> His office sacred, his credentials clear.
> By him the violated Law speaks out
> Its thunders; and by him, in strains as sweet
> As angels use, the Gospel whispers peace."

"We have, also, a great and goodly company of
Local Preachers, who cannot be estimated at less
than 20,000; with 80,000 children in our Day
Schools, and more than half a million in our Sabbath
Schools, brought under the influence and instruction
of 100,000 Teachers. There is, too, the vast
multitude of our Leaders, and Tract Distributors,
and Visitors of the Sick; besides a membership of
more than 300,000 in Great Britain alone. But,
taking into account all the prayer, and faith, and
labour, that have been exercised, and all the learning,
and eloquence, and enterprise, and devotion, that
have been expended, during the year," (1864,) "we
feel that such an aggregate result to show as the net
increase of only 300 or 400, is a matter that calls for
anxious attention and searching inquiry."

We have a numerous, wise, and wealthy laity,
many of whom adorn the doctrine of God their

Saviour, and are princes in our Israel, and among the brightest ornaments of the Churches of Christendom. We have a Normal College which annually sends out its band of well-trained Teachers, and which is said to be without a rival in the wide world. We have at its head a Principal of whom we may justly be proud; one whose calm, clear, and cautious mind may be compared to a bright, clear lake, and whose Inaugural Addresses seem to flow up fresh every year as from a living well. And this Principal is aided by an able and vigilant Secretary. We have two well-manned Colleges, with their Governors and Chaplains, and a competent staff of Commercial and Classical Masters, to whose care and tuition the children of our wealthy friends may be safely confided. We have two first-class Schools for the godly education of the children of our Ministers and Missionaries, where, by means of sanctified learning, and the union of the "pair so long disjoined,—knowledge and piety," they may be prepared for prominent posts of usefulness, both in the Church and in the world; schools from which some of our most eminent Ministers have arisen; and in one of which the much lamented and noble-minded Attorney General, Sir William Atherton, received his education; a fact which, in honourable contrast with some others, he was never ashamed to own. We have two most important Institutions for

the mental and moral discipline of men, who profess
to be moved by the Holy Ghost for the work of the
Ministry; in which, as the soldiers of Christ, they may
be more fully equipped for their good and glorious
warfare ; more skilled to wield the Spirit's sword, to
pull down the strongholds of Satan, and to storm
the citadel of the foe in this and other lands.

We have a commemorative Centenary Hall, and
monumental Mission House, with its energetic and
eloquent staff of Secretaries, with their ready pens,
their "thoughts that breathe, and words that burn,"
as from "Tongues of Fire," which have thrille
through all our Churches. We have an extensive
Book Room, which has for many years been managed
with consummate tact, indefatigable industry, and
the most rigid economy, by that venerable man,
whose worth, whilst with us, was not well known,
nor wisely enough appreciated. " We do not know
the value of water till the well is dry." We have
this mental store-room, pouring forth its multitudinous
publications and periodicals throughout the year,
and throughout the land.

CHAPTER II.

WE have a wise and wary Chapel Committee, under whose cautious consideration have passed a vast variety and a prodigious number of Chapel cases during the last few years. Let any candid person take up a Chapel Report, and cast his eye over the Chapel cases of a single year; and we think he will marvel much at the wondrous workings of this part of the Methodist machinery.

Take the cases which came under the consideration of the "Committee of Review" at the Camborne Conference in the year 1862. These cases comprised ninety-two new Chapels, twenty-three School-rooms, forty-nine enlargements, twenty-three modifications of previous cases, seventeen organs : total, two hundred and four cases, involving an estimated outlay of £122,363, towards which the parties concerned engaged to raise at least £103,185, within twelve months of the opening.

These numerous and varied cases, let it be borne in mind, opened up at a time when the condition of commerce in this country was very depressed. Now, if there was such a vast outlay for chapels in our Connexion at a time when the land was clouded with commercial gloom, what may be expected when it shall be cheered with commercial sunshine? If contributions for one department of the cause of Christ rose so high when commerce was at zero, what may be expected when it shall once more attain something like summer-heat?

We will suppose one of the Clergy, of the High Church school,—who has been moving all his life long in too lofty and sublime a sphere to see such a speck as Methodism on the face of creation,—emerging from the monkish mists and clouds that have gathered around him, and getting into a clearer field of vision than he could possibly command amid the subdued light of mediæval churches, in the long-drawn aisle or the dim cloister. Suddenly there pass before him, as in panoramic view, thousands of these great buildings, lovely temples, elegant edifices, Gothic structures, cathedral-looking chapels and schools; some, too, with lofty spires and pinnacles, in all their architectural beauty and glory. With bated breath, he asks, "What great buildings are these?" And his informant answers, "These are palaces of the King of Kings; these are the temples of His grace; these are the habitations of God's House, where His name is recorded, and where His honour dwelleth. But in the school in which you have been brought up, they are contemptuously termed ' conventicles,' and their worshippers are consigned to the uncovenanted mercies of God, which may, in fact, be no mercies at all." We think every line and expression of his countenance would betoken surprise, perhaps *sad* surprise. He would be led to feel, if he did not own, that there was something bordering upon the marvellous in all this panoramic array of Methodist "conventicles." If, besides these material temples, the tens and hundreds of thousands composing the congregations that gather in them from Sabbath to Sabbath, and including the true worshippers who form the lively stones and the spiritual buildings, were to pass in procession before him, singing some of the songs of our Zion ; to what would he attribute this marvellous march of Methodism, these wonderful results, flowing as a mighty and ever-widening river from the preaching of one man?—that man who, little more than a century ago, was driven from the consecrated churches of this land,—driven from "*the* Church," as our supposed spectator is pleased to term his own "dear mother ;" that man who was persecuted and pelted from place to place, as a man unfit to live, but whom hundreds of thousands are not ashamed to call their "venerable Founder," yea, their "father in the glorious Gospel of God's dear Son," whilst they humbly

but confidently claim to be "the children of God in
Christ Jesus."

Could a candid Christian observer of such remarkable results,—an observer free from the blinding
influence of Church bigotry,—fail to look higher
than the human instrument? Would he say, "This
is only *man's* work, and it will soon come to nought?"
Hardly could he *now* have the hardihood to say so.
The old pseudo-prophets, who loved thus to prognos-
ticate of Methodism,—the "wish" being "father to
the thought,"—have long since passed away. Must he
not see the mighty moulding hand of the Great Builder
of the militant Church? It surely could not require
a very copious measure of Christian candour and
charity, to constrain him to say, "What hath God
wrought! This is the Lord's doing, and it is
marvellous in our eyes."

Yes, such doings are doubtless marvellous.
"Great marvels" have been wrought by some one,
and no mere man could have wrought them. Aud
these great marvels have been performed, too, beyond
the narrow preciucts of the Papist's devotion,—
performed beyond the petty province of the Puseyite's
prayer,—performed beyond the boundary of the
Bishop's diocese,—performed beyond the pale of the
bigot's temple. Who, then, hath wrought them?
Who is this great worker? Dare any say that they
are the doings of demons? Some have been bold

enough to place themselves on this pinnacle of presumption, and, pointing the finger of scorn at these proscribed temples of God, have declared that they belonged to Beelzebub, and that those who went to them were going "*down* to the pit," instead of going *up* to their Father's house. But if to say that such mighty works as these are wrought by *man* is something worse than puerile bigotry, to ascribe them to the power of *Satan* is nothing less than bold blasphemy.

We would remind those, who dare thus to presume, of the solemn preamble of the prayer which they have presented a thousand times over : "O Thou who alone workest great marvels, send down upon our Bishops and Curates," &c. And then, we would ask whether greater marvels than these we have named have ever been wrought, in answer to the oft-repeated but exclusive petition on behalf of Bishops and Curates. We trow not.

We point not so much to the material structures, great and manifold as these buildings are; but chiefly to the "lively stones," raised from the roughest quarries, dug out of the deepest pits, hewn out of the hardest rocks, now smooth and precious stones, "polished after the similitude of a palace." To these we point, as bearing, in their fashion, their beauty, and symmetry, the most manifest proofs * of the

* Psalm cxliv. 12.

matchless skill, the grace, and the power of an almighty Architect; proofs as plain and positive of wisdom and power from on high as the finely moulded, the curiously and chastely fashioned clay bears of the potter's power. We may surely point to these sacred spiritual structures, and say, These are "God's building." We point to the congregations of faithful men: we point not to inert masses of material stone, but to living Churches,—to those who are "created anew in Christ Jesus," who are "changed into the same image, from glory into glory," by the Lord the Spirit,—and say, These are the "epistles" of those whose apostleship ye deny: these are "lively stones built up a spiritual house," cemented and compacted with the "living Stone" which the foolish builders of old, both scribe and priest,

> "Rejected with disdain."

> "Scattered o'er all the earth they lie,
> Till Thou collect them with Thine eye;
> Draw by the music of Thy name,
> And charm into a beauteous frame."

Boast not against the branches thus "graffed in;" cast not a burning brand into those temples, which are sacred and dear to them, as thy own "dear mother" is to thee; lest haply, in seeking, like the mad prophet, to curse them, thou shalt be found fighting against God, and, whilst unchurching these, thou shalt uncovenant thyself, and falsify all thine own high claims to apostleship.

We see in connexion with this mighty Chapel movement much sanctified talent and consecrated substance, compassed about, of course, with some of those human frailties which so closely cling to the best of our services in the present imperfect state. It may well excite surprise, that so complex and extensive a machinery, so vast an annual expenditure, should have such continuous and careful oversight, such able and vigilant attention, for so little additional outlay in connexion with its secretariat, and its managing Committee.

Calls and claims upon anxious thought, upon time and talent, must indeed be manifold and multifarious. And many of these chapel cases are exceedingly complex and perplexing, with conflicting opinions to adjudge upon, and conflicting interests to consider and adjust. These, in their details, are very dry, prosaic, and sternly practical; here and there, it is true, relieved by some flights of fancy, some poetic soarings of the imagination, some romantic and Utopian schemes, which the cautious Committee prudently dispose of as a kind of aërial castle-building, and as the projects of those who, finding no plausible plan, no suitable site or solid ground upon earth, on which to build, rise on the wings of fancy into the

regions of space. Such flighty eases are summarily
dealt with in sober and stern reality; the Committee believing, as a certain nobleman has said, that
"there should always be some foundation of fact for
the most airy fabric."

The Committee and the Connexion may well be
congratulated on having so able and attentive, so
diligent and devoted a Secretary. It is a pity that
his untiring energies should be overtaxcd and over-
burdened, as, we think, they must be in his present
position : toiling and struggling comparatively alone,
the burden is too great for him.

Jethro's admonitory advice to Moses, we regard as
not altogether inapplicable : * " Thou wilt surely
wear away: for the thing is too heavy for thee.
Thou art not able to perform it thyself alone."
Economy in some respects, both as to men and
money, seems to be the watchword of the Committee :
but, " to overdo, is to undo ; " and the ease of one
valued but now disabled brother should serve as a
warning in this matter.

In Committees, especially Financial Committees,
where there are conflicting claims and clashing interests, human nature is often seen, not in its sunniest,
but in its sternest, bleakest aspect. Such Committees meet to discuss the dry details of business, to
" pay tithe of mint," as some have said,—to take

* Exodus xviii. 18.

care of the £. s. d.,—and are in danger of omitting weightier matters. When certain cases come under their consideration, they have conscientiously to close their ears, and to steel their not too tender hearts, against pathetic appeals to the finer sensibilities of human nature. Relief from our very Contingent Fund may sometimes, from the too stern necessity of the case, be not only too scanty, but too tardy, if not too late. The failing may fall, and the " weary wheels " of the well-nigh " worn out " may "stand still," before the needed help in any form arrives. How different are the ways of God from the ways of man ! His " willing mercy flies apace."

On Committee-days, when finances are chiefly concerned, members seem to move in a colder clime, and to call into exercise the more northerly part of the complex and wonderful nature of man,—the head rather than the heart. The cold and calculating, the logical and intellectual, rather than the emotional part of the soul's subtle essence, must now be brought into play. And if some stealthy influence would creep into the soul to touch it with tenderness, and to move the bowels of compassion, there must be a' manly application of something stringent, and mere emotional feelings must be promptly and prudently repressed. For this reason it, perhaps, is, that the official or collective conscience of Committees has not generally been held in very high consideration

for its sensitiveness, although it may be for its stern-
ness and soundness. And for this reason, too, it
probably is, that whilst Committees can conscientiously convict others, they can but too seldom
be convicted in their own conscience. A large
amount of artillery, in paper warfare, may be aimed
against a Committee; but how gently, and almost
gracefully, it glides down from the Committee's
shoulders, as water from the back of an aquatic bird !
All such missives are as harmless as flashes of pow-
der, and as fumes of smoke, aimed as an assault
against the crocodile's scaly coat of mail. They are
as blank cartridges.

As it regards the *Chapel Committee*, in particular,
it is perhaps as securely intrenched and as well
guarded as any; and has little to fear, except a few
stray shots from a " small band " of "irregulars,"
on whose cases the Committee sit, as it is termed, as
a kind of court-martial.

Some of this little detachment, we are told, have
been totally irregular. These we do not defend, as
their case looks like a defiance of rule and order.
Others, we feel sure, have had regard to rule, and
have aimed at the mark, though they may have
missed it, as the best marksmen sometimes do.
Some, no doubt, have striven to do the best their
circumstances allowed; and angels, it is said, " can
do no more."

The just and well balanced precept, " Be ye wise as serpents, and harmless as doves," is not always found in its full force, even in the best-formed Committees. There may be the serpent's sagacity, where there is not the dove-like meekness, but a sting. Doves may decline to nestle there. Hence the old proverb may be verified, that " the doves are often censured, whilst the crows are spared."

Our Connexional Committees, in general, may, we think, be advantageously compared with any in this great country, with its multiplied institutions, its many Churches, and multifarious committees. For wisdom, for strict integrity and impartiality, for well and wisely balanced influences and interests between Ministers and laymen, few Church committees could compare with them. Our Chapel Committee is formed for the purpose of removing and preventing heavy and distressing debts,—to give prudent counsel in all chapel plans and projects,—to insure economical expenditure in the erection and enlargement of chapels and schools,—and to afford what aid its funds will allow in this great and general chapel movement. It is well known that these laudable objects have been accomplished on a grand scale, and to an almost incredible extent, during the last few years, under the skilful supervision of able secretaries, and the careful consideration of a cautious Committee.

E

" To err **is** human." It would be too much to assert on behalf of a Committee, composed though it be of shrewd financiers, of wise and worthy men, that they have never made a mistake. No claims of infallibility are set up on behalf of the Committee; and it is an awkward dilemma for any to be placed in, neither to be allowed to make a mistake, nor yet to be infallible.

The Chapel Committee have had, as far as they could, to cure a great existing evil. They have had to sweep away a vast heap of old and offensive chapel debts. They have had also to administer the better, though to some, perhaps, the bitter, cure, in the prevention, as far as possible, of new debts on new chapels. This could hardly have been done, despite tender appeals, peculiar circumstances, and pressing claims, except by a stern will and a strong hand, such as committees, in their joint capacity, can command.

It is, however, but too common a case, in seeking to shun one evil, to run to the opposite extreme; and, in guarding, when in narrow straits, against one dangerous rock, to steer so closely as to dash against the opposite one. It is easier far to talk of the *via media*, than it is to find it, and to walk therein. One extreme, indeed, is sometimes necessary to cure another. To make the curved paper flat and even, it must be rolled back to the opposite side, or placed for some time under a heavy pressure. " The pen-

dulum pushed to one extremity of its arc, will re-
bound to the opposite extremity."

The extreme of republicanism is not far from the
iron hoof of a stern despotism; and a pretty sure
way to make murmuring peoples patient, for a time,
under the latter, is to give them plenty of the former.
A perfect reign of liberty, fraternity, and equality,
may soon end in a perfect "reign of terror;" and
the "tender mercies" of a reign of terror may make
a nation, steeped in anguish and reeking in blood,
long for a Louis Philippe, or a Louis Napoleon, or
any despot that may deliver confused and conflicting masses of men, wearied with bitter and bloody
strife for mastery, from their own demon-like
selves.

Chapel affairs, in our Connexion, had got lax and
loose : they must therefore be held with a firm hand, a
tight rein, and curbed by bit and bridle. Chapels
had been built without counting the cost. Goods
had been taken up, without the probability of prompt
payment. Debts had been contracted, and left for
simple faith and hope to discharge. The works of
faith, the required offerings of charity, the ways and
the means, had been left, in a large degree, to gene-
rations yet unborn. It was, therefore, natural, if not
necessary, for the Chapel Committee, under such circumstances, to exercise a very strict control over the
cases which came before them,—cases concocted by

those whose motto was, "Onward, Onward, at any risk, and at any rate," and who seemed to forget that, whilst in this material world, and in the militant Church, religion itself required that there should be a due regard to things temporal, and especially to the temporalities of the cause of God.

Of course, where credit is tolerably good, it is found far easier to get goods, and to build chapels, than it is to pay for them. These loose and almost Antinomian chapel-builders, whose *faith* was to do everything, must be controlled by the Committee's curb, and kept back from running into that Slough of Despond, the Court of Bankruptcy. But often, in this world, the innocent have to share the sufferings of the guilty: and this arises not only from the general arrangements of Providence, but, in many instances, from man's utter lack of power to discriminate between the two. How often parks and pleasure grounds have had to be closed, or kept open only under the strictest rules, because meddling visitors would touch the curiosities, pluck the flowers, get out of the proper path, injure the fence, and thus use a licentious liberty !

The Chapel Committee has no divining rod, no infallible oracle to consult, by which it can certainly foretell how the case on the *tapis*, for which large credit is claimed, may turn out in the end. Those

careful riders who would curb *all* horses, would curb
too many, as it is known full well that *all* horses do
not need the curb. The Committee's curb has, no
doubt, proved a most salutary check, in many which
may be termed " neck or nothing " cases. At the
same time there can, we think, be quite as little
doubt that there have been many cases, coming up
from the country, which were as slow, but as sure, as
the cart horse which brought our friend the farmer
to the Minister, to see if anything could be done to
raise a new chapel, in that part of the country
where he lived. He would give so much, and they
would raise so much, and in so many years could pay
off the debt. They had been a long time thinking
about the matter : now a suitable site offered, pro-
spects brightened, a " wide door " was opened, and
they would be glad to begin to build as soon as
possible. They could not, however, come up in time
with the case to the requirements of the Committee's
rules. That our slow and cautious friend the farmer
should have felt it a little hard to be *curbed* so
tightly by the Committee, when he wished to begin
to build, and *spurred* so sharply to *give*, we can
hardly wonder, especially as he and his friends would
have to bear their own burden, and were, perhaps,
quite careful enough that they did not take too heavy
a load. Curbed very tightly, they will not perhaps
go on with the case at all ; for, although our country

friend has not studied logic, or sat at Gamaliel's feet, yet he thinks it reasonable that those who have to bear the burden, or to drag the load along, should have their feelings consulted a little as to the curb and the spur, and be allowed to say which of the two they prefer. They could and would go at their own rate, but would not be too firmly bound to go at the Committee's pace; and therefore they did not go at all, or, if they did go, it was quite an " irregular ease."

Times of trial, of pressing and painful pecuniary claims, have come to many trustees, such as some people call " rainy days." And at such times these trustees have found in the Chapel Committee, and in the Chapel Fund, a very merciful provision for advice and assistance. They have had the Committee's counsel and aid ; they have come under the Committee's canopy ; and have found a shelter in the storm, and a kind protection against these rainy days. But, of course, there have been many cases that have not needed the same shelter; they have had no unpropitious weather ; they have not been so exposed; they have had but a very " limited liability ; " they have incurred but little risk ; they have perhaps been more weather-wise ; there have been no dark clouds in their sky, portentous of rainy days. And these cases have not, therefore, had the same, if any, stern need to come under the sheltering shadow and capacious canopy of the Chapel Committee.

Extreme "rigid right is not far from wrong." The stringent rules of the Chapel Committee, to make all cases regular, have, no doubt, made too straitened paths for the feet of some. In striving to make all move in one particular way, according to rigid rule, the Committee has probably kept some—it may be, many—of the little ones from moving at all. Some cases, possibly, have been so ruled, and over-ruled, that they have been somewhat like the pages of a blank copybook, consisting of nothing but rules, and having this premonition on the cover, "No stroke must be made, except such as will be as correct as the copper-plate copy itself." So strict a rule for new beginners, enforced by a severe penalty, by smart strokes of the ferule, would, we suppose, make many boys tremble to begin at all; and, perhaps, cause such a general strike in the school as would prevent, in some cases, any line from being written in imitation of the copy.

"To overdo is to undo." "Fire," it has been remarked, "is a good servant, but a bad master." So, as we have often heard a distinguished Minister state, it may be said of rule and order: they "may and should serve us, but none should be their slaves."

There is an eastern fable of an elephant, that was

marched in solemn state and gay trappings to pick up a pin. For a great Committee to exercise too strict a circumspection and control over the minute details of those smaller cases which arise far away from the sphere in which the members of the Committee move,—cases which perhaps no schedule can fully set forth in their local interest and importance,— too much resembles the stately elephant in the fable; except that the elephant *did* pick up the pin, and not, with its ponderous proboscis, prevent the pin from being picked up.

A committee cannot be ubiquitous, any more than it can know all things. And, as a great body marches slowly, whilst a small one moves nimbly, the two cannot well walk together. One will have to wait for the other; and whilst waiting, the work may be hindered. "The King's business requires haste."

Surely some of the smaller Chapel cases,—cases of erection, enlargement, and modification,—could be as skilfully, as safely, and more swiftly dispatched by a Circuit or a DISTRICT *Chapel Committee*, with the Chairman at its head, the Superintendent concerned, and a respectable layman from the locality to explain and urge the case.

Moreover, in many instances, local committees are impatient under the very stringent control of the Chapel Committee. Some *local* committees, as well

as the General Committee, combine strong wills.
They may be, as some stubborn men are,
prone to leave undone that which they are imperatively required to do, and *vice versâ*. They are like
the "gals" of whom Mrs. Stowe's Sambo speaks,
that "allays go by the rule of contrar;" or like a
spirited, mettlesome horse, that spurns the bit and
bridle, that rears and kicks when held with a close
curb and a tight rein. The spirited must not be
too strongly curbed; nor the gentle, that have gone
almost beyond their power, be goaded to go farther
still.

A dozen villagers, or so, have given of their
time and their labour, and of their hard-
earned money, to raise a house for God. They have
done what they could. Of course, to those who
move only in cities and in the midst of great things,
who worship in capacious and cathedral-like chapels,
these country people and their chapels may seem but
small affairs. But to simple Christian people in the
provinces, to build or enlarge a house for God,—
though, compared with others, that house may
be small,—is a great work and a grand
idea. It sets them all astir, minds, hearts, and
hands; they are inspired with noble purposes, and
cheered by the brightest hopes for the cause of God,
though they be "little among the thousands of
Israel." To have those purposes thwarted, and

those hopes dashed, for prudential reasons which they cannot see, is to them a dreadful disappointment which they cannot welcome. From the Chapel-Committee they have received nothing but rules and regulations, restrictions and requirements, counsels, checks, control,—and, in the end, it may be, censure. And they, in their turn, begin to complain, and perhaps to kick against these goads, and are in danger of getting into a habit of kicking; for they think their case is as hard as it is irregular. Could they receive trifling pecuniary aid,—had they but a little *cash* to sweeten the counsel or censure of the Chapel Committee,—they would be better able to bear their burden. Special circumstances have arisen, which loudly call for a speedy erection or enlargement. The Spirit is poured out from on high; many "hear the word gladly;" the people fly as a cloud. Some chapel in the neighbourhood has been closed or abandoned : their own chapel is crowded. Delays are dangerous. The set time to favour this little Hill of Zion seems, to those who are on the spot, now to have come. Everything seems to say, "What thou doest, do quickly;"—everything, except the decision of the Chapel Committee.

We know that prudent provision is made for any case of proved urgency; but unless in the smaller cases a larger debt be allowed, with longer time to pay it in, where the utmost local efforts have been made, the benefit of this provision, we think, is greatly modified and minified, if not in some cases altogether neutralized.

A small sum per annum may be paid for a series of years towards the liquidation of the remaining debt, which cannot, without overstraining, be grappled with at once, or within a year or two of its erection. And further pressing appeals, without a little breathing-time, may tend to sour and prejudice the minds of the people who have a mind both to work and to give, and who will pay the debt if those who press them will have a little patience with them. Stringent rules, in such cases, may, instead of being promotive, prove obstructive of the Church's great mission. They may shorten the cords which should be lengthened, and weaken the stakes which should be strengthened. Rigid rules, in these cases, may but hem up, as with icy barriers, those who, in the warmth of their first love, and the ardour of their zeal, are impelled in their evangelistic efforts to go to regions beyond. Such stringent rules seem scarcely to leave sufficient scope for the exercise of faith, hope, and charity ; and may contract and circumscribe the outposts of an aggressive Connexion, which has a world-wide parish and a world-wide commission ; in the fulfilment of which commission we may not always wait till we can see our way quite clear, but must be guided by the moving of the cloud. We must, when all proper means have been tried, trust the God of the future, as well as of the past. We must confide in God's changeless covenant on behalf of His own Church and cause. We must, when walking in darkness, take God's hand, and lean on His arm, as we wend our way through the wilderness. We must not forget that "He leads the blind by a way which they know not;" nor must we make too much haste ourselves, or hurry the Providence of God, but wait His time, and meanwhile embrace the passing opportunities, enter the open doors, as He prepares our way.

> "Still achieving, still pursuing,
> Learn to labour and to wait."

Some one has said, "We are prevented by those very stringent restrictions now in force." Is there no danger lest the country parts, at least, of our Connexion should be cramped and confined by these rigid rules, as it respects those cases which have had in a liberal degree the Committee's counsel and control, but none of its charity in any form? If there be a danger, in the quiet country, of our children being too credulous, or too childlike and simple in their trust, as to chapel matters, such a simple faith is perhaps less likely to be confounded in the end than the over-prudent policy, and the too cold and careful calculations, of some of our friends in the bustling cities,

whose terms are, " Ready money," "Cash only," or
who give but little credit, and leave little for faith,
little for the future to work out, little scope in these
chapel cases for those instructive and interesting
specimens, which we find in the old magazines, of
" the Providence of God illustrated."

> " Blind unbelief is sure to err,
> And scan His work in vain."

If the stringent chapel restrictions have, in some
respects, been as bonds too firmly fixed around our
body, let those bonds be loosened a little, lest they
be burst asunder, as by some they have been. Whatever may be done with those who are of full growth
and of expanded powers, let the buoyant and bounding energies of the younger branches of our great
family have, in the warmness and freshness of their
first love, free, fair, and full play. Let them not be
cooped up and confined; let them not be closely compressed, as with steel around their chest; let there not
be too tight lacing; let them have room to breathe, to
grow and expand, room for a full muscular development;
and then, instead of being stunted and dwarfed, as, in
more respects than one, we are in danger of being
in these modern days, they may become equal to the
giants of former times. Then, should a little more
freedom of action in the present bring them into

some financial difficulties at some future day, may we not justly hope that they would have strength to grapple with those difficulties in proportion to the day? A little relaxation would, we think, be both safe and salutary.

We suppose that the Metropolitan Chapel Committee found it convenient to get a little loose from the rigorous restraint of the General Chapel Committee, and to have more freedom of will and action in its grand chapel extension scheme. And it would require too consummate stickling for rule and order to check those clear and cautious brethren in their boundings forth to civilize and Christianize the heathendom and moral barbarism of the modern Babylon.

Of course it was meet and right that the metropolitan see, in this noble project, should have, as far as possible, an unchecked course and an uncontrolled will; but that freedom which was found convenient for the mind and will of the metropolitan District, it would, we think, be both politic and prudent to extend in some due degree to all the Districts of the Connexion. A great portion of those cares and responsibilities which now crowd upon and over-burden the General Committee, and over-tax its able secretary, may, doubtless, not only with safety, but with much advantage, be distributed among the different District Chapel Committees, having the Chairman at their head, and being vested with power to commence and to complete their own chapel cases, subject simply to a general review, as other District matters are, at the end of the year.

We should suppose that, in so large a Connexion as our own, there must be ever and anon arising a number of small cases, of some kind or other, too small for so great and important a Committee:— small chapel cases; small organ cases; still smaller harmonium cases, which, despite their tuneful names, do not always tend to harmonious concert in the Church. These small chapel and organ cases, whilst of local importance, are hardly large enough, or serious enough, for the grave deliberation of our great Chapel Committee. And it seems to us that a more manageable machinery is much needed,—one that can adapt itself to the required time and season; which will move with swifter speed, and throw off with greater velocity the cases which may in quick succession rise.

Would it not be well, too, that one or more of the parties specially concerned in the chapel case should have the opportunity of coming into closer contact with the Chapel Committee which may have to consider and control their case? As it is, what more can many of our trustees, personally at least, know of our Chapel Committee, than if their meetings revolved around the North Pole, or were among

the great and mysterious Northern Lights? They
do not know enough of the members of that Committee to cherish toward them that love and respect
which, it is likely, they would cherish if they could
be favoured, were it but once only, to see and to hear
them. From many of the trustees, of course, the
members of the Committee live at a respectable distance, and in dignified seclusion; they are to them
quite unknown. Distant objects, which often assume
strange and startling appearances when seen through
a misty medium, reveal, when we approach them,
nothing to excite our surprise or dismay. That
which, on the distant mountains, seemed to be some
monster form, may be a friend and a brother. Thus,
different sects often look at each other through the
mists of prejudice. Afar off, they appear as aliens;
but brought into close contact, they are led to say,
"Let there be no strife between us, for we are
brethren." So hard thoughts, harsh opinions, dread
ideas respecting the Chapel Committee, which some
seem to cherish, might be dispelled, could the Committee be seen, approached, spoken to by a representative trustee, and the *pro* and *con* of his chapel
case be *heard*, and not simply *seen* sketched on some
schedule. Both parties might then arrive at a better
understanding. A disappointment would be better
borne by the trustees, if the case had not been too
sternly and too summarily dispatched, and if it had

been thus represented by one of the trustees themselves, as well as by the Superintendent. The
Superintendent would thus be relieved of a great
deal of his burden of care and responsibility. Now,
the Minister sometimes stands alone, to bear the
brunt of the battle. He is subject to a kind of
cross-fire, and is often a target for both the Chapel
Committee and the trustees. Heavy missiles may
come from the Chapel Committee upon the Minister,
as though he were one of the offending trustees; and
heavier and harder still from the uncontrollable and
chagrined trustees, as though their Minister were a
condensed and censorious Chapel Committee, cen-
suring and controlling their case.

We have one case in point of this class, which has
just come under our notice; and one of considerable
importance. The Minister has the mandate of the
Committee as to the maximum of debt allowed, and
echoes, before the trustees, the decision of the Committee. The trustees complain, and almost rebel.
They ask, and almost demand, that some hundreds
more of debt be allowed. The Committee, of course,
as we understand, remain unmoved; so large an additional debt cannot be allowed. One " cannot " often
confirms or creates another " cannot." The concur-
rent reply of the trustees appears to be, " We cannot
wait any longer. The building must be begun. The
fine-weather opportunity will be passing away."

The Superintendent may remind the refractory brethren, that even if the chapel be built, unless the chapel conditions be complied with, it cannot be opened by any Wesleyan Minister. "Then we will have another," may be the prompt reply of the trustees. Is not the Minister, in such a case, between the horns of a dilemma? And though he "have all his wits about him," he may nevertheless be "at his wits' end." He would fain comply with the will and gratify the wish of the trustees, for they are among his leading friends; but he *must* keep the rules, and observe the order, or expect the censure of the Chapel Committee, as a promoter of an irregular case.

After some nights of sleepless solicitude,—for, besides this critical case, there are other "cares of the Churches" which crowd upon him,—our esteemed brother may consult the Chairman of the District; but he can hardly advise what to do. Of course, the Chairman cannot contravene the rules of the Committee. These *must* be kept, or this will have the odium of being added to the list of irregular cases already too long in his District.

Would it not be a great convenience, under such circumstances, to have a DISTRICT *Chapel Committee,* which might be convened within two or three days' notice? For a month may be more than three weeks too long to wait in such a case,—too long for the work to wait, too long to keep a Minister in unpleasant altercation with the trustees. Such a Committee, being within a reasonable distance, could be attended by the Superintendent, and one or two of the trustees proposing the outlay; and might be fully empowered to decide doubtful and disputed points, and to guide and govern critical cases.

This, we fancy, would be a safety valve for the escape of a little surplus steam, or any explosive material. Let the trustees, who think they have reason and right on their side, bring forth their strong arguments then and there. Let them courageously, but Christianly, contest the case with the Chapel Committee; and if they come off victoriously, well; if not, let them be content to be beaten. Let them now speak, show cause why, or "for ever hold their peace."

In this way, we think, many cases might be saved from becoming irregular. In this way trustees might be spared from bearing what we know some feel to be a brand as irregulars,—saved from a rankling sore which though a Committee may have power to inflict, it should, we think, have Christian prudence and policy enough not to inflict either upon Ministers or trustees in any of our Connexional Churches, except when imperatively required by the evident culpability of the case, and by no means for monetary inability.

It is well to allure, and as little as possible to alienate, those who form essential, integral, and important parts, as trustees, of our great Connexion.

And last, though not least, it may save Ministers from being somewhat too rigorously required to render an account before an august assembly, as though they were schoolboys or serious defaulters, —to render an account of cases, which, by the combined purpose of a large majority of strong-willed trustees, may lie altogether beyond the prudent control of a Superintendent, however judicious, who is left solitary and single-handed to cope with such critical cases. As it now is, many worthy trustees have simply to secure the site, project the plan, raise the money, rear the building, subject to the rules and restraints of the invisible but overruling power of the Chapel Committee somewhere in the North.

The Chapel Committee has done well and nobly during the last few years. A large sum has been expended in aid of this great chapel movement,— very large when compared with the doings of former days. Three-quarters of a million for the erection of chapels, and more than half a million for the liquidation of chapel debts, are no mean sums of money to raise for these objects within the last ten years, among the many other monetary claims of the Connexion. There may be some just reason for congratulation in all this. Yet, what, after all, are these sums, compared with the vast outlay in this so-called Christian country for "that which satisfieth not?" What is it compared with the enormous expenditure for snuff, tobacco, and drams? What is it, compared with the large amounts annually absorbed, among even professing Christians, in needless indulgences, luxuries, superfluities, in the lust of the eye and the pride of life,—our own Churches not excepted? What is it, compared with the mighty capabilities, the marvellous resources of the Methodist people? What is it, compared with the pressing and imperative claims of home heathen-dom, the dense darkness and deep depravity of vast masses in our beloved country?—a darkness too dense, a depravity too deep, too demonlike, to be credited, did not school statistics, the columns of newspapers, and calendars of crime too clearly con-firm and too amply authenticate, the growing preva-lence, even under the shadow of our multiplied sanc-tuaries, of all manner of ungodliness. And what is it, we may further ask, compared with what is now being performed and projected in that Church whose regular clergy it was one part of the mission of Methodism—a part which she has well accom-plished—to "provoke to jealousy?"

Many have done much to aid in this required mul-tiplication of Methodist schools and sanctuaries, by their large subscriptions or donations, by gifts of chapels, or in some form or other. But many more, and these quite as well able, have done but little in the tithing of their substance for God's cause. There have been, ever and anon, many covetous lepers in Israel, and but comparatively few completely cleansed. Many, it may be, have day by day prayed, "Thy kingdom come," whilst, as a self-sacrificing missionary has strongly remarked, "the jewellery on those hands that have been lifted up in this prayer has cost more than they ever gave to promote the coming of this kingdom in all their life." *

Of course, people may most expensively adorn themselves; they may elaborately decorate their drawing-rooms with superb furniture and pleasant pictures; they may thus wish to encourage trade and the fine arts. They may present a stained glass window, a lofty pinnacle, a stately spire, to the house of God. They may liberally lavish their Lord's goods on a superfluity of splendour, if not of naughtiness; whilst stern necessity, rigorous requirements, the pressing claims of the perishing, are overlooked, slighted, or but very scantily heeded. But whatsoever people may do with their money, we suppose most Christians are agreed that we "*must* give an account," and a "strict account," of our "stewardship;"—an account, too, to that God who, whilst He gave glory to the heavens, splendour to the rain-

* Dr. Duff.

bow, exceeding loveliness to the lily, a rich fragrance
to the rose, and delicate pencilling to the flowers of
the spring, yet has filled the peopled earth with *good-
ness*, and crowns his dependent creatures with *tender
mercies*, and would never give a gay flower as food
for the famishing, nor a gorgeous rainbow instead of
the fertilizing rain, nor smooth stones or serpents as
substantial aliment; nor tantalize his needy children
with the mockery of magnificence, instead of nutri-
tious milk for babes, or strong meat for men of
mature growth.

If, in the diocese of London North, a million of
money is to be raised, in the South a million, and in
the diocese of Worcester a million; and if, in other
dioceses, there should be doings on a similar scale,
to promote the Church Extension scheme; then
what might Methodism do, if it yet be " Christianity
in earnest ? " What might Methodism do in her
different Districts, were she to arise and shake herself
from the dust, arouse all her dormant energies, call
up from their graves all her buried talents, employ
all her vast resources of wealth and influence, enlist
the sympathies and co-operation of all her gifted and
godly lay members, marshalled, as their time would
permit, as Home Missionaries, as volunteers against
the army of the aliens? What might she not do, in
her onward march toward the millennium, and in fulfilment of her great commission on behalf of the

world that yet lieth in wickedness? How far may the next ten years leave the last decade in the rear, instead of leaving Methodism in its decline! How many millions may be raised and cast into the Lord's treasury! How many souls may be saved from death, and won to Christ! How many a multitude of sins may be for ever hid!

The movements of the Church of England at the present time seem to us, in some respects, as remarkable as were those of Methodism at its early outset. Not only are large *sums of money* being raised, for Church extension; but *lay agents* in large numbers are being employed; hired rooms, temporary buildings, in an experimental way, are being used; Scripture Readers are sedulously working, and stealthily seducing sheep from our fold, and with proffered benefits vigorously prosecuting, at every nook and corner, the work of proselytism. Meanwhile earnest Evangelicals hold open-air services, dispense with forms and ceremonies, do not wait for the parish clerk, or the churchwarden, or the country squire, nor for the time "when the wicked man shall turn from his wickedness," but step on some stone at the corner of the street, and try at once to "convert the sinner from the error of his way." They draw the bow at a venture; they sling the stone; they wield the Spirit's sword, and sow the seed beside all waters.

Thus, whilst some of the modern *non*-conforming Churches are disposed to *conform* a little more to the Church, the Church is copying the past well-doings of Noneonformists. These evangelieal Churehmen are beeoming more earnest : Noneonformists are growing more formal. Churehmen are beginning to pray and to preaeh without a book : Noneonformists are essaying to pray and to preaeh with books. Chureh- men can preaeh in the open air with only one short prayer before the sermon : some Nonconformists must have three prayers before the sermon, in pre- seribed and punetilious ordcr,—little, larger, largest, —positive, comparative, and superlative. Churchmen are stooping : Noneonformists are soaring. Church- men can preaeh in a humble upper room : Noncon- formists—many, at least—must have vaulted roofs and steepled sanctuaries. Churchmen now think it is *good* to copy some of the old Noneonformists in their evangelistic efforts : Noneouformists think it is *grand*, after all that has been said and suffered for conseienee' sake, to be a little like the old Chureh, and to copy her in her forms and ceremonials. " You are losing the poor," said a Churehman, of catholic views and a wide range of observation, to the writer a short time ago ; "and your ground, if you do not mind, will be swept from under you."

Would it not be well, sinee these modern Church- men have taken a few leaves out of the old book of the Nonconformists, for the modern Nonconformists —the Methodists not excepted—to take a few leaves out of the new book of these zealous Churchmen?

There is a way of stooping so as to soar higher in the end; and a way of soaring so as to sink lower at the last. "For he that humbleth himself shall be exalted: and he that exalteth himself shall be abased."

In addition to our other manifold chapel schemes, we have our energetic and eloquent Mr. Punshon's beautiful and benevolent project for the erection of chapels in watering places; a scheme which we hope will well succeed; for in such places many of our people, in their annual recreations, are much in danger of straying from us.

Let us, then, suppose that all these means are in constant and active operation; that all the wheels within wheels of this vast and wonderful machinery are at work, and always at work. If so, it is surely for some grand practical purpose. It is not for self-aggrandizement, as a body of people. It is for the extension of Christ's kingdom, for the enlargement of the Church of Christ, for the glory of God, for the salvation of souls.

Then, let us ask, is there anything like a proportionate and corresponding result? What work is wrought? What spoils are taken from the foe?

What aggressions are made on the world that lieth in wickedness? What strongholds of Satan are pulled down? What moral victories are achieved? What sheaves are gathered? What souls are saved from death? Work is wrought; trophies are won; sheaves are gathered; souls are saved. God has not left His servants without witness, without seals to their ministry. Zion has not been forsaken : " God is in the midst of her." " The shout of a King " has been heard in the camp of our Israel. The glory has not departed.

But is the glory declining? Is it *departing?* Is the true glory of old Methodism, with its venerable old men, passing away? Is our sun going up to a grand and a glorious meridian; or has it been at its meridian height, and is it now going down, while it is yet day? Whilst we walk about our Zion, " tell the towers thereof, mark well her bulwarks, consider her palaces," let us enter her inner sanctuary, and inquire how burns the sacred fire on her altars. Whilst the sun of worldly prosperity is blazing without, is the celestial fire burning dimly within? Is the sun putting the fire out? " Watchman, what of the night?" Churches many, great, and fair, have arisen, flourished, and faded away. We have greatly flourished : is it not possible that we too may fade away? Who dares say that it is not? Is Methodism, then, in the sere and yellow leaf? Is the old tree to be looked upon, year after year, in vain for fruit, and then after that to be cut down? Is our venerable Methodism, like many of its men, well nigh worn out, and soon itself to be put on the shelf, or sit down as a Supernumerary? Is the candlestick soon to be removed out of its place? Is the day of its " defection and degeneracy," the day of its decline and decay, the day of its darkness and dearth, the day of its death and its doom,—O, is it at hand? God forbid! The God of our fathers forbid! The God of our venerated founder forbid! The God of the unnumbered hosts, of the great cloud of witnesses, that have passed away from our militant Church to the Church triumphant in heaven, forbid!

CHAPTER III.

CAN CHURCHES BE STATIONARY?

CAN Christians or Churches be stationary?
We have been wont to say they cannot. Then, as
a Church, are we *advancing?* Scarcely so, if adding
"daily to the Church" be a fair and true test of the
advance of a Church. Whether it be a fair test or
not, it is one which we have long used. We have
rejoiced when there have been large accessions, and
have called our friends to rejoice with us; and we
have mourned when we have been minished and
brought low, and have asked our friends to mourn
with us.

If there be decline in this respect, is there not a
cause? And if there be a cause, where are we to
look for that cause? Certainly not in things that
continue the same as they have been from the beginning, but in things that assume a *changing* aspect.
What is changing? Thank God, we have not a
changing creed. Our glorious doctrines remain the
same. But our circumstances are, doubtless, mightily
changing; and people, we know, often change with
their circumstances. And with their circumstances

have not Christians, and Christian Churches also, greatly changed? We have seen that, as a Church, we have much more money than we once had. And we have not failed to think on these things, and to talk about them, and that rather loudly sometimes, and to give many thanks, as perhaps it was our duty to do. And it may be that of money, if not of "means," we have "made our boast," if not an "idol made."

It may be worth our while to inquire,

. First: *Are we not, as Ministers and as Methodists, in danger of being satisfied with generous gifts, instead of looking for genuine grace?*

Some may think, if they do not say, that great gifts are signs of grace. We say, No; at all events not infallible signs. It is true that he who has grace must and will give, though it be " of his little." Yet it is no less true that many may and do give who have not grace. This is as true as that whilst " godliness is great gain," great gain is not godliness. And as it regards great gifts for God's cause and for good objects, the righteousness of Pharisees, Papists, Puseyites, may more than equal that of Evangelical givers in our own and other Churches. Yea, even profane and profligate persons, publicans and sinners, when they have to pay the last debt of nature, have at the same time hoped by a large bequest to pay off a long score of sin and crime. Ay, and may not many among the wealthy Methodists, who, in their life-time, have so many "good things," hope by mere money—which Ministers so much need, to meet the pressing claims of various funds—to "cover a multitude of sins?" And who dare deny that there is danger of our smiling upon subscribers, and at the same time suffering sin upon them, passing it by without rebuke or frown? Then, whilst *gold* is gained, though it be for God's cause and a good object, yet *grace* will be wanting. Then, as with the wedge of gold, there will be sin in the camp. Then with our wealth there will be a woe. Then with secular prosperity there will be spiritual penury. Then, whilst religious revenues advance, religion itself will retrograde. Then, whilst the *funds* go up, the *faith* will go down. Then, as people and preachers, we may plume ourselves that we are progressing greatly; but whilst there is progress in mere monetary matters, progress in sheer temporalities, there will be the progress of spiritual decline. Then our "Body" might become in time a mere bloated material system, with little life-blood, and with languishing vitality, doomed to a connexional collapse. Then, instead of the wheels of the Gospel chariot going on gloriously, they would, like the wheels of Pharaoh's chariot, drag heavily. Then, as is most significantly said in a late Pastoral Address to our Societies, (1864,) " Methodism would be clogged with its own weight, and stayed in its movements, if the Spirit of Life were not in the midst of the wheels." Then, if money be given to God's cause, and hearts be not given to God, as the danger is, instead of soaring as the aëronaut does with lessened ballast, we should gravitate down to a spiritual sepulchre, splendid though it may be,—"Earth to earth,"—and should "see corruption."

Should any among us be disposed to pooh-pooh the probable perils from pecuniary prosperity, and paramount attention to it, we should be inclined to regard this as next to a positive proof that "blindness had in part happened" to them, and as a sure sign that there was a worm in the bud, a cankerworm at the root. Scripture cautions against self-security and self-deception are addressed to us in solemn tones; as, also, admonitions which warn us of the dangers which attend worldly wealth. "When thou hast eaten, and art full, then beware."

Surely the flaming eyes of Him who walketh in the midst of the golden candlesticks see not as man seeth. And to shrink or shy away from the irksome and humbling, but safe and salutary, task of searching and self-suspecting scrutiny, would be a sad and sure omen of the decline of a Church whose religion began not with condemning others, but with condemning ourselves. "Let him who thinketh he standeth," and who assuredly does stand, "take

heed lest he fall." Let, then, money-begging Ministers, and money-giving Methodists, value the money
so given for just what it is worth, and no more.
Let us more "earnestly covet the best gifts." Let
us not rest, till they who give their gold to God's
cause, get grace, and give their hearts to God. This,
ye generous givers, ye should have done, and not
have left the other undone. This, thank God, many,
yea, most, we trust, have done. Howbeit, not all.
Let us not, then, congratulate ourselves on the
increase of subscriptions, the advance of funds, the
great influx into the Lord's treasury; let us not
thank God, and thank the givers, and thank ourselves, for these great gifts for chapels, for Missions,
&c., without solemnly remembering that greater gift
which God Himself imperatively requires,—He, to
whom the silver and the gold belong,—and without
which the swelling reports of all other givings will
be but a mere flourish of trumpets, waxing louder
and louder, as sounding brass and a tinkling cymbal:
"My son, give Me *thy heart.*"

Let us not, either as pastors or as people, indulge
in anything that savours of vain boasting. Let us
not, even in the secret self-complacency of the soul,
say, "We are rich, and increased in goods." Let us
observe the very proper and prudent caution of the
President in his Jubilee address, and not indulge in
self-laudation, lest, while in temporalities we are rich,

in things spiritual we be wretched and poor and blind. Let us earnestly strive, with increasing revenues, to have advancing religion in, and large accessions to, our Churches ; more souls, as well as more subscriptions ; that we may be made glad by seeing the grace of God in all those who give their gold to God's cause. Let none have a shadow of just reason to say,—as some do malignantly,—that we care more for subscriptions than for souls ; that Ministers are always after the money. If any perverse and persecuting men say that we are sent chiefly to take care of the funds, let it be " falsely." Let none settle down into a self-satisfied state as shrewd financiers, " good business men,"—not the highest compliment for the Minister of Christ ; but let us vividly remember that our great business is to save " souls out of the fire, to snatch them from the verge of hell." Let us be able boldly and truly to say to those little givers and great grumblers, who freely give little except their frequent taunts about money, " We seek not yours, but you."

Surely those who have to attend so much to the funds, and perhaps too much to " serve tables," would be gladly released, if they well could, from this heavy addition to their arduous duties. They must mourn that *monetary matters* claim so much of their precious time. All of us must sadly sigh, if, whilst more sovereigns annually swell the subscription list, souls are but sparsely " added to the Church." Come, then, ye wealthy laity, a little more to their help. Help by giving more of your *time*, if possible, as well as of your money, that they, as Ministers of Christ sent forth to PREACH Christ, may give themselves more fully, yea, " *wholly*," to the work of the Ministry. Come to their help : haste to the rescue. Come, and relieve them by your free, spontaneous, " systematic beneficence." Come, and let your systematic giving supersede their systematic begging. Come, and do a little more of the work, not only of giving yourselves, but of begging from others, which some of you blame *them* for doing so much, but which *some one* must do. Many of them think it is hard both to " dig " and to " beg." Hard enough to beg, without being blamed for begging. Try yourselves both giving and begging on a larger scale.

And, above all, give yourselves. Give your hearts to Him who claims you as His own. " For a man is more precious than fine gold, even a man than the gold wedge of Ophir." And then, whilst we have to rejoice over more money cast into the treasury, we shall not have to mourn over minished numbers of souls saved from death. May there be an equal advance of temporal and of spiritual prosperity !—tithes brought into the storehouse, and the Spirit poured out from on high ! May the spiritual orb not go down, whilst the temporal orb goes up! If it be possible that both suns can long shine together, may it be so! But let the money perish, rather than souls. Lost souls the great and good Shepherd came to save, and has sent the under shepherds, who are in Christ's stead, to save.

" It is not reason that we should leave the Word of God, and serve tables. Look ye out men of honest report, full of the Holy Ghost and wisdom, whom ye may appoint over this business. But *we* will give ourselves *continually* to prayer, and to the ministry of the Word." *

> " I would the precious time redeem,
> And longer live for this alone,
> To spend, and to be spent, for them
> Who have not yet my Saviour known;
> Fully on these my mission prove,
> And only breathe to breathe Thy love."

Closely connected with the former, there may be another inquiry.

Secondly: *Are we not just now, as Ministers, much in danger of being swayed, in various ways, by mere monetary influence?*

O the mighty, more than magical, power of money over the minds of mortals! How potent are the spells of this sorceress! Under her enchanting wand what transmutations take place! How blinding and

* Acts vi. 2–4.

yet bewitching are a few grains of gold dust, when they get into a corner of our vision! Hold up a prism to the eye, and the most ordinary objects, objects on which you would not think it worth your while to dwell one moment, are suddenly bespangled with the most beautiful and brilliant colours of the rainbow. A gloomy scene becomes gay and gaudy as fairy-land. That which annoyed now attracts the eye, and you are compelled to exclaim, "How beautiful!" Take away the prism, and these objects are as suddenly stripped of their borrowed beauty. They assume once more their ordinary aspect; they are clad in their old costume; they have lost their coat of many colours. Let a man of rather doubtful character, and of suspected friendship, minister the needful supplies, give of his gold; and how doubts are dissipated! how cherished suspicion yields to the sentiment, "A friend in need is a friend indeed!" How the guilty are gilded over! the wood is as brass, the iron as silver, and the brass as burnished gold! The character is gold-washed. "Wealth maketh many friends, and every man is a friend to him that giveth gifts."

Such changes surpass those which take place on the surface of things, by borrowing the beautiful rainbow tints, or clothing them with prismatic colours. And yet it would seem strange to put such questions as these to a Christian man or a Christian Minister :—

Can mere money mitigate moral evil? Can gold given lessen guilt contracted? Can contributions cancel crime? Can silver or gold soften the grim aspect of sin? Can money mask that "monster," which is

> "Of such frightful mien,
> That to be hated needs but to be seen?"

Can money change a pretty pebble into a precious pearl? Can money change chaos into a new creation? Can money make a mass of moral loathsomeness lovely and of good report? Can money so clothe a corpse with the mere "mockery of life" that the dead cannot be discerned from the living, and so that we shall seek the living among the dead? Can money give so striking a semblance and similitude, so imposing and finished a form of life, to a dead and delusive figure, —such as may be seen in Madame Tussaud's Exhibition,—that you cannot find out the cheat, till you walk up to the draped statue and dumb show, and essay to converse and commune with it, knowing not, for a moment, whether to smile or to blush at the deception? Can money clothe sin with the beauty of a serpent's skin, and then, fixing its fascinating gaze upon us, make us quite forgetful of the fatal poison "concealed in its crooked fangs," and of the death to which it dooms us?

One or two of such a series of questions, if pointed at a professing Christian, or a Minister, may call

forth the indignant inquiry, "Is thy servant a dog?"
And yet, after all, though not to the same extent,
yet to some extent, are not most of us, in these days,
in danger, if we may so speak, of an optical monetary
delusion,—in danger of deceiving and of being deceived? "For a gift doth blind the eyes of the wise,
and pervert the words of the righteous." * One cannot but regret that so wise and so great a man as
Lord Bacon should have been bribed and blinded.
Sir Robert Walpole said, "Every man has his price."
Doubtless Sir Robert had found many political men
who could be purchased for a paltry and pitiful price;
so he thought all men might be bought, some at a
higher price, and some at a lower. Many in our day
seem to cherish this carnal notion concerning even
good men. Money, with them, is such a power, and
has so potent and seducing a spell, that they think
none are proof against its charms. We remember
sitting, some years ago, by the side of one who
appeared to have seen better days. He held in his
hand a splendid gold-headed stick, and bore about
his body the outward signs of an inward scapegrace.
He could fluently descant on the lovely scenery of
the Garden Isle, which he had visited, and on the
architecture of its venerable churches. Biding our
time, we gently glided to graver topics, until we
passed from the material edifice, called "a church,"

* Deut. xvi. 19.

to conversation on the character of those spiritual
structures which are called the "building of God."
There was soon a sullen gruff "Ugh! You talk of
your Christian men, but I never met with one of
them who wouldn't cheat if he could." We eyed
him askance, and looked a little reprovingly upon
him and his prodigal garb, and simply said, "So
much depends upon the kind of company we keep, as
to our impressions concerning Christian people."
These words seemed like a sharp arrow, that winged
its way into a wounded conscience. We told him of
one whom we knew, a good but poor man, of intelligent mind and honest report, who had the "poor
man's wealth, a large family," of well known repute
as a mining captain, who was offered many hundred
pounds simply for his signature to a swindling
Mining Report. He, however, promptly and sternly
spurned the tempting sum, which to him hardly was
tempting, as a barter for the truth, and as the bribe
of a good conscience. This great price could not
purchase this poor man. And we much doubt whether Sir Robert Walpole himself could have bid high
enough for the stern stuff which composed the conscience of this honest man, who had found that, the
gain whereof is far better than fine gold, and who
had often sincerely sung,

> "Wisdom to silver we prefer,
> And gold is dross compared to her."

That upright and noble-minded man soon passed away to the inheritance above, and to his reward in the skies, which his faith had long looked at, and his soul long tasted of. Having overcome the world, he entered into the enjoyment of the enduring substance, and the undefiled inheritance. And we hardly need say that the weeping widow and the fatherless family were not forsaken or forgotten by the faithful God of that father whose loss they mourned. He had not left them the gains of dishonesty, but the legacy of his earnest prayers, and the bequest of a bright example ; and they were not allowed by the faithful Promiser to lack any good thing.

Our prodigal companion seemed much struck with this stubborn fact, and forced to feel and own that the old Book was true, and the religion which it revealed, not of man, but of God. Still he had never seen such a case, though, as he told us, he had travelled much. We thought he had,—into "a *far* country," and "a great way off." "As is the earthy, such are they that are earthy." He heartily shook hands with us when we parted, and said, with a deep and tremulous sigh, that his parents, too, were godly Methodists. And the influence of his sainted mother, it was evident, yet lived in the dead soul of her prodigal son, and she being dead yet spake.

There is, then, a spell far stronger than silver, a

motive power more mighty than the love of money or
of life, a gain the good man has gotten greater than
gold, and compared with which gold is counted by
him but dross and trash. All have not, like Demas,
left Christ because they loved the present world; all
would not, like Judas, sell the Saviour for a few
pieces of silver. Monstrous man! thy love of gain
has left on sin-stained humanity the darkest, saddest,
foulest blot! Better had it been for thee, hadst
thou never been born, than that thou shouldst have
bartered away the precious blood of the Blessed One
who came to ransom thee. Monstrous act! blackest
of all barters! A Saviour sold for silver! The
Prince of Life for the pitiful price of a slave! The
price for which Jesus was sold by Judas to the Jews,
was the price for which Judas was bought, both soul
and body, by Beelzebub. Satan entered into Judas
as into his peculiar property; and who could dispute
his right to do what he would with his own? Yet
it is saddest of all to think of Judas as one of the
Twelve; to think of his dipping his foul red hand
into the same dish as his Lord. One of the Twelve!
worse than any one of the legion. The foul apostle,
the false accuser; which has the greater sin? which
is the fouler of the foul? which the blacker in the
blackness of darkness?

Yet how sad and long the list of those who, since
that dark day of sale, have sold the Lord of Life,

sold the Son of God, and put Him to an open shame, —sold Him for even, a less sum than Judas did! Bad as was the bargain of Esau, who bartered away his birthright,—and of Judas, who bartered away the precious blood,—the one for "the pottage," and the other for "the price;" yet Esau did get the pottage, and Judas got the price; he had the silver; he got the "cash in hand." But the terms of some who are sold under sin, and sold to Satan, are not for "cash only," it is all trust. And they promise to give: to give pelf, to give pleasure, to give pomp, to promote to honour. But the promise has never been performed; the pottage has never been prepared; the price has never been paid. "He would fain have filled his belly with the husks which the swine did eat: but no man gave to him."

" Man never *is*, but always *to be*, blest."

We are tempted to diverge for a moment to refer to the offer of "advantageous terms," coming from the college of a certain saint, to any Wesleyan Minister wishing to become a Clergyman of the Church of England. Whoever wishes to covenant for this charming change can have particulars from the Principal. He is, we opine, a perfect pattern of principle,—the principle of proselytism. In this, we suppose, he could scarcely be surpassed. But the flimsy "fly-sheet" from St. Aidan's College forcibly reminds us of puffing placards which we have seen near St. Paul's Cathedral. "Immense Reduction!" "Tremendous Sacrifice!" "A Bankrupt's Stock at less than Cost Price!" "Admitted to St. Aidan's College on advantageous terms!"

"Now the serpent was more subtle than any beast of the field." And the serpent is most subtle when he comes under the seducing form of some patron saint, or as an angel of light. For then he deceives, not the reprobates, but, if possible, the very elect. And now, my dear young brethren in the ministry, will you not be caught by this charming bait, the subtle snare of St. Aidan's? Will you not sell yourselves to this so-called saint? Will you not violate your solemn vows, cancel your church covenant, barter away your birthright, break the bonds of brotherhood, "wherein thou hast laboured from thy youth, if so be thou mayest be able to profit?" For what profit? Better bread? a richer reward? more money? higher honours? Nay, for nought. For that which does not profit, and which is not bread. The immense reduction shall be on your side, and the balance in the wrong scale. "A vanity tossed to and fro." You will exchange your birthright for a miserable "mess;" and be shorn, as silly sheep, at once, if not of your strength, yet of your status.

But, to return, how many souls is Satan daily

seducing by silver snares, by gilded baits and golden gins! And there seems to be not only a feeling among the foes, but a fear among the friends, of Zion, that the spiritual power is waning within her borders, and the secular and monetary power waxing stronger and stronger; a fear that in her balances there should be as a makeweight "the metal of merit." " Not only in John Hearn's flock and fold, but in many others, is not their god their gold? I am afraid that their case is not by any means peculiar; I am afraid that we are all sadly given to worship wealth,—I mean as a people. Of course there are thousands among us who can and do estimate us by what they believe to be our real intrinsic worth, and not by the establishment we keep up, or by the vast amount of Income-Tax we are reluctantly compelled to pay to Her Majesty's Government. Still, without doubt, one of the great and increasing sins of the age is this money-worship, which estimates a man not at his true moral and intellectual worth, but at his £. s. d. account at the banker's; and the British nation, like Nebuchadnezzar of old, glories in its golden idol which it has set up on 'Change, in the market-place, on the social hearth, and, alas! in the sanctuary itself; and 'at the sound of cornet, flute, harp, sackbut, psaltery, dulcimer, and all kinds of music,' or without any music at all, old and young, rich and poor, the Church and the world, Nonconformists and

Episcopalians, are all equally ready to worship it, lest they fall under the malediction of that arbitrary and mysterious thing, commonly known as 'public opinion.' For, to be under the ban of society is to some people almost as bad as being cast into a fiery furnace seven times heated." And is there not a profound moral in Hood's witty poem, which many Christian professors of our day may profitably ponder? We mean " Miss Kilmansegg and her precious Leg." Let us quote a verse.

> " The very metal of merit they told,
> And praised her for being as ' good as gold,'
> Till she grew like a peacock haughty;
> Of money they talk'd the whole day round,
> And weigh'd desert, like grapes, by the pound,
> Till she had an idea, from the very sound,
> That people with *naught* were *naughty*."

One of the grandest triumphs of the grace of God is seen in those who, when riches increase, set not their heart upon them ; in those in whom there is no sordid selfishness, no supposed superiority, no vain show, no empty parade, no expectation of homage, no exaction of supreme deference to their opinion, no connivance at sin, no conformity to the world, no idol-worship. But how few did Wesley find, through his long life-time, who, when they rose to riches, retained their religion, and rose with Christ !

CHAPTER IV.

WE may refer, farther, to several points of danger from mere monetary influence, leaving abler pens to portray them more fully, or to show that our fears are groundless. Are we not in danger of *laxity of discipline,* and of *viewing moral and religious character through the medium of monetary givings?*

Meeting in Class with us constitutes Church membership. The ticket is the token. At least so it *was.* But is it not now notorious that many who seldom or never meet in Class receive the token,—have their tickets taken to them? They are not always sick, or always distant, or always at business; but they are always or almost always absent. If they take a ticket for a tea party, or a ticket for a lecture, or a ticket for a concert, they can go. But they can have a Class ticket, and yet not come to the Class. They " with one consent begin to make excuse."

What a puzzle and a pain these nominal professors are to all parties concerned,—men who have, as one candidly said, " just religion enough to make them miserable;" who receive a Church token without Church communion! That Class ticket, or Church token, once so highly prized, has a chosen portion of God's truth upon it, and also the *name* of the nominal member, and the initials of the Minister. This is the solemn *sign* so attested. Where or what is the thing signified? Examine the Class books for many months, and many quarters past, yea, perhaps, "for many long rebellious years," and what see you? "Absent: Absent: Absent." Blank: Blank: Blank, —from beginning to end.

Here our system of "numbering the people," and taking the average amounts to be paid to divers funds, if it have its advantages, has, unquestionably, its dangers and delusions too. One of the weightiest words of warning, as to the future of Methodism, given by the faithful and "able historian of our Churches," is thus stated:—"One thing is certain, that in the system of *averages* we have gone quite far enough." For Leaders, and perhaps Ministers too, having to make up their amounts and averages, are tempted the more to strive to keep enrolled on the Class book those who pay their money, which is so absolutely required, although not walking quite worthy of their vocation; whilst others who cannot pay, or cannot pay so much, though walking, it may be, more worthily, some Leaders have a strong propensity to drop, or not to re-enter in their books;

considering them, perhaps, as not worth keeping, for they " pay little or nothing to the cause." *Sheep* may possibly thus be left out, whilst *goats* may be kept in.

Let not, then, this word of warning concerning the system of averages, given by one who has well and valiantly fought our battles, pass unheeded by the financiers of our body. Here, without doubt, there is danger; danger lest matters of higher moment should yield to monetary claims; danger of discipline growing lax ; danger of contributions being considered, instead of character; danger lest, whilst taking tithe of mint or money, weightier matters should be merged or minified ; danger lest we " have respect to persons," and so " commit sin ; " danger of losing the poor, whilst we keep the rich; danger lest, whilst gold and silver are pressed in, godly sincerity should be pressed out; danger thus of dearth, and decline, and death ; danger of having dead men's bones, instead of living souls; danger of having mere names, instead of new creations; danger of having splendid tombs, instead of spiritual temples ; danger of having a church organization, and monetary claims, in which " rich men shall be a necessity," and then, if our Founder was right, our doom is sealed; danger of our striving together and contending earnestly for the funds rather than for the faith, and so by our multifarious monetary matters,

II

calls, and claims, cooling down to a Christianity " at ease " in its spiritualism rather than "in earnest;" and so by stealthy and unsuspected degrees making Methodism, instead of " Christianity in earnest," and the means of life to others, a vast monetary machinery, and a magnificent mausoleum.

And, meanwhile, is there not danger with us as Ministers? Danger there has always been, but danger, we mean, in proportion to the pressing claims which Ministers have to make for money;—danger of soothing our consciences, softening our speech, and smoothing our tongues. Is there not danger of healing slightly? danger of healing before we have probed the spiritual sore? danger of daubing with untempered mortar? danger lest we "bear them which are evil," and sanction as members with us those who are of the synagogue of Satan? danger of dealing, in some sort and degree, in indulgences? Is there not a danger lest we look through the medium of money upon the negligences, the follies, or even the sins of these nominal members? Shall we practically lower the standard which our sainted Founder set up? Are worldly diversions, dancing, and divers kinds of dissipation, less worldly because wealth is offered at the shrine of a jealous God? Shall we sacrifice to idols?

But what shall be done with merely nominal members? Many, we know, shrink from the Class-meeting, who are as worthy of a place in the Church as those who are regular in their attendance. And many, perhaps, as conscientiously stay away, as some do conscientiously go. They know that they do not walk worthy of so high a vocation. We must rather respect those who shrink away from the semblance of hypocrisy, than those who, influenced by sinister motives, wear the livery of the court of heaven to serve the devil in. We respectfully but earnestly put it to the prudent and powerful among us whether it would not be far better either more strictly to enforce, or else a little to modify, the rule as to the meeting in Class. Let us not keep up the strange anomaly of giving a token of membership to those who, according to our rules, as they now stand, are not members, and yet whom it would be perilous, perhaps, in more respects than one, to "drop." If these *must* have a piece of paper from a pastor at the end of the quarter, let it be a blank, as blank, at least, as the columns of the Class-book opposite their names. Let us not have three witnesses to attest an anomaly, a falsity. Or, let us have some sign which would serve as a scale to signify the rate of attendance, and which would be in some harmony with the thing signified, similar to those given to Sabbath scholars for their good attendance. But though we thus speak somewhat as Elijah, when he said, " Cry aloud, for he is a god : he is in a journey, or peradventure he sleepeth, and must be awaked;" yet we are serious on this grave and solemn subject.*

We certainly may have, and ought to have, a large class of *communicants*, amongst whom may be properly and consistently comprised many of those who, according to our rules, as they now stand, are improperly and inconsistently called "members," and are quite an anomaly. Very many others may be included among these communicants, who as yet are not disposed to meet in Class, yet who are equally worthy with many of those who do, or at least are *said* to, meet, and whose Methodism consists chiefly in their being simply *called* Methodists. But are not many others, too, found worthy of some recognised place among us? Could not many, without any anomaly, and with incalculable advantage to themselves, and to the church, be carefully enrolled as communicants with us, and taken under general pastoral oversight? Let not these be subjected to the strictness and rigidity of our monetary system, but left to freer and fuller scope, according to their own conscience and their own way of "systematic beneficence,"—giving " as the Lord hath prospered them." These com-

---

* Would it not be better, whilst it would relieve the consciences of those concerned, to consider and enroll these simply as communicants, who, though now not meeting in Class, receive their tickets as though they did ?

municants would then have, on a wider scale, the
privilege of a means of grace, which has Christ's
express sanction and solemn command; a means of
grace which, by the eminently blessed influence that
so often pervades it, would be likely to draw them
into closer communion and church fellowship with
us; a means of confessedly Divine authority, and
about which there could be no carping, no complaints, no such exceptions taken, as are now so
common against the Class-meeting, and are weaken-
ing what were once our strongholds. This course,
with proper pastoral care, may bring converts into
the Church, and members into our Classes, by being
directly brought by this solemn ordinance into close
and immediate contact with the cross of Christ, and
led to "behold the Lamb of God" as *their* Lord and
their God. Have not many Ministers seen on these
sacred occasions eyes overflow and hearts melted?
Have they not seen evidences of the presence and
power of the Saviour, and of the unction of the Holy
One, which they have witnessed at no other times?
And for this sacred means, we have the mighty
moving power and authority in our Lord's own
express and solemn yet loving command, such
as we cannot so decidedly and definitively affirm
concerning the Class-meeting, important though
it be, and which no rules in the Class-book, no
Conference decision, can possibly give, or, we sup-

pose, wish to claim. "THIS DO in remembrance of Me." *

Should we not, with judicious care, have thus a good preparation, a safe and scriptural stepping-stone, in many cases at least, into our own form and system of Christian communion in our Class-meetings?

But be this as it may, let us not have a guilty compromise, a plain contradiction, and something like a solemn counterfeit, by continuing to give tickets to those, as members, who, whatever they may contribute to the cause of God, violate this rule of membership? "Be not deceived: God is not mocked."

Is there not danger lest modern Methodism should be modified, and should wane from its primitive power, its spiritual might, its vital and earnest simplicity, with the increasing splendour and magnificence of its temples? We are no advocates for sanctuaries in the style of secular establishments. We wish no barn-like buildings. Some of the miserable muddles called Methodist chapels have been, we think, a libel on the good taste of John Wesley as seen in the chaste style of the mother chapel at City Road. Yet Christians and Churches are prone to run to extremes. We scarcely avoid one rock before we are in danger of dashing against another. And, in

* Luke xxii. 19.

the midst of material magnificence, we must not
forget, as we may perhaps the more easily do, that
"God is a Spirit," that the dispensation under
which we worship is eminently spiritual; that whatever may be the *style* of the structure, *spiritual
worship* is that which God solemnly requires, and
which, wherever it be offered, He graciously delights
to accept. Nor must we forget, or practically ignore,
the fact,—as perhaps just now we are prone as a
people to do, in the midst of our modern grandeur of
style,—that God gave a far greater glory to the
humble "upper room" by the descent of the glorious
Spirit than Solomon's splendid temple ever saw. A
celebrated writer remarks, that "a Church will seek
to supply its declining spirituality by external
splendour, and its decaying life by more imposing
forms."

Is there not danger arising from the *motive* by
which some may be moved to seek greater splendour
and magnificence in the sanctuary? We know that
this is a very delicate and difficult question to decide,
and we would not be dogmatic. It is not for us to
judge, except by fruits. Yet it may be well, in this
as in other respects, to cherish

> " A jealous godly fear,
> A sensibility of sin,
> A pain to feel it near;"

and with godly sincerity to say,

> " I want the first approach to feel
> Of pride, or fond desire :
> To catch the wandering of my will,
> And quench the kindling fire."

We much admire many of the munificent subscribers to these our splendid modern sanctuaries. They, the "lively stones," "built up a spiritual house," are more "precious" than the lifeless structures. Many of these temples, if not lively, are lovely.

> "These temples of His grace,
> How beautiful they stand !
> The honours of our native place,
> The bulwarks of our land."

A dirty, dingy, dilapidated dwelling of God, whilst the worshippers live in style, is distasteful to the Minister, a discredit to the people, and a dishonour to God. We have had not a few of these, and we want no more. In them we have had to close our eyes to things seen, in order to say, How amiable are these tabernacles ! Yet, even in these nondescript, obsolete specimens of antiquity, these marvellous medleys of style, these fantastical fabrics, God has deigned to dwell, and in these He has been worshipped in "the beauty of holiness." "Look not on his countenance, or on the height of his stature ; because I have refused him. For the Lord seeth not as man seeth; for man looketh at the outward appearance, but the Lord looketh on the heart." "Neither in this mountain, nor yet at Jerusalem," is the only sacred site where God can be worshipped. The "true worshippers" everywhere "shall worship the Father in spirit and in truth." A godly clergyman, in opposition to the high and haughty apostolical claims of some of his brethren, referring to the time when he was in the navy, says, "Methinks I now see that humble house of prayer, where for the first time I ate bread and drank wine in remembrance that Christ died for me. And if ever I felt the presence of God, it was then and there; although the place was simply a wooden frame covered with tarred canvas, and the Minister who dispensed the elements was simply a Protestant Missionary, pretending to no succession, except the succession of faith and love and holy zeal. The only succession," he adds, "that can pass current in heaven, or avail to any good purpose upon earth. And from that time to the present I have been led to say,

'Jesus, where'er Thy people meet,
   There they behold a mercy-seat;
Where'er they seek Thee, Thou art found,
   And every place is hallowed ground.'"

Scorn as ye will, ye simple ones, those old stuccoed sanctuaries, and those old barn-like buildings, the

old women with their old bonnets, and the old men
with hoary heads as their crowns of glory; yet there
were "times of refreshing" there, heavenly influences
were shed there, which made them "heavenly places;"
influences which thrilled through the hearts of pastors
and people; influences from heaven, which attracted
the soul thitherward, far away from things seen, and
which absorbed those spiritual worshippers in the one
great, glorious, realizing idea, "Lo, God is here!"
The Lamb was their light and their sun. They were
bright in effulgence Divine : and they were "warmed"
with "live coals from off the altar." There was
something around and about them after the pattern
of the heavenly. For "God glorified the house of
His glory, and made the place of His feet glorious."

There was one which Wesley opened at early dawn,
and oil was poured upon the top of the pillar; and
surely God was in that place. And there was the
one in which Watson's eloquence soared, and where
Clarke read and gave the sense, and Benson was so
thrilling, and Bunting so lucid in preaching and so
mighty and overwhelming in prayer. And there was
the "sunny corner," where the heart of "old Glory"
glowed within him, and whence the hearty "amen"
arose, with the ardent aspiration of the soul, entering all ears, and striking many hearts, and where
"Bless the Lord" broke out without a book. And
"John sang" on in his "heart," though "out

of tune." And "Come, Holy Ghost," couldn't wait
for the chant; and the "celestial Dove," the "Source
of the old prophetic fire," came; and "Praise the
Lord" sat not very silent on their tongues; and
"Hallelujah" came off before the close of the service and the end of the chorus. For "the King
himself" came near, and the shout of a King was
heard in the camp. They sat under His shadow with
delight, and His fruit was sweet to their taste.
They sat in heavenly places in Christ Jesus.

And now let the beautiful Gothic structures, with
the Gothic worshippers, of modern times, surpass
these "glorious scenes," and match in their mighty
power the Methodism of the past, or at least emulate
its glowing worship. Instead of these humble but
earnest devotions, have we not in some, it may be
many, places mere formal worshippers, with their
perfect propriety in repose,—the decorum of death;
with the beautiful liturgy, and the semitoned service;
the skilful choir, composed of gay young men and
giggling girls; the fine toned organ, with the frequent fingering of note-books during prayer; stealthy
whispers, self-complacent smiles, all *preparing to rise
and lead the devotions of the congregation* in singing
to the praise and glory of God? And then, perchance,
as a *finale,* comes the exclamation, "O, what a sermon! What a pretty piece of poetry! What a fine
peroration! What an effect! Quite dramatic!"

The congregation have doubtless there heard of heaven and of the living way: for Christ must be preached there. But if they have not learned that way, or if, amid the splendours of the sanctuary, the grandeur of its forms, the punctilios and proprieties of worship, and all that was sublime and beautiful, they have lost sight of the simple saving plan, and the good old way, may not their vagrant thoughts, as they leave the sanctuary, be recalled by looking—as certain Church people, not to say Roman Catholics, do—on some form of a cross, be it wood or metal, or on the soaring spire affixed to the front of the elegant edifice, which, like a long "stony finger," points them to the skies.

Tell us, ye sainted fathers and brethren who have passed away to the skies, and who from your "lofty seats" may now look down upon us in these our "lower courts," and, if possible, would mourn with us over minished numbers, tell us the secret of your mighty and matchless strength. Tell us how you gained that "power from on high." But stop: we have not only Moses and the Prophets, but Christ and the Apostles, and also the lives of those earlier labourers in that vineyard once so fruitful. And we may read the words of the faithful Promiser: "Whatsoever ye shall ask the Father in My name, He will give it you;" and call to mind the gracious admonition: "Ye have not because ye ask not; or ye

ask, and receive not, because ye ask amiss." Was it
then, after the prayers were over, after the sermon
was preached, after the day's duty was done, that ye
sang?—

"My company before is gone,
And I am left alone with Thee:
With Thee all night I mean to stay,
And wrestle till the break of day.

In vain Thou strugglest to get free,
I never will unloose my hold!
Art Thou the Man that died for me?
The secret of Thy love unfold:
Wrestling, I will not let Thee go,
Till I Thy Name, Thy Nature know."

CHAPTER V.

It must be gratefully admitted that, whether in majestic magnificence or mendicant meanness, man may worship God in spirit and in truth. Yet it is surely worth while for those who are so fond of expensive elaboration, " outward adorning, and costly array," whether it be about " themselves " or their establishment, or the place where they worship, to ask, " What is my ruling motive? What is my true object and aim?" "O," say some, "I cannot worship God in such a place! God ought to have a better house." In this statement there may be two words for man and one for God. There may be more in the " cannot " than in the " ought." There may be more for man's honour than for the glorification of God. " The heart is deceitful." At any rate most of us know from observation, if not from experience, that man is a very fussy, showy little creature. " Man walketh in a vain show." Although so many godfathers and godmothers have promised on his behalf that he should renounce the pomps and vanities of this wicked world, yet, alas! how many failures have there been in the performance of these promises! "Simplicity," Dr. Johnson said, "is the order of God, and is impressed on His works." But it is the aim of erring man to depart from this order.

This seems to be an age for great things, grand doings, and gorgeous display. In business there are bewildering speculation and maddening competition. Men make breathless "haste to get rich." Each strives to outvie the other, not simply in practical business, but in pretentious and pompous display; in splendid and ruinous extravagance, and mere tinselled grandeur. Each strives to have the most splendid shop, the widest window, the most extensive establishment, the handsomest horse, the finest carriage; to make the fairest show in the flesh; to blow, it may be, the most brilliant bubbles, blinding an enlightened public, which loves to gaze upon them till they burst in their eyes. There must be a luxurious table, a magnificent mansion, "a palace of a place," before the cost of building is counted, before it is well considered whether it will be *within*, or *without*, and far *beyond* the means, or not.

In too many instances all this worldliness comes under the solemn sanction of the Christian name. A kind of working capital is made of the Christian profession. Worldly gain is made *pro tem.* of the name and form of godliness; until the true character

comes out, credit is gone, the terrible collapse and
crash take place, scattering consternation among
creditors, bringing ruin and regret, shame and sorrow, to the wretched insolvent, and inflicting incalculable mischief and almost irrecoverable damage
upon the Church of the living God, under whose
shadow the cheat and corruption had taken place.
" How men blow great bubbles, and God bursts
them with the slightest touch !" What a series of
disastrous failures, little less than death-blows to
some Societies, have our Churches struggled and
staggered under, during the last few years ! How
many could we calculate, that have occurred within
a small compass and in a short time ! Failures
which have made foes scoff and blaspheme; failures
which have made friends hide their diminished heads ;
failures which have been a foul blot on the Christian
name, and have swept like a dark and fearful blight
over the Church ; failures which, like a cloud of
locusts, have consumed the fruits of past years of
faithful preaching and pastoral labour, and will
doubtless paralyse the efforts and energies of years to
come.

If this insatiable avarice, this eagerly grasping
worldliness, this craving covetousness, this grave-like
cry, " Give, give," be found among a few leading
men, or *the* leading man, in a Church, they become
something like scarecrows in the garden of the Lord,

which do not frighten the birds of prey, but scare
away those that should "fly as a cloud and as doves
to their windows." They are as an "abomination of
desolation in the holy place;" and the minister is as
"one that beateth the air." "One sinner destroyeth
much good." Who can tell to what extent Zion has
languished, and bowed her head as in widowed desolation, while ministers have had to mourn over
minished numbers and religious retrogression on
these accounts? If Christian professors did not take
up goods without a fair probability of paying for
them, if men did not launch out beyond what their
capital will command, "beyond their capacity of
mind, and beyond the bounds of prudence," how
vastly different might be the state of spiritual things
among us! Then we should be spared some of those
taunts, "We would rather do business with those
who make no profession at all;"—"If a man makes
a profession of religion, I keep a sharper look out in
business matters:"—and these rebukes proclaimed
not by the malignant tongues of worldly men only,
but uttered with shame and sorrow by Christian-
minded professors themselves. Let not any to whom
such strictures may apply, any who have deserted
Christ and damaged the Church, because, like Demas,
they have loved the present world, think that Ministers
are disposed to be harsh in word or deed towards them.
It is often to them a matter of great grief and bitter

regret, and they " tell them weeping." " Count them
not enemies because they tell you the truth ; " but
remember, that " faithful are the wounds of a friend."
Men will strive to stem or turn the torrent which
threatens to inundate them. They will set bounds
by the sea wall to the overflowings of the surging
tide which would steal away their land. They will
skilfully and strongly bank up the mighty reservoir
whose waters, when under due restraint, are almost
the life of the peopled parishes around, but which,
alas! if there be some secret break in the embank-
ment, seem surcharged with an awful mission of
wholesale death; swollen waters which with one
terrific slaughterous sweep carry with them dreadful
desolation into hundreds of happy homes, and bury
both old and young, rich and poor, the carking
worldling and the careless spendthrift, the prayerful
and the profane, the father and his family, the
buoyant son and the bending sire, the sweetly
slumbering child and the startled shrieking mother,
in one wide watery ruin. O, had they but known
what hour of the night that wasting flood would
have broken from its bounds, would they not have
watched? Yet how slow are men to set timely
bounds to that treacherous torrent, that desolating
tide of worldliness, whose fatal flow, when it has been
suffered to gain strength, has broken through all
restraints, overleaped the most sacred barriers, and

drowned myriads of "men in perdition!" How many a worldling lingers, like Lot's wife, till it is too late, and sudden destruction comes!

Let us, then, ask, Is the spiritual tide flowing from the Church into the world around us? or is the temporal tide, a fatal flood of worldliness, in some form or other, flowing from the world into the Church? Is the Church saving the world, or the world secularizing the Church? Is the Church giving the light of the glory of God to this dark world? or is it gathering to itself the gaudy splendour of the kingdoms of this world and the glory of them?

Let us ask ourselves, Is modern Methodism moulding, as it once did so mightily, the men of the world after its own type? or is it being modified in any way, and moulded by worldly men? Is our own Church being changed more fully into the image of Him who created it? Is it waking up after the likeness of God? or, with its wealth, is it forming itself more after the fashion of this world? There are great things, grand doings, mighty movements, in the Methodism of modern times. There have been some signal instances, of late, in which worldly ways have been adopted in connexion with schools, and schemes to raise money for sacred objects: and they have met with a well-merited rebuke. There has been sometimes a great flourish of trumpets about little matters, which has reminded us of

> " The ocean into tempest wrought
> To waft a feather, or to drown a fly."

The country has lately been visited with the great Shakspearean sensation, and has been edified with a sermon from lawn sleeves in solemnization of the ceremony; the religious part of it ending in that sublime climax of an actor's devotion, that graceless prayer before meat, that the spirit of Shakspeare might rest upon the meeting! An utterance which ought to have been " positively the last " farce in that serio-comic scene. Surely this was blowing a most brilliant bubble; one, too, that has burst in a way which signally illustrates the Eastern fable of the elephant that was marched a mile in gay trappings to pick up a pin! Whilst there is much that is truly good and great in the onward march of things around us, yet with regard to many of these grand movements, when the sensation is passed, when the scene is closed, when the curtain drops, and the transient splendour has gleamed away like the crackling of thorns under a pot, or as the fading flash of a falling rocket that comes down in such a contrast of style with the way in which it went up, leaving things more gloomy than they were before; we are ready at the end to ask, " What went ye out for to see ? "

Splendour, and not *simplicity*, seems to be the order of the day. *Grandeur* is sought rather than *grace.* Many wish to enter the kingdom of God, not as little children, but as great men, if not as little gods. Like the aspiring Baruch, they seek *great* things for themselves. As the proud Naaman, they would do "some great thing" rather than as lepers simply wash and be clean ; something that would minister to pride rather than mortify it. Some new thing is sought rather than the good old way, some wandering star, or flashing meteor, to dazzle, rather than the steady shining light, to guide them into the way of peace. And if, as Methodists and Ministers of Christ, we have a right to look for spiritual results, on a scale corresponding with the magnificence of the means employed within the last few years, thén is not our hope cut off? And are we not led to ask, "What went ye out for to see?"

We have had a long list of chapels erected, of elegant design, of noble structure, with commanding front, and some with costly decorations, with tower-ing turrets or lofty steeples, as though they were meant to rival the churches of our land. We have had long advertisements, a splendid programme, a series of sacred services from men of superior talent, who have come from afar. There have been crowded congregations, good sermons, large collections. Every thing has gone off well. Every body has seemed more than pleased, even proud of the whole affair, which was

pronounced "a grand success." A cheering report
has been recorded; and yet, when the whole has
been wound up, in full many instances, we have
scarcely heard whether there was any Holy Ghost,
whether the Lord was among them, or not. And if,
on such great occasions, we had a right to look for
spiritual results, for souls saved, then our hope has
been cut off, and we have been ready to ask, "What
went ye out for to see?" Fervent and faithful
Ministers were there; earnest and eloquent sermons
were preached; Christ crucified was set forth: but if
other thoughts than those of Christ and things Divine
filled up the "foolish heart," and choked the good
seed,—if there was little or no fervent prayer to pre-
cede the service, no present faith in Christ; then,
had Christ in the flesh been there, many mighty
works would not have been wrought by Him. And
yet these were great days. It is possible, if not probable, that on these occasions God was, if not lost
sight of, but dimly seen by the dazzled assembly. It
is possible that the great truth, "Not by might,
nor by power, but by My Spirit, saith the Lord of
Hosts," was utterly forgotten. It is possible that
thoughts about men and means and magnificence
were revolving and mingling in the mind from early
morning till the midnight hour. And though all
these thoughts were about God's house, yet *God's
house* is not *God Himself.* And the means of grace,

or the servants of God, are not greater than their
Lord, and should never cloud our vision of Him.
Means are not *the end*, and must not intercept
between the soul and God, or dim the mental eye
which sees the King invisible.

> " Whatever passes as a cloud between
> The mental eye of faith and things unseen,
> Causing that brighter world to disappear,
> Or seem less lovely, and its hope less dear ;
> This is our world, our idol, though it bear
> Affection's impress, or devotion's air."

There have been, thank God! cheering spiritual
results on some of these great occasions.   Some souls
have been saved from death, some signs have followed ; but, alas! how few and far between !

CHAPTER VI.

WHY and wherefore the contrast? What author among us will take up his pen, and write well on this subject, and solve this problem? Little that has been satisfactory to the mind or safe for the conscience of Christians and Christian Ministers has, we think, yet been written upon it. "Has the old rod lost its conjuring power?" Has the old sword of the Spirit, once so mightily wielded, and so wont in our fathers' days to strike dismay down to the depths of the deceitful heart, dividing asunder soul and spirit, become blunted? Has it lost its massive might, its piercing power? Cannot it now wound and kill?

How is it that the reporters of chapel openings have not to dip their pen again in the ink, and to superadd, to their pleasing account of services and subscriptions, so many sinners startled from their deadly sleep, so many souls saved from death, so many added to the Church, as well as so much money collected for the chapel? Why is it that we never witness now, or only at rare intervals and with doubtful resemblance, any reproduction of the scene of

Pentecost? Why is it that we never hear of thousands converted by a single sermon, of the simultaneous movement of souls stirred and swept together, as the multitudinous waves of the sea, by the same wind of heaven? Oft in olden times there has been a simple unlettered man, destitute of intellectual culture or rhetorical art, by whose words—wherever he went, in hamlet, town, or city—the hearts of men were strangely stirred. Masses and multitudes felt "the soul-converting power." In our day our ablest and most cultivated minds, after long and laborious training, armed with all that learning, eloquence, and dialectic skill can lend to human lips, will, in too many cases, fail, throughout the course of a long ministry, to elicit any such marked authentication of their teaching.*

And are Methodists, who are the gracious fruit of "the Great Revival" more than a century ago, and whose great revivals have been their glorious proverb of reproach,—are they about to settle down into a sedate frame of mind and a self-satisfied state, into an exclusive and expensive establishment, worshipping God in splendid sanctuaries, amid frigid formalities, cold ceremonials, and decorous proprieties, whilst " souls still are perishing and need to be saved," and still the world is slumbering in sin, and has need to be startled as with thunder-tones from its fatal sleep? Are we about to have magni-

* "Good Words."

ficent chapels as a sort of adjunct to the warehouses
of large mercantile firms? one building in which
business shall be most diligently done, and another in
which *worship* shall be most properly "performed?"
Are we about to rest in great means without seeing
the grand end? Whilst our means and agencies are
multiplying, ministers multiplying, chapels and congregations multiplying, gold and silver multiplying,
shall *members* be diminishing? Shall these splendid
sanctuaries be as painted sepulchres, burying-places,
the places of the dead, rather than the birthplace of
souls? May not advancing architectural adornments
among us lead to architectural adoration, and
material splendour be regarded with a sort of religious reverence, and usurp the place of a spiritual
God? Is there not danger lest the style of the
sanctuary be thought of rather than the unseen
Spirit that dwells there? danger lest the chapel
should be so magnified in the mind that it shall be
considered as "the Church," and senseless stones be
substituted for spiritual structures? And does not,
in some instances at least, our great chapel-adorning
seem to claim a religious adoration?

Do not our chapel *decorations* already absorb a
vast amount of attention, fill up a great space in the
records of our proceedings, and withal involve an
excessive outlay of money which might be better
employed for the Great Proprietor? Let the reader

peruse the lengthened reports of some of our chapels, built in the style of the decorated Gothic of the thirteenth century; let him mark their minute details, and note the mighty absorption claimed by their architectural adornments; and he may well imagine himself to be on his way to St. Paul's or St. Peter's; or to be carried backwards to some shadow of Solomon's temple. Shaking off the illusive dream, he will rise with a conviction that our excellent architects hold us in leading strings, and that we are following them whithersoever they will.

We may read of a *cruciform* plan; of *choir stalls* on each side of the nave beyond the transepts; of a pulpit in the centre of the nave, in front of the chancel screen; of carved capitals lighted by a trefoiled arcade; of a highly enriched doorway, richly carved cornice from which springs a spirelet; of carved finials, and *a cross*, graceful carved figures, noble tracery, and *finely toned colours* of the windows; marble columns supporting the roof of the chancel, the elegant organ screen, the elaborately carved pulpit in pure Caen stone, with the communion table and fittings, which produce a rich chastened effect which is very rarely attained. "All the fittings of the building are in harmony with the general design." *

Again, we are informed that the pulpit is quadrangular in form, and skilfully carved in the early

* "Chapel Report," 1863, p. 99.

French style. The communion is enclosed by a railing of polished and carved oak, resting on nine supports of elegant design. The communion table is covered with a cloth of rich velvet. The communion linen is of rich damask. And what may be named last, though not least, we read of " crocketts on each angle, and terminated by a carved finial, from which rises a *wrought metal cross*. The height from the ground to the top of the cross is ninety-three feet." The cross to which Mary clung, we suppose, was not quite so high. The total outlay, exclusive of land, is about £10,000.*

There may be things, in this mere extract, which are very right and proper; but, as a whole, does it not savour of the sensuous, and tend towards the sensuous rather than the spiritual? What a striking contrast does such a report offer to the sublime spectacle presented before us in the simple record of St. John!† There we see the great Architect, the "great Builder of the Church below," sitting

---

* "Chapel Report," 1863, p. 101. The total expenditure, the same year, of the great Home Mission and Contingent Fund—comprising grants for ordinaries and extraordinaries, grants for Supernumeraries and widows, grants to Ireland and Welsh Ministers, grants for Aldershot, Chatham, Shorncliffe, Portsmouth, and Zetland Missions, and the entire expense of FIFTY-THREE Home Missionary Ministers—amounts to only about double the outlay for ONE such chapel,—£20,997. 18s.—" Home Mission Report, 1863," p. 80. Such is the consistency of our Connexional givings. Thus do we lavish on the superfluous, and neglect the necessitous.

† John iv. 6.

unsheltered "on Jacob's well," speaking or preaching to the Samaritan woman, spiritualizing the water
of which she drank : and—as though to sweep away
every sacred relic of the worldly sanctuary, and all
those carnal notions which so fondly and so closely
cling to sacred mediums and sacred places of worship
—after teaching that "neither on this mountain nor
yet at Jerusalem is the place where men ought to
worship," our Lord places at the very antipodes of
all that is carnal, earthy, material, sensuous, in worship, that short sublime sentence of rebuke : "God is
a Spirit: and they that worship Him must worship
Him in spirit and in truth."

Within the memory of some who are not very old,
Methodists would have marvelled to have seen any
cross in connexion with our chapels, save that which
many have heard so eloquently proclaimed, as the
only object of glorying, by the musical and majestic
voice of one of our noble fathers who now rests from
his labours, but who, being dead, yet speaketh.
How did he denounce the exhibition of any material
cross, whether of moulded or wrought metal ! If the
sight of any cross, save that which faith sees, would
administer any aid to the infirmities of the worshipper
in public, may it not also in private? If so, it may
possibly find its way before long, with advancing
externalism, into the houses, the closets, and the
Classes of some of the people called Methodists.

In the case of sentient beings, who look at things seen with eyes of flesh, and test that which is tangible by the touch, it is no matter of marvel that the carnal should have the ascendancy over the spiritual, and the things of the flesh over those of the Spirit. A trustless Thomas may want to thrust a finger into the nail prints, to aid his faith; and he may require to probe with a hand of flesh, rather than of faith, the riven side of his risen Lord, to help his own doubting heart to believe: but we must not forget that "rather blessed are they that have not seen, and yet have believed."

Faith never lends so fully "its realizing light," never so clearly sees the Invisible,—never so sensibly surveys "the wondrous cross on which the Prince of Glory died," never so blessedly beholds the Lamb of God, as when the mortal eyes are quite closed to the things which are seen.

If Peter, when he proposed, in his sublime transport on the Mount, to build three tabernacles for those celestial visitants,—Moses, Elias, and Christ,— had been furnished with a Divine pattern, which should serve as a specimen of a style of sanctuary suited to the new and spiritual dispensation,—as Moses on Mount Sinai had been shown a pattern of the tabernacle of old,—and as a model of a future St. Peter's at Rome, and also of all church structures for spiritual worship to the end of time, we doubt

much whether any pattern on so grand a scale as
some now reported would have been presented, for
the true worshippers, by Him who did not abhor the
Virgin's womb, who was born in a stable, cradled in
a manger, grew up in the cottage of a carpenter,
wandered in a wilderness; who came lowly riding
upon an ass; who sat with publicans and sinners;
who mingled with the common people; who washed
the feet of His disciples; who preached the Gospel
to the poor; who humbled Himself to the death of
the cross, and was laid low in the grave; and who,
when God had highly exalted Him, sent down His
glorious Spirit into an humble upper room; thus
holding in supreme scorn all semblance and show of
tinselled earthly splendour, and thus writing, in
large, legible, and life-like letters, on His own royal
banner, as the glorious Prince of a spiritual Israel,
" My kingdom is not of this world." One would
like to know, if it were possible, from any portion
of the New Testament, now that the carnal ordinances and worldly sanctuary, the glorious temple and
material magnificence of the old dispensation, have
passed away, how far these " neatly carved corbels,"
" gracefully carved figures," " skilfully carved French
style pulpit," " finely-toned colours," with all the
other things that " are dealt with in similar style,"
" all combining to produce so rich and rarely attained
an effect,"—to say nothing of the wrought metal

cross lifted up ninety-three feet from the ground on the outside,—delight Him who humbled Himself; how far they attract the admiration and approving smile of Him whose eyes are as a flame of fire, whose wondrous cross is designed to be the attraction of all hearts, the object of all glorying. How far? Is it right or wrong to ask this? Is it pert or pertinent to put such a question? Are these rich decorations, these elaborate and costly ornamentations, too low for the Lofty One, or too lofty for the Lowly One? Is all this church furniture, are all these things about His Father's house, the house of prayer, too grand or too grovelling? Are they too magnificent, or "too mean delights for Him?" Are they not car-nal? Are they such things as concern Christ? If a spiritual God sees these splendours of style from the cloud of His own glory, does He smile upon them? If the cry of a raven and the fall of a spar-row, if the hairs of the head and the cup of cold water given to a prophet or a disciple, if the sighs and tears of the lowest and the least of His people, are all noticed by our Heavenly Father, then that which is so great and grand, so rich and rare in the Father's house, cannot be quite lost sight of; and, viewed in connexion with the motive which has thus arrayed them in their glory, they must have, as good or evil, either God's smile or His scorn. Which is it? Who will tell? What is the object and aim?

When other houses have to be furnished and ornamented, how carefully and considerately is the taste of the parties concerned consulted! And if, whether we eat, or whether we drink, or whatsoever we do, we are to do all to the glory of God, then it would seem right and reverent to ask, What would most please God? What is most likely to suit the taste, and harmonize with the mind and will, of that God who is a Spirit? Do these things strongly savour of the things that be of a spiritual God? Are we minding in them the things of the Spirit, or the things of the flesh,—the lust of the eye and the pride of life? Are they things that taste of the powers of the world to come, or of the power of the world present? What answer does the conscience give? Is it, "That in simplicity and godly sincerity, not with fleshly wisdom, but by the grace of God, we have our conversation in the world?"

> " I want the witness, Lord,
> That all I do is right,
> According to Thy will and word,
> Well pleasing in Thy sight."

O, could we know how much more sunny the Saviour's smile would be upon those who had built and beautified so splendid a sanctuary, than if it had been simply chaste and commodious! Could we divine how much richer the tokens of His grace would be, that should rest on those who have so richly adorned His house, than if the costliness of its charms had flowed into other channels where claims are urgent, where chapels are few and far between, where His people are in pinching poverty, where Pastors, too, have pressing claims with a scanty stipend,—smaller, perhaps, than the salary of the single young governess in the Day school,—where supplies, though not quite stopped, are scant and stinted; where there is no stalled ox, but the dinner of herbs; where pining sickness is wasting away the life of some loved one, and the nurse and the physician's bill must be paid; where large demands are made upon little means; and from whence shortly that Pastor will come to the annual gathering at the District Meeting, with the poignant pangs of bereavement, and whilst the wounds of a bleeding heart are yet fresh, to plead for a few pounds to meet in a small measure the expenses of " protracted family affliction," or for " fatal family affliction," and, alas! towards "the funeral expenses" of that loved child, or for the sympathetic sharer of his chequered lot; where he has to plead for a paltry sum in the presence of those princes who,—although they have kindly given their one pound to the Worn Out Ministers' Fund, or to the Contingent Fund, which is intended to comfort the distressed, solace the sick, to minister to the suffering and sorrowing, and in so doing to minister to the Saviour Himself,—

have given perhaps from £100 to £1000 towards, not the erection simply, but the expensive elaboration and adorning of a chapel, with its "costly carved capitals," its "gracefully carved figures," and "finely toned colours;" whilst the morning flowers, whose silken leaves, sweeter than the virgin rose, have faded, and the graceful form, whose "human face Divine" but lately bloomed in the pride of its beauty, and in colours fairer than spring, has been blanched and chilled in death:—

> "Or worn by slowly rolling years,
>   Or broke by sickness in a day,
>   The fading glory disappears,
>   The short-lived beauties die away;"—

and those short-lived beauties, so sacred and so dear, as the desire of the tearful eye that gazed upon them, had far less perhaps to preserve them from fading, and to prolong their short and dying life, than was expended upon "the finely toned colours" of the chapel window, (which could admit nothing finer than the homogeneous light of heaven,) or on "the gracefully carved figures" of cold Caen stone!

There are instances among some Churches, it is credibly said, in which Charity seems to be stranger still and more contradictory in its exercise, as though it had become cold, benumbed, paralysed, and almost petrified on one side, by coming so much in contact with stone. It seems to be past feeling, except it be brought against some marble column, or carved figure of stone; or if it have light aud heat and motion, it seems subject to fits and starts, and strange phantasies, as though it had St. Vitus's dance, or was afflicted with spasmodic action. It will impulsively stretch forth a large and liberal hand to rear a turret, raise a spire, colour a window, adorn a church or chapel; but will suddenly draw it back from a brother in need. It is almost stoue-blind to the scene of suffering, stone-deaf to the tale of woe, to the widow's and the orphan's cry. It cannot stoop, like the Good Samaritan, to heal the wounds of those who have been left weltering in their blood; and can scarcely give more than the cup of cold water, or more than the cheap, "Be ye warmed," to the disciple of Christ.

It has been often said that for every sovereign given on behalf of Foreign Missions, a soul has been gained from heathendom. It may be doubted whether there has been success on such a scale as this; yet, supposing the statement to be approximately correct, it goes to prove that there has been prosperity in the foreign field greatly proportionate with the Christian benevolence of the Churches at home. Means have been multiplied, and cheering results have followed. Seed has been sown over a wider space of the arid moral waste, and shcaves have been gathered.

We know sovereigns must not be put in the same scales as deathless souls :—

" Heap worlds on worlds, one soul outweighs them all : "—

but if the cost of the means may be counted in the one case, may it not be considered also, in some degree, in the other ?

How many more sovereigns would it take, then, at the rate we are now going on, to save a soul from the heathendom of home, and the barbarism of our modern Babylon, than from idolatry in the Mission field ? Could the able and devoted Secretary of the Home Missions tell us ? And could the equally able and indefatigable Chapel Secretary tell us about what has been expended, within the last two or three years, in the expensive elaboration, the costly array, and showy splendour of our sanctuaries, above that which has been necessary, or which would have pro-duced structures of chaste and beautiful simplicity ?

Indeed, one seems disposed to vie and compete with another in this march of magnificence. We will assume that the great and generous givers towards the erection and expensive adorning of our chapels give from principle ; that they give as unto the Lord, as His stewards. We will assume that those who delight so much in the ornamental style, have " the ornament of a meek and quiet spirit ; " that they devoutly desire to please God, and to adorn the doctrine of Christ. If so, they will meekly receive what is kindly meant; and will not at once scold or scorn those who are chary in their estimate of the benefits of earthly splendour to those who profess to be strangers and sojourners on the earth, and who form a spiritual house.

Of course it is a maxim with the man of the world to make as much as he can of his money. He would much rather make five than three, and ten than five, *per cent.* He would rather get cash than give long credit. He is generally glad to preserve a long friendship by short reckonings and quick returns. At any rate, he likes to be as sure as he can that he shall have some returns. He does not like to do much business of doubtful profit, or to make much outlay when it is likely he will not see his money again. Some, alas! are so ensnared by seducing speculations that they have inextricable " entanglements beneath," in the shape of mining and other shares, with many calls, but no dividends. Some of these concerns partake of the financial condition and the convenient scruples of Sheridan, who, when waited upon for the interest of some money lent to him, said, " It is not my *principle* to pay *interest :*" and then, being asked for the principal, shrewdly replied, " It is not my *interest* to pay the *principal.*"

One of the most solemn questions which the servant and steward of Christ can put is, " Lord, what wilt Thou have me to do ? " Now, to this serious question the Scriptures on many points give no doubtful answer: and the nearer we keep to the *decided,* and the farther from *doubtful* matters, in religion especially, the better. That men must repent, believe, be born again, bring forth fruits meet for repentance, and prove their faith by their works,—all this is plain. That the ministry should be supported, that the " workman is worthy of his hire," that the forlorn widow and the fatherless of Christ's flock must not be forgotten, that we should have compassion on our brother in need, that we should pity the *heathen* abroad,—all this is clear. And that we are not strangely to neglect our nearest neighbours at home,—those over whom darker clouds are gathering, a more dreadful doom impending, a severer scourge threatening, than over those who perish without the law,—this is a claim which cannot be disputed.

All these duties are plain, positive, imperative. We *must* " haste to the rescue." We *must* " come to the help of the Lord." We *must* by all means strive to save those from perishing, for whom Christ died. Precept upon precept, upon these important points, is as plain as those two laws of the Ten that came down with thunder peals from the terrible mount, " Thou shalt not steal," " Thou shalt not kill."

"Lord, what wilt Thou have me to do?" Now, whilst the steward who thus asks has so many plain and pertinent answers from the Great Proprietor and

Governor on the solemn subject just stated, what we wish to know is, whether, in the excessive expenditure, the great outlay to which many seem disposed to go, both in the inward and outward adorning of our material temples, it is as plain that the servant is doing what his Lord wills. Is the steward expending his Lord's money just as his Lord wishes; so that when He who says, " Occupy till I come," shall call him to reckoning, that Lord shall have His own with the right rate of usury ; and so that, in the fiery scrutiny of "that day," the steward shall have the heaven-inspiring plaudit, " Well done, thou good and faithful servant ? " There must be no self-seeking, where God should be sought ; no self-glorying, where God alone should be glorified. No sinister motives will serve, where the eye should be single. There should be no self-satisfaction in the sanctuary, in the worship of God,—a state of mind which, as the profound Watson says, is utterly displeasing to God. There should be no defrauding God, in the midst of much money given, of the *honour* due to His name ; —no robbing God of the greater gifts and sacrifices of self, of the heart, of prayer and praise, whilst we have rendered the lesser gifts of gold and silver, of frankincense and myrrh ;—no keeping back a part of the price,—no making the chapel more of a memorial and monument for man, for Mr. A. or Mr. B., than a place of prayer, and a sanctuary for the

service of the living God. Or, though that house be
high, and that wrought metal cross be " more than a
hundred feet from the ground," and though the
towering turret and perilous pinnacle be so lifted up
that there may be nests there as high as the eagle's,
yet this house which is high, with its crosses, and
turrets, and spires, shall be " a proverb, a byeword,
and an astonishment, to every one that passeth by,"
God-forsaken, Ichabod-marked, without living glory,
and with this fearful question and answer engraven
on its costly *façade*, " Why hath the Lord done this
unto this house ? Because they forsook the Lord
God of their fathers, and laid hold on other gods,
and worshipped them, and served them. Therefore
hath He brought all this evil upon them."

Who among us does not most devoutly pray that
this day of darkness and doom Methodism may never
see ? There is no such prayer, it is true, in the
Litany, which some so much love to introduce among
us ; and if there were, comparatively few of the
Clergy, whom some seem inclined too closely to copy,
would be disposed to offer it. Whilst a few devout
and godly Clergy, some of whom we know and
greatly esteem and love, would deprecate, how very
many desire, the downfall of Methodism ! It is
reported of one Clergyman, that complaints were
made against him that he would not bury any Methodist. On hearing it, he said it was a great mistake,

for he should be glad to bury them all. But this, we think, he would find far too heavy a duty, and would hardly survive to bury the last.

Are we, then, we may again ask, in so closely con- forming to the Church style, in the architecture, the towers, the spires, and the costly decorations of our chapels, pursuing the plain path of duty, or straying into some bye-path from the good old way? Are we making a useful or a useless outlay of the Master's money? Has he who contributes largely to rear a metal cross, to raise a high tower, to put up a lofty pinnacle, which, for all practical purposes, are not worth as many pence as the hundreds of pounds expended on them, and which may be perverted, in time, to identifying us in some degree with Puseyites; —has the steward, in this excessive outlay, a plain right to expect the plaudit to be pronounced upon him, " Well done, thou good and faithful servant? "

Are applications for HOME MISSIONARIES urgently pressed? Are men and means wanting? Would it be a calamity not to meet these claims? Should all (and there are many) be met? Then, shall we con- tinue to spend large sums on lofty towers and " stony fingers," to the amount perhaps of four hundred pounds at least each?—a cost enough to support five single men, better than many young Ministers are supported, as Home Missionaries. And whilst the high tower, or the metal cross, or the lofty spire, would serve chiefly as a roost for birds of the air, these Home Missionaries, these messengers Divine, might, like their Master, be going about doing good, gathering in the outcasts, paying thousands of visits to wretched homes, to the chambers of the sick and dying, *preaching Christ*, and Him crucified, to the perishing for whom Christ died; charming the scattered stones into beauteous frames and spiritual buildings; lifting up many who are now low in the dust, and placing them as living and lasting pillars in the temple of our God, to go out no more for ever.

But suppose ten lofty towers to be raised during the year, at a cost of four hundred pounds each; then you have towered and soared away aloft in the air, in empty space, with enough of the Master's money to support FIFTY *Home Missionaries* down in this lower world. Now, whilst these ten towers or spires were standing in still and solemn grandeur, lifting their cloud-capt heads in the aërial regions, simply to be seen of men, to how many thousands of men during the year might these Ministers of Christ, our Home Missionaries, have been showing the way of salvation! How many sermons might they have preached in the cottages of the poor! How many visits of comfort might they have made to the needy, the naked, the stranger, the sick, the fatherless, and the widow! How many souls might they have saved from death! What a multitude of foul sins might have been hidden and forgotten for ever! How many trophies won to Christ! How many sparkling gems added to His royal diadem! Or, if the cost of these towers were to flow into the chapel current, how many distressed chapels might have been relieved! Ten or twelve good country chapels might be built by the cost of these ten towers, whilst substantial aid might be rendered to forty or fifty urgent cases of chapel debt. And so on in good and grand proportion. What succour might be given, were these many thousand pounds, now subscribed for superfluous splendour, given to supplement the scanty stipends of some of our Ministers who have scarcely a subsistence, whose livings make theirs but a dying life, or a daily and desperate struggle to live! What vast comfort and help might be administered to worn-out Ministers,—to weeping widows, whose tears are their meat day and night,—to fatherless children, whose noble sires early fell a sacrifice on the Missionary altar, and were early laid in a Missionary's grave in a distant land!

Which, then, of these is the better thing to do? Which the more excellent way of giving? Which calls the louder for help?—the lofty tower to be reared, or fallen men to be lifted up from their low and lost estate? Which has the stronger claim?—the senseless spire of stone, or the stony-hearted sinner? The spire, or the servant of Christ? The spire, or the salary raised? The spire, or the school supported? The spire, or the sick and suffering saint? The spire, or the half-starved Supernumerary? The spire, or the Saviour Himself? Concerning which is the righteous Judge at the last the most likely to say, "Inasmuch as ye did it unto one of these, ye did it unto Me?"

And yet there may be some who would subscribe their hundreds of pounds to these structures of stone, to an ornamental edifice, to a memorial and monumental building, who, lacking an enlightened charity, would grumble to give as many pence to meet the just and righteous claims of Ministers, Missionaries, Supernumeraries, and widows; and who would "pooh-pooh" at Mr. Prest and his pressing claims for Home Missionaries. But we appeal to candid and reasonable men, to the stewards of the Lord, to those who must shortly give an account of the outlay of that silver and gold which are the Lord's: where is the common sense, where the Christian charity, of this scale of giving?

It would seem as though, in such cases, a process of petrifaction had been going on. Instead of stones being converted to flesh, flesh has been almost converted to stone. Instead of stones being turned into Abraham's sons, Abraham's sons seem almost turned into pillars of stone.

We know there are many wise and generous subscribers, to whom such strictures would not apply; who have something like a scale of systematic and

•

proportionate giving; whose charity has a single eye, and is far from being blind, partial, or misguided in its exercise. May their number be increased tenfold; and may their spirit be caught by all who give!

"Lord, what wilt Thou have me to do?" Untold numbers of deathless souls are straying as sheep without a shepherd. O for Christ-like compassion towards them! When the clear and solemn claims of the Chief Shepherd, and of these lost sheep, are fully met; when the great commission of Christ is fully discharged, "Go ye into all the world, and preach the Gospel to every creature;" when there is no plaintive cry, "Come over and help us," without a response; no "One wanted;" no "One earnestly requested;" no "One to be sent," without the money to send him;—when all the vast wastes of heathendom have been traversed by the feet of him that bringeth good tidings; when the dismal dens of depravity, which surround us in this land of light, shall be transformed into pure and happy homes :— when all these clear calls and *imperative* claims are met, and there is money yet to spare, then, having done all the works of stern necessity, we may begin the works of supererogation. Then, when we have nothing better to do, let us begin to build high towers, and prepare to send forth from them merry peals of praise, and to set upon them waving banners as signals that the wide world is won to Christ. Then may some perhaps lift up their voices from them, to meet the great voices from heaven, saying, " The kingdoms of this world are become the kingdoms of our Lord and of His Christ."

Till then, may we not more safely wait to search out some shadow of *Scripture sanction for costly spiral structures*, and turn the silver stream of subscriptions which they require into some almost dry and deserted channel, to fill up and replenish exhausted funds ? Should we not be on our guard lest, while we are doing that which we need not do, and leaving undone the things which we ought to do, these towers prove little better than small Babels, and, instead of being memorials of our wisdom and glory, be but monuments of our folly and vanity, and end in strife, confusion, and shame ?

" Lord, what wilt Thou have me to do ? " " He that doubteth is damned if he eat, because he eateth not of faith : for whatsoever is not of faith is sin." * Let us not linger in any doubtful domain, but persevere in the plain path of positive and practical duty. Whither are we tending ? Are any among us unsuspiciously wending their way, in the time of their wealth and worldly prosperity, with an orthodox creed and the glorious · doctrines of our fathers, towards the material splendour, the meretricious

* Romans xiv. 23.

adornments, and the cold ceremonials of a carnal
Catholicism? Can it be in the course of time, that,
with our costly chapels, supported by worldly wealth
and worldly-wise men, who, as rich merchants, may
traffic with the best article in the market, and bid for
the best talent in Methodism, the Connexion shall
gradually change—without doing any damage to the
old Model Deed, and without any apparent violation
of Wesley's wise and almost prophetic provisoes—
into a splendid array of Congregational Churches?—
like some which we know, that can boast of having
no poor in them, and where the members are rich
enough to pay for the best of everything,—to pay
for prayers said and service performed by proxy.

Can it be that, step by step, stage by stage, and
stone by stone, we shall pave the way for the suc-
cessors whom we leave behind,—instead of being as
flames of fire, speaking as with fiery tongues the
living word,—to become by a petrifying process like
cold marble columns, or carved capitals,—like
" neatly carved " pillars of stone, in " finely carved "
pulpits of stone in French style, pointing, as with
fingers of stone, the people with hearts of stone to
some " skilfully carved " figures of stone, as " symbols " of the Church in her chasteness, purity, and
glory? with no breath of life ; no live coal from off
the altar ; no " thoughts that breathe," no " words
that burn ; " no heart strangely warmed, without its

seeming to be some "strange thing," and one of the "great marvels!"

Whither are we tending? To St. Aidan's? O, no. To an intoned or a full cathedral service? From reading sermons and reading prayers, to the practice of praying, if not in Latin, yet only in a prescribed form? It has been well asked whether we have not long enough done deference to the deep-rooted prejudice of Wesley in favour of the Service of the Church of England. How much more of *material* splendour, and how much less of the *spiritual*, shall be found among us? How much more of the *form*, and how much less of the *power?* How much more are the *senses* to be pleased, and how much less is the *soul* to be profited? How much of architecture and symbolism, of the pealing organ and the echoing response, filling the long-drawn aisle? Will symbolism keep the Saviour in, and the serpent out of, our sanctuaries? Where did Joseph and Mary lose their Son, but "in the temple?" *

A few days ago, we read the report of the opening of a Methodist chapel, the sum and substance of which was that the "rich tone of the organ, combined with the skill of the performer, rendered the services very attractive." We suppose *prayer* was offered, and *sermons* were preached; but these had no record. We were reminded of an announcement

* WISEMAN'S " Christ in the Wilderness."

L

said to have been made by a certain Minister, to the effeet that, on the next Sabbath evening, he shonld "consider the effect which the playing of David's harp had on the mind of Saul." We hear of some among us statedly praying that He who alone works great marvels would "send down upon our Bishops and Curates the healthful Spirit of His grace." Now, of course, Bishops and Curates need our prayers; but why should they be prayed for, in this stereotyped style, in our chapels, unless those who thus pray suppose that many of them would not be comprised in the more general phrase, "Ministers of the Gospel?"

We have heard some who, if they offered a short prayer, were sure to make use of the short sentence, "Vouchsafe, O Lord, to keep us this day without sin;" which is a very proper petition, certainly; but its constant repetition leads us to fear lest we should so closely copy the Church prayers, as to become as punctilious and stereotyped in our petitions as one of the two men that went up into the temple to pray.

CHAPTER VII.

WE have no doubt that God will shortly visit us in His mercy, and give us proofs of His love. We have begun to mourn over lessened numbers and declining spirituality. Times of Church chastening will come, as they have come aforetime. There will be a time to mourn, as well as a time to dance; a time for fast-days, as well as a time for feasts; times to pluck up, as well as to plant; to break down, as well as to build up; a time of war, and a time of peace : for to everything there is a season. And in this low and languishing spiritual state of our Zion, amid abounding worldly wealth, with silver and gold multiplied, multiplying temples, multiplying Ministers and hearers of the word, but fewer conversions to God; advanced revenues, but religious retrogression; temporal prosperity, but spiritual decline; is not this a time when it would be meet and right to weep and mourn before God? right to turn aside for a moment from the crimson cushion, the rich hassock, and the warm and comfortable "kamptulicon," and, if any sackcloth can be found, in that and in the dust to humble ourselves before God? Is not this a time to bow our faces toward the earth, and on the bended knees both of our body and of our soul, and not so much from the Prayer-book as from a penitent spirit, to confess, that "we have followed too much the devices and desires of our own hearts?"

Let us humble ourselves, and in due time, when we are low, God will lift us up. First there must be humiliation of ourselves; and then exaltation by the Lord will follow. We well remember a stern but spiritually minded Supernumerary, one of the old school, on whom it is so refreshing to gaze in our annual gatherings, a friend and fellow-labourer of the devoted Bramwell, who has often been summoned at four o'clock in the morning to engage in fervent prayer with him on behalf of the family under whose roof he was lodged, and on behalf of the Church which he so much loved and adorned. We remember in by-gone years to have been often present with this Supernumerary in prayer meetings, when the Spirit has been moving in the midst, and the arm of God has been made bare; and when during prayer, as he went to and fro among the penitents to direct them to Christ, he has seen some standing on the one side, and gently inclining one knee toward the pew or the form; and regarding this as an outward sign that the knees of the soul were not bent before God, he would shout with a stentorian voice, which was enough to startle a sinner in Zion, "Why, man, you are kneeling UP: kneel DOWN!" Alas! have there not been many among us who, when they have risen up in the world, have neglected to *kneel down* before God? We do not think the former days were better than these: we do not long for their return: we do not sigh for the times of old stage-coaches, though we confess that we like now and then to see one of them, and to think of some of the noble men among us who travelled in them up and down this land, preaching the word, and scattering the seed of life. There were giants in those days. We are often reminded of the story of an old Waterloo veteran, who attracted the attention— on some review day, we presume—of an officer, who came up to him, examined him, looked at his coat and the buttons upon it, and then remarked, " These are singular buttons. Why, we hav'n't such buttons now-a-days." The old soldier smartly replied, " No, Sir, nor such *men* either."

We are a little too old to crave for anything new in Methodism, and rather too young to yield to be carried whither we would not,—back into the old and obsolete economy, into its worldly sanctuary and its carnal ordinances. Can we not discern the signs of the times? Can we not call to mind the corruptions which with worldly wealth and costly array crept into the Church in Constantine's time? And have we not some reason to pray, not formally, but fervently, "In all times of our wealth, good Lord, deliver us?"

Whilst we do not, like the Catholics, so called, covet much material splendour, yet we are not Cromwellian. We would not, like Cromwell, open a cannonade upon a church, or leave the trace of a bullet on a buttress, such as we have seen in Salisbury cathedral,—a memento of the war which Cromwell waged. We would not mutilate a limb or mar a feature of a graceful statue. Those that have been so curiously carved, may remain; and those that have been broken or bruised in their fingers, or their feet, or their nose, should be bound up with new plaster, and so left that you could distinguish the new from the old. We have gazed with great admiration on splendid specimens of architectural skill,—chapels, churches, cathedrals,—in this country and on the Continent. We do not envy those who cannot admire the grand old cathedral of Rouen, the palace of Versailles, the Pantheon at Paris, the magnificent St. Peter's at Rome, or St. Paul's in our own metropolis. Though we cannot endorse that transcendental sentiment of Lamartine, that "St. Peter's gives us the grandest idea of the immensity of God," yet as, time after time, we have walked within the noble edifice and under the wondrous dome of St. Paul's, we have thought that these give sublime ideas of the marvellous skill of man, and that Sir Christopher Wren did indeed need no other monument to his name.   But neither at St. Peter's nor at St. Paul's would we wish to worship.

Surely no one has any right to say, as some have been prone to do, that we have Puseyites among us. There may, however, be some who are *Puseyitish*. Many who have not quite arrived at Rome may be " *Romeward.*" *   And, alas! not a few who have got to Rome did not at the outset expect to go quite so far.   It is too notorious to conceal that some of those who were once in our schools, our sanctuaries, and our social circles, have forsaken the fold of their fathers, and have become the rankest Puseyites, the greatest sticklers for the Church, and the most stealthy seducers from our fold.   Does the sin in any degree lie at our door ?   Are we preparing the way of such ?   The Establishment is running after Rome : are *we* not running after the Establishment ?   Are not the first germs of a *sensuous worship* being intro-duced among us ?   Is not our church architecture in danger of losing all appearance of simplicity ?   Is

* See an excellent article in the " Methodist Recorder " for June, 1865, p. 204.

there not a tendency to an exaggerated *use of music*
in public worship, departing from the idea of congregational psalmody, in which the plain and unlettered, as well as the musically uneducated, may join
with heart and voice? The exigencies of the times
seem to require from us something like a practical
protest. Modes and forms of building and worship,
harmless enough under other circumstances, may
become inexpedient when all around us there is such
a tendency *Romeward.* We stand almost aghast at
the audacity of St. Aidan's; and, instead of the
sanctity of the saint, we suspect the subtlety of the
serpent, and the snare of the fowler. But are we
not, by Church prayers, cold proprieties, prescribed
forms, by a punctilious Pharisaism, by a kind of symbolism that seems to be stealthily creeping into our
splendid sanctuaries,—are we not preparing for a
more general falling away from the godly sincerity, the true simplicity, the deep spirituality, the
sacred fervour, and the earnest power of primitive
Methodism?

May we not, then,—to say nothing of economy for
nobler purposes,—more wisely, more safely and
spiritually, adopt, in the style of our chapel architecture, whatever would combine comfort and convenience with the chaste and the elegant, and yet
have temples worthy of Him who built the skies?
And let us consign over all that is expensively elabo-

rate, superlatively splendid, and gorgeously grand, to a carnal Catholicism, the Scarlet Mystery, with all the costly and attractive array of her abominations,— her gilded tombs, her painted sepulchres, and her dead men's bones.

CHAPTER VIII.

THE PIOUS POOR.

Do we not suffer, as a people, *for want of proper provision for the poor?* It has been said in past days that Methodism has a special mission to the poor. "The poor," Christ said, "ye have always with you." And we think Methodism has had some of the noblest, the most pious and princely poor, whom God has ever chosen; poor who have been proof against the strongest spells to seduce them from the Church of their choice; poor who could neither be allured nor alarmed, drawn nor driven, flattered nor frowned, bribed nor buffeted from the despised conventicle, from the place where they found the "pearl of great price." With what keen and terrible severity has their godly sincerity been tested in pinching poverty! Beset with seducing smiles and scathing scorn, promises and penalties, they have remained "firm as the beaten anvil to the stroke," "faithful among the faithless," unshaken, unterrified, and unseduced.

They could go to church, and get gifts many; they came to chapel and to Class, and chiefly, when they came, to give out of their little. Bread and blankets, loaves and legacies,—the soup, the silver, and the day-school,—curates, clubs, coals, and divers chari- ties,—all combined to conjure or to cajole them to church. Class-money, collections (often), pew-rent, charitable appeals neither few nor far between, have all combined to make full proof of the purity of their motives, the strength of their piety, and the ardour of their attachment to the sect spoken against. But *all* the poor are not equal to so severe an ordeal : and if we are to have conversions among the poor, we must have the prayerless and the profane, as well as the godly among them, that to these the Gospel may be preached from Sabbath to Sabbath. If, however, as Wesleyans, we get our Church chapels, and Church prayers, and cold Church formalities, *without any Church charities*, then the odds are against us ; and what wonder if the masses of the poor steal, or are stolen, away from the chapel to the church ? For what, in many respects, is the difference ? The Church chapel is much like the church, except a little finer than some of the old churches are ; and the Church prayers are much the same in every place, and at all times and seasons ; and likely still, it would seem, to remain the same through this changing world to the end of time.

" What is the difference ? " ask the poor. " There's only one way to heaven ; and we be all serving one Master ; we has exactly the same prayers. It is true

I likes the preaching better at chapel, and always did; but, you know, there are many collections there, and I never likes to come without giving, and we be but poor people, you see; and if we go to church, we gets coal at Christmas, and soup and blankets beside, and every little helps; and so as we gets safe to heaven at the last, it will be all right. And then the Clergyman is a very nice man, and a very learned man too; and her ladyship is a very nice woman, and so are the young ladies; and we never meets any of them in the road but they stops and speaks to us; and the chapel people be got so mighty stiff and cold and such fine folks of late, you may go to chapel for years, and nobody never stops to speak to you, except to ask you for something."

If, then, the regular Clergy, who have been provoked to jealousy, with their staff of Curates, their copious charities, their Scripture-readers, their schoolmasters and mistresses, and a host of satellites, are ever ready to compass sea and land to make one proselyte, and to meet more than half way any who are disposed to leave the conventicle for the church; is it any wonder that, being repelled by coldness of conduct and almost constant collections at the chapel, and allured by the courtesy, the condescension, and the almost ceaseless current of charity, all of which, as in harmonious concert, join to welcome them to the church,—is it any wonder, we ask, that so many of the poor should cross the narrow stream which separates the chapel from the church; and that whilst we have to rejoice over advanced revenues from the rich, we have to mourn over minished numbers of converts from among the poor? Must not this be an occasion of great sorrow to Ministers among us, especially when they remember that the preaching of the Gospel to the poor was one of those marvels of mercy so near akin to those glorious miracles which attested the Divine mission of Christ, and was also one of the glories of primitive Methodism? Whatever glory Methodism may have in her material temples and in the splendour of her sanctuaries, or from her multiplied silver and gold, and from her great institutions, yet if the *poor* are permitted unheeded to pass away from us,—the *poor*, who are the chief objects of the care and compassion of Christ, the Great Head of the Church,—then, with the *poor*, we think our *true glory* also will depart.

We may refer to one or two cases, to show how the poor are sometimes pressed, in some form or other, to pay when they lack the power. I do not now refer to the weekly pence in the Class. I remember the case of a poor, but respectable, mother, with a large family, and withal but recently left a desolate widow; who, with her late husband, used to attend the Wesleyan chapel, with several of their family. He had been much esteemed by respectable mem-

bers of the Church of England, who, with the
Clergyman, paid frequent visits to the widow, as did
also the Wesleyan Minister. So far the race seemed
to be fair; but an offer was made on the Church
side, to send one or two of the sons to a school, free
of charge. The Wesleyan Minister, not liking to
lose this widow and her family from the congregation,
promised to see that the school pence for two other
of her children should be paid: and they were paid.
But a pew also was offered gratis at the church, with
sundry courtesies and charities, all such as would
save that widow's heart from the wounding thought
that she was " not wanted there."

The Wesleyan Pastor, too, though much perplexed, remembering the rigid pew system at his
chapel, promised that her pew rent should be paid
there, if she and her children would come.* She

---

* May not the present pew system, in many instances at least, be
relaxed with safety and advantage? May not pews be paid for, in
part, by the rich for the poor, or let at a lower rate? Let truth be
made as accessible as error. In the race and contest between them,
let truth have fair play. Let not error have all conceivable facilities
for progress, whilst truth has all the dead weights and heavy burdens
placed on her back; and then wonder why she does not march along
more swiftly and triumphantly. If error has so many *bribes*, let not
truth have too many *burdens*. In several places where pew-rent has
been abolished, "the income from VOLUNTARY WEEKLY contributions
has been more than doubled. There may be cases among us in which
this could be tried without risk."—" Watchman," Sept. 6th, 1865,
p. 293.

could, of course, have sat on the free seats ; but she did not like to go there. The old Adam, or the old Eve, was not, we suppose, quite dead; for " pride and poverty," it is said, " often go together." She, however, with several of her children, did come to the pew, the rent of which the Pastor had promised should be privately paid. He had promised it should be paid, although he scarcely knew how, as it could not properly be paid from the Poor Fund ; and there was no other applicable, and the Pastor himself had pressing family claims. So far this widow seemed to be secured to the sanctuary where she wished to worship ; and the Pastor was pleased to see the pew filled up by this respectable but poor family. But what was his surprise and sorrow, when he heard, on one of his visits, that widow's tale of woe, told whilst bitter tears chased each other down her care-worn cheeks ! Rude words had been sent to that widow in a rude way, warning her that in no form and on no condition whatever was she to come to that pew ; and this strange and unfeeling message was sent to that widow by one reputed to be a respectable Wesleyan, who had of course the pew rents to look after, which, it is fair to say, was a duty he strictly and sternly discharged. .

That widow, as she told the Pastor, spent the wearisome hours of that night in bitter weeping. She wept, as she thought of a kind husband, and the

father of her family, gone; money, and means of
support, gone; and, as is wont, friends also gone.
And would not that widow's " wailings pierce the
skies ? " O spirit of the poor-befriending Wesley !
what wouldst thou have done on behalf of that poor
widow, driven from a chapel that bears thy name so
prominently on its front? Surely, rather than she
should have gone, thou wouldst have sold one or
both of thy " two silver spoons."

After having paid many thousands of visits to the
poor of our churches and congregations, we look upon
this as but a part of a *too stringent monetary system,*
which keeps or drives out tens of thousands from
fellowship with us; and as one among several reasons
that, whilst we are rich and increased in worldly
goods, and have temporal prosperity, we are in danger
of spiritual decline.

We know that in some of our large circuit towns
the poor are well visited and relieved. In such cases
we have, besides the Society Fund, Dorcas and
Benevolent Societies, and devoted visitors of the
sick and poor. But what of many of the country
Societies, where there is, perhaps, no counter-current
to High Church influence? What power have the
Pastors among us, except from their own private
purse, to show to the poor people committed to their
charge, that their love for them is not in word and
profession only ? Scarcely will their allowances suffer

them to do more than say, " Be ye warmed," or to give them, as it is significantly termed, " the priest's blessing."

These poor people have perhaps heard of a *Poor Fund*; but what relief have they had from it in the season of sickness, in the day of trouble, in the time of need, when out of employ, in the severity of a long winter, when death, as well as dearth, has entered their dwelling, when want has rushed upon them as an armed man,

> " When health and strength and friends were gone,
> When joys were withered all and dead,
> And every comfort was withdrawn ? "

What help *could* they have from the Poor Fund of that Society, of which they were the needy and suffering members ? What help could they have from the few shillings, or it may be the few pence, collected at the Lovefeast or the Lord's Supper, in a country Society, among whose members these few shillings were to be distributed ? Yet their next-door neighbours who went to church could have coals and soup and blankets, and charity in various forms came to their help ; whilst ours has been a POOR FUND indeed, rather than a FUND *for* the poor.

One pound, or two, would, perhaps, purchase all the Poor Funds in all the country parts of many Circuits which have much hoarded wealth at their head. Does not such a state of things too strongly tempt our poor people to desert us? You may as well call egg-shells eggs, a dessert-dish a dessert, or expect to fill the lungs from an exhausted receiver, as to obtain relief for the poor from our Poor Funds in many of our country Societies. They are what both nature and grace abhor,—a vacuum. "Inasmuch as ye did it *not* to one of the least of these, ye did it *not* to Me."

Could not cheap Hymn Books * and Bibles be purchased, in part at least, for the poor? Could not *pews* be taken for the more respectable and worthy of them? and in the winter, instead of simply saying, " Be ye warmed," might not coals and blankets be obtained for them at a cheaper rate, soup-kitchens be established, visitors engaged to see them during the week, and a list of their names carefully kept, which should comprehend, not the poor of our Society only, but the poor of the congregation also?

Young persons, *chiefly females*, as true sisters of charity and angels of mercy, might be appointed to this work, the circuit town being the centre and head of this visiting and benevolent society; the Pastors taking the oversight of the whole, and being made, as much as possible,—on a far larger scale than they are at present,—almoners to the poor of their flock.

Would there not be formed, by such a system of

---

* This is in some places now being done; and a right step has been taken in printing cheap Hymn Books, of good type. Could not these be purchased in part by the rich, and given to the poor?

benevolence, a sympathetic bond of union between Methodist Pastors and their people; a bond which, from their respectable vagrancy, their frequent wanderings to and fro, their short sojourn in any one sphere, it is very difficult to form, and which, when formed, is too soon broken by their next removal? For, scarcely do they well know their people, before they have to preach from, "Finally, brethren, farewell." Whilst, then, these Pastors have to preach the Gospel to the poor, let better and more systematic provision be made for the poor of their flock and of their congregations. Let some better practical proof be given to the poor of our Churches, and to the hearers of the word, that they are thought of, and cared for, as it regards the life that now is, as well as that which is to come. Shall we not then have many more of the poor among our hearers? And will the poor thus provided for be the less likely to prove the Gospel to be the power of God to their salvation? Have there not been salutary effects, of a spiritual nature, flowing from a relief of the great distress amongst the poor in Lancashire?

Christ, our great Pattern, who, though rich, for our sakes became poor, cared for the bodies as well as the souls of those whom He came to seek and to save. He wrought miracles of mercy on their behalf; He healed the sick, fed the hungry, had compassion on the multitude, went about doing good.

M 2

He caused the widow's heart to rejoice, and brought
upon Himself the blessing of those who were ready
to perish. Let Ministers have the power in these
respects to be more fully the imitators of Christ.
They cannot, besides preaching the Gospel to the poor,
work miracles on their behalf: they cannot multiply
the barley loaves and fishes of the poor. They would
be glad to be able to multiply their own : and it requires almost a miracle for some of them to subsist
on their scanty allowances without such multiplication. Let, then, the rich who have not time to visit
the poor and relieve them personally, do it by proxy,
—do it by their Pastors, making them their almoners.
This, happily, to some extent is the case; but the
custom should be universal.

And is it not *possible* that a more extended system
of benevolence towards our poor should be practised
among us? Are our respected laity unable or un-
willing to do this, if they will but duly consider the
matter? How soon could twenty or thirty thousand
pounds be paid to treasurers at Centenary Hall, as
was done towards the mitigation of the Lancashire
distress! How soon could a great Central Benevolent Institution be established, active agents be
employed, and, possibly, some Florence Nightingales
or John Howards be brought to light, were the
thoughts of our wealthy people to be turned towards
this laudable object! How soon could a depôt be

formed, for the reception of clean cast-off garments, cheap apparel, cloaks and coats, for our worthy poor to wear by day, and warm Witney blankets to comfort them by night! How many attacks of rheumatism might thus be warded off! what grateful emotions might be inspired! Instead of tossings to and fro on bare boards, balmy sleep would be induced; and the poor family would each night give warm thanks to God and blessings to their benefactors, ere they " sink in blissful dreams away." Again we ask, Cannot these things be done by our noble and wealthy laity? Let the cost of our expensively adorned chapels, of the highly decorated Gothic, and of our lofty towers and needless spires, answer this question. Without more regard to the temporal wants of the poor, our wheels, we think, will drag heavily, and our great and good Home Mission scheme, which has so much to do specially with the poor, although of vast benefit, will be a *comparative* failure ;—compared, we mean, with the vast and widely extended blessings which it might otherwise diffuse in the wide world parish of our Founder. Do not Home Missionaries tell us of a pretty sure way by which they can gain the poor man's ear, and get to his heart? If he have an empty stomach, " feed him : " let him have something in this sense inwardly to " digest," and he will not be the less likely to " mark and learn " the saving lessons of truth.

If our Pastors have nothing more to do with tem-- poralities in their connexion with the poor than to ask them what they can afford to give,—to give to their Class,—to give for their ticket,—to give for the Worn Out Ministers' Fund,—to give to the Yearly Collection,—and to give at all the other collections through the year; then would it not be far better that the rich should unite these Church temporalities with their own, and that Ministers should give themselves "*wholly* to the ministry?" Not indeed that we think the poor *give* too freely or too much of their little, but that they *receive* too little.

Attention to the poor on a more liberal scale would greatly tend to neutralize the prevailing pernicious notion, that " Ministers are so much after the money," —an idea which is as calculated to check the course of the word among the poor, as are " the cares of this world" to choke the precious seed among the rich. We have heard of one elegant and commodious chapel, in which ample accommodation is made for about five hundred of the poor; and which, more- over, is situated in the midst of a poor and populous part of a large town. And yet we were informed that no poor attended. How is this? " Is there not a cause?" What is that cause? Such a state of things demands a close, cautious, and searching in- quiry. Some will say, "This must be a very extreme case." Certainly it ought to be. But why, within

the wide world of Wesleyan Methodism, should there
be such a case at all? And are there not other cases
too near to this extreme? Yes, we know there are.
Men of position, men of property, of extensive business and influence, ay, and of Christian compassion
and benevolence, can take their comfortable drive on
a Sabbath morning from their calm and lovely country
retreat, and, when they are softly seated in their
crimson-cushioned pew, can open their beautiful book
of thrilling psalmody, and sing in sweet and well
skilled strains,—

> "These temples of His grace,
> How beautiful they stand!
> The honours of our native place,
> And bulwarks of our land!"

But what of the dense masses of the poor that surround these beautiful temples? "O, they were
not intended to be shut out." Certainly not, or such
ample provision would not have been made for them,
and there would not have been those vacant seats for
the poor inside. They have not been, however, by
any cause *compelled* "to come in." Let it not be
supposed that we chide the rich, or that we cherish
a censorious feeling toward these wealthy Wesleyans
for choosing a calm country residence away from the
scene of pressing business, and away from the sight
of pinching poverty. All this is very *natural*, we
freely allow; but it may be doubted whether, for

sojourners and strangers upon earth, it is very
spiritual. And it may also be strongly doubted
whether in the end it will be well for them, and well
for their families,—if for the life that now is, yet not
for that which is to come. Are not these families
very likely to go away from the Church of their
fathers, as numberless Methodist families under such
circumstances have done? They are far away from
the social sphere of Methodism, far away from any
Wesleyan chapel; and the Clergy and their Curates
keep a close and careful eye upon such cases, and
can and do exhibit a very courteous and alluring
demeanour towards them; and they have not to compass any sea, and but little land, to make them
proselytes. And so, whilst the grandparents of these
children were among the good old-fashioned Methodists of primitive times, these their grandchildren
will probably pass away from the pale of Methodism,
the Church of their fathers and mothers, over to
"Mother Church;" especially as the separating
stream is so very narrow that they can soon step
across.

What, then, is it, we would still solemnly ask, that
prevents these poor people from forming a part of the
congregation? What is it that keeps them outside,
whilst the wealthy are within? It used to be quite
the other way. The poor in primitive times chose,
and the rich eschewed, Methodism.

Whilst we have been breaking down the mighty barriers of caste in India, are we not in danger of rearing up something too much like caste in our own Christian community; or at least of marking too strongly the line which divides the rich from the poor,—and this, too, even in God's house, "where God alone is great?" Our general pew system, at its best, marks this difference quite plainly enough; and have we not much reason to mitigate this offensive distinction? Should we not, as far as possible, remove this iron fence, melt away this icy barrier, break down this "middle wall of partition," trample over this thorn hedge, that separates the two classes in God's great family, as we would tread down Satan, the world, and sin, and triumph over the lust of the eye and the pride of life? Let us do this, by all that Christian consideration, that Christlike compassion, and comprehensive charity, which we can possibly show towards those whom Christ is not ashamed to call His brethren.

Cannot we, without coming to a community of goods, contract or bridge over by Christian charity the wide chasm, which even in the Church of Christ cleaves so far asunder the two classes of rich and poor? classes which should be joined in the one fold and in one body, be cemented as one in the Christian temple, and become one with each other, as Christ is

one with the Father? Judge Talfourd thought that
if, by condescension and charity, the great gulf
between the rich and poor were spanned, the calendar
of crime from year to year would be greatly diminished. The poor would have more self-respect, if
they had more sympathy from the rich,—as well as
respect for their benefactors; and both of these sentiments would restrain them in the path of vice and
ruin. Let, then, the lofty on a more liberal and
general scale stoop to lift up the poor around them
from the dust and from the dunghill, as God has
lifted them up and placed them among the princes of
our Israel. It was whilst fervently and eloquently
pleading on behalf of the poor, the fallen, and the
condemned, that the learned judge breathed his last,
and sighed away his spirit into the hands of the
righteous Judge of the whole earth, at whose bar
rich and poor, small and great, must stand at the
last, and with their works be weighed in an even
balance. Happy for those who in that day will not
be found wanting in acts of Christian charity!

Let not the bridgeless gulf in the other world,
across which the rich man cast his despairing glance
toward Lazarus, cast its sombre shadows athwart the
distance which divides the rich from the poor in the
present world. Let the rich, on whom God has so
liberally lavished the good things of the life that now
is, bless with their fallen crumbs, their surplus stores,

and overflowing bounties, the poor and peculiar people whom God hath chosen; and thus "use this world
as not abusing it," and make to themselves "friends
of the mammon of unrighteousness." As Stephen-
son's skill spanned, by his suspension bridge, the
Menai Straits, and as by one continuous line of rail
we connect the cold North with the genial South,
join John o' Groat's house with the Land's End, and
form a friendship and fellowship with the far off
which we could not otherwise enjoy; so, by a sympathetic bond, by kindly and daily communications, by
Christian condescension, compassion, and charity, let
us more closely connect and clasp these wide extremes
of rich and poor, of high and low, as members of one
common family.

Especially should this be done in our own Churches,
which are *not congregational*, but *connexional*. Then
will our great Connexion be greater, yea, and grander
too, in the future, than it has ever been in the past;
and we shall be bound with stronger cords and more
sacred bonds,—the bonds of a wide and blessed
brotherhood; bonds which will never be broken, but
will be renewed, perpetuated, and eternalized with
the one family in heaven.

We cannot cherish too jealous a care, or take too
earnest heed, amid so much material prosperity and
worldly wealth, and amid the smiles and blandish-
ments, the "pomps and vanities of this wicked

world," that the congregations of our wide Wesleyan
Connexion come not under the merited chiding and
condemnation of the faithful James. (James ii. 1–4.)

Think, then, dear readers, on these things. Do
not scorn them as needless cautions, nor sleep, as
do others ; but wake up, ye stewards of Christ, and
of the unrighteous mammon : ye who have sometime
slumbered amid the wants and the woes of a sin-
stricken world, and the *claims* of suffering humanity,
wake up to the dignity of your duty ; wake up to the
greatness of your honour, and to the richness of your
recompense, as the visitors and helpers of the sick
and the poor, the widow and the fatherless of Christ's
flock, who are as Christ Himself. "Hearken, my
beloved brethren, Hath not God chosen the poor of
this world rich in faith, and heirs of the kingdom
which He hath promised to them that love Him ?"
(James ii. 5.)   To you let it never be said, "But ye
have despised the poor."   "Pure religion and undefiled before God and the Father is this, To visit the
fatherless and widows in their affliction, and to keep
himself unspotted from the world." (James i. 27.)

CHAPTER IX.

Is there not, even in large Societies, a lamentable lack of right men for Leaders? Any one who has long been a Pastor among us, must perceive how very far short many of our Leaders are of the lofty standard set down in the Class-book. A Minister, on a visit to the barracks in a certain town, where one of the finest regiments in Her Majesty's service was stationed, remarked to an officer of gigantic stature, " You have some very fine men in your regiment." " Yes, Sir," was the .reply, " we have." " You are rather tall yourself." " Sure an' I am six feet four without shoes and stockings." Dr. Clarke remarked that Ireland was the only country that produced giants, and this appears to have been one of them. " Have you many men of that size in your regiment ? " " Not many now, Sir. We used to have ; for it was considered the finest regiment in Her Majesty's service ; but we had to lower the standard during the Crimean war, when there was such a demand for

men.　We take shorter men now,—men we shouldn't
have locked at before the war, Sir." And have not
we, since some of our connexional struggles, lowered
a little our standard of Leaders, because perhaps we
could not get better? It has been said, "There
were giants in those days." It may be added, There
are dwarfs in these.

Many devoted and godly men have we known as
Leaders, in whose steps we have desired to follow.
And members should be able safely to follow their
Leaders. But have there not been many Leaders
appointed, whom it would not be safe or wise to
follow?

It would have been well for many of our members,
in times of connexional strife, had they taken a like
cautious heed to their steps. Alas! how many have
been led sadly astray by those to whom they looked
as their guides in the good and the right way!
We heard but a short time ago of about eighty
members being led away, by one erring Leader, from
the Church of their choice. Some Leaders read
regularly every quarter the Rules to the members of
their Class; and it would be well for all to read
frequently, also, the grave and solemn cautions given
to Class-leaders.

Some Classes remind us of Bunyan's great chasm
of shame, which cart-loads of rubbish could not fill
up; or of Pharaoh's lean kine. Put member after

member with them, yea, merge one Class after another in theirs, yet somehow they never get full; they wane away and dwindle down in the course of time to about the same narrow span. Whereas another begins with two or three, whom he has gathered from the world; but how soon they multiply, so that it becomes necessary to divide the Class! Who does not see that if we go on to increase the former kind of Leaders, our number of members will continue to diminish? And are there not many Leaders who are a little disposed to give long lectures to their Ministers on the duty of visiting the people, whilst they are notorious for their neglect of visiting the absentees from their Class? Some even of their sick members we have known left for a whole quarter without a visit. And some Leaders, strange to say, we have heard declare that they did not and would not run after their members; whilst they were very fervent in their pleadings for pastoral visitation. But no visit of a Pastor will supersede the necessity of a visit from the Leader to the absentees, and especially to the sick of his Class. For what confidence in the Leader, or comfort in the Class, can that member have, who has been kept to his house or shut up in a sick room for several months together, and never been visited by the Leader, although the name of that member must be under the eye of the Leader week after week? "I have not been able to get to Class

for several months," complained a member, "and my
Leader has not called to see me once." "I was ill
for many months, and living near in the same yard
as my Leader; and he never came to inquire after
me; and I have not met since, and that has been
more than a year." But that member, by the visits
of the Minister, was restored. "I have been kept
at home for fourteen weeks, and my Leader has had
to go near to my door many times in a week, but
has never called; and if I were to be ill for a year,
I should not expect a call from him, as he never does
visit his members." Such are some among many of
the jottings of a Pastor. And yet some of these
Leaders are perhaps the loudest and longest in their
complaints of the lack of pastoral visitation, as though
they wished to lay the cause and the sin of the
decline of their Class at the Minister's door.

Perhaps such a Leader some time ago was a pious,
humble, zealous, Christian man: his business has
prospered, not so his soul: his care about many things
has increased, not so his care for the one thing, for
that which should be his chief concern. He has
enlarged his borders, extended his worldly business,
customers increase; but his Class meanwhile is contracting, his members drop off one by one, his love
for Zion declines, and his zeal waxes cold. There is
temporal prosperity and *spiritual* decline.

Many devoted, zealous, and successful Class-leaders

we know, who are also plodding men of business, and engaged in extensive commercial pursuits, who hold in solemn and sacred regard their duty to their Class, and who can scarcely be allured from that weekly gathering by any call, however inviting, from the world or even the Church. The Classes of such will generally be found to be in prosperity. We have a goodly company of Class-leaders in our Connexion, many of whom would make far better *lay agents* for the Bishop of London in his great Church scheme on behalf of the metropolis than any he is likely, we think, to obtain. At the same time we have doubtless many who have become wealthy and worldly, and whom it would not be safe or prudent to follow; for they are running more for the corruptible and the perishing than for the incorruptible and eternal. It is almost as delusive and dangerous to be led by a careless and a covetous as by a blind Leader. Those who are so led are not less likely to fall into the ditch, and to be drowned in perdition.

We remember some time ago being induced by the noisy howl of a dog to look out of our window. We saw in the street a dog crouching and howling most piteously at the extreme end of his chain. Not far off, at the other end of the chain, stood a poor blind man against a lamp-post. He had his hand pressed against his brow, which, it seemed, had come bang against the iron post; and when the blind man took his hand from his bruised brow, it was to beat the dog which had led him against the post. As he smartly applied the stick indiscriminately upon the poor brute's back and sides, he gruffly said, "*Lead me right, then; lead me right.*" "Give me Thy hand," said quaint old Herbert, "since Thou hast both mine eyes." How many members have the Methodists had, who seem to see only with the same eyes as their Leaders! They look to the Leader, and especially in "times of trouble," quite as much and a little more than to the Lord, to lead them; and by perverse men they have been led astray, and have run their heads against a post. Hence how often it has been said, "Such a Leader went off with all, or nearly all, his members!" Have they not had reason to say to these Leaders, who have had "both their eyes," as the poor blind man to his dog, "Lead me right?" We may be excused for referring to the line which often forms the conclusion of epitaphs in some of our country churchyards:—

> "Prepare by death to follow me;"

under which, in one instance, a humorous friend wrote,—

> "To follow you I'm not content,
> Until I know which way you went."

How many thousands of our Israel have, in times of strife, been led sadly astray, simply because they did not take the trouble to know which way they were being led! How vastly important, therefore, to have enlightened, sound, devout, and godly Leaders, if they can possibly be found! *

Some Leaders we know who seem rather disposed to keep out and lop off, than add to the numbers of their Class. They keep for years almost as stereotyped a number in their Class as is the number of Wesleyan Printing Establishments on the Mission field,—which, who does not know, is eight? Now and then they get one in, to fill up a vacancy created by death or removal; but filling up the lines of the small Class-book, and getting from the small to the large one, is an expansion of ideas which seems never to come within their " faith's capacity."

And are there not others who have strong, stern *financial* reasons for keeping the number down as low as they can? They are the men who look after things in the Quarterly Meeting, and to whom simpler minds look up. Have they not been seen sagely sitting down at the Quarter board, with those far-seeing spectacles before their eyes, and with pencil in hand? They know the price of the last tray or tea-kettle that was had for the preacher's house, how many sermons have been preached, how many sovereigns have been paid, and how much it has cost them

* Since the above was written, some excellent articles on this subject have appeared in the " Watchman " newspaper.

N 2

for a sermon; and thus they compare the spiritual with the carnal, and weigh them [in their own scales, and often find the former wanting. Ay! and they know, too, full well that such a Society should pay so much per member; that the Circuit has to average sixpence per member for the W. O. F.; and how many members are allowed for a child or half a child or a quarter of a child. What sifting, searching scrutiny, as though the Pastor were about to palm a child upon them!

> " Heap worlds on worlds,
> Amazing pomp ; redouble the amaze,
> Ten thousand add, and twice ten thousand more;
> Then weigh the whole,—one soul outweighs them all,
> And calls the astonishing magnificence
> Of unintelligent creation poor."

But here, alas! paltry sixpences seem to be often placed in the opposite scale with priceless souls. Pastors are made painfully to feel at such times that, if not in numbering the people, " in our system of averages we have gone quite far enough."

We have many aged and godly men, filling the office of Leaders, who retain the freshness and fervour of early piety and the warmth of their first love; whilst there are others whose many worldly cares engross their time and energies, and render them less efficient than they were. Some of the latter are quite indisposed to have new Leaders appointed, when there have been clear and strong calls for them. Whilst there are many Leaders at whose feet it would be a privilege for even a Minister to sit, to listen to their pithy sayings, wise counsels, and warm and pointed appeals, we have at the same time too many sing-song, ding-dong Leaders of die-away Classes; and if the two or three who meet with them are not dead already, they cannot be expected to survive long at such a " dying rate."

It has been well said by Dr. Doddridge, that John, our Lord's forerunner, knew how to set as well as how to rise. He was glad to have his own little light as a morning star eclipsed in the greater light and richer lustre of the Sun of Righteousness. "He," John said, "must increase, but I must decrease." There are, however, many who, though they know how to rise, do not know how to set. There can be no doubt that if our Class-meetings are to be kept up in truth, in spiritual interest, in Christian intelligence, in vigorous reality and power, and not in form, in semblance and shadow only, our Class-leaders must be men of enlightened mind, of increasing knowledge, men of pure morality and consistent deportment, men of sterling piety, men of prayer, men of mighty faith and burning zeal.

O, could we find or create in sufficient numbers

such men as Father Reeves, and let them begin Classes, or have two or three to commence a Class, we doubt not but that soon our mourning would be turned into joy, and God would greatly comfort the waste places of our spiritual Zion.

CHAPTER X.

" That there may be equality."

THIS is a subject of such extreme delicacy that the writer almost trembles to touch upon it. He would refer to it with much modesty and care in a suggestive way ; and would abstain altogether from an allusion to it, were it not that he entertains a deep and solemn conviction of its great importance, and a hope that it may be much more prudently and profoundly thought out by others than he has any pretensions to be able to do.

Is there not, then, too great a disparity in the salaries or allowances of Ministers among us as a Connexion ?—a disparity ranging, with single men, from about £50 to nearly £100 ; and, among married men, from about £80 to, we suppose, nearly £300. The *maximum* need not be such a matter of marvel as the *minimum.* It may be truly said that there is also a great disparity of talent among the Ministers. No doubt, there is, and always must be. But there is one talent in which all men, Ministers included, are pretty much on a par :—that, we mean, which,

being mercifully implanted in them by their Maker,
leads them instinctively to look for a similar flow of
daily supplies; and which is closely connected with
the petition, " Give us this day our daily bread." A
talent this, which, while it does not lift up man, in his
material and mortal nature, to the top of the ladder
which Jacob saw, so that physically he can live on
angels' food, neither levels him so low at the foot of
the ladder that he may not only " feed *beside* " but
on the same verdant aliment as the beasts that
perish.

This was the talent to which one of our sage
fathers referred, who succeeded in an important Circuit one of the most popular Ministers of that day.
When the Steward proposed a reduction of the salary
of the new Minister because of the superior talent of
his predecessor, the meekness of that Minister's
reply—and he was no ordinary man—was quite
equal to the modesty of the Steward's proposal. It
was, we believe, to this effect: " None could call
in question the superior talent of the Minister who
had preceded him; but there was a talent in which
he, and the family God had been pleased to give
him, would not be a whit behind those who had preceded him." This seasonable stroke of wit well
served him, as it generally did in circumstances of
perplexity which might have seriously baffled the
graver wisdom of others. The Stewards perceived

the propriety and felt the pungency of the Minister's reply, and suffered the supplies to flow on the same scale as before, and did not mete out material support according to a subtle metaphysical sliding-scale.

We would not abate one jot from the salaries of the more talented Ministers, if as a general rule these, in a financial sense, are the most favoured. Be this as it may, we would respectfully ask our wealthy and worthy lay friends gravely and generously to consider the just claims of those whose limited salary scarcely suffers them to live ; and to consider, too, that these claims of our common humanity are on a similar scale throughout the whole of our Christian brotherhood.

To some extent, it may be said, these claims have been considered and met by the Contingent Fund, which owes so much to the skill, the indomitable energy, and the plodding perseverance of the Rev. Charles Prest. But has all been done that ought to be done? Has all been done that stern justice demands? Has all been done that the wisdom and wealth of our lay friends would enable them to do, if their minds, their hearts, and their hands were brought to bear in mighty unison on this important matter?

Is it a right and seemly thing that some of our young Ministers should have to strive to subsist upon a salary of £50 or £55 *per annum ;* and from this have to draw supplies for board and lodging, clothes, collections, books, and to meet the various other demands made upon them; whilst there are others, not wiser or worthier, but, it may be, wealthier, who have £80 or £90, and in some form perhaps £100? It is not improbable that with the smaller salary there are larger demands. The youthful Minister has, it may be, left at home a widowed mother, who needs some little help from her only son; whilst the larger salary of the wealthier brother is perhaps supplemented with frequent maternal supplies and liberal paternal donations.

This small salary of £50, or £55, seems the more strangely small when the single young Minister pays his visit to one of our day schools, and finds that in the *infant* department the salary of the single young governess is over £70. Yet she is employed but about six or seven hours on five days of the week in charge of these little lambs; whilst he, in reading, studying, travelling, pastoral visits, pulpit preparations, and preaching, must be almost wholly engaged from early morn till beyond the dewy eve, each day of the seven.

Of course, in Congregational Churches, commanding talents will, in general, meet with their reward; but in our Connexion, in the cases of single men, to whom we now refer, such difference of stipend exists where perhaps no plea as to transcendent talent would be set up, or, if set up, could be sus-

tained. Are, then, such inequalities, where no
sufficient reason can be shown, likely to cement our
Connexion as it should be cemented? Are they
likely to keep young Ministers, just entering our
ranks, from envying, from jealousy, from evil surmising or evil speaking? Are they likely to lead
them to regard with becoming respect those on whom
rests the responsibility of their appointments? Are
they not in danger of attributing these inequalities to
other influences besides those which are perfectly
pure and solemnly sacred, and in some degree, at
least, to another wisdom than that which, being first
pure, is also " without partiality ? "

To profess ignorance of such whisperings, both
among Ministers and laity, would be folly indeed.

Could not, then, a fund be established somewhat
similar to the Sustentation Fund in the Scottish Free
Church? or could not our present Contingent Fund—
as yet too contingent—be so replenished by the ample
resources of our Connexion, that, after the utmost local
efforts had been put forth, the shamefully low salaries
of some of the junior brethren, and those of the married
Ministers below £110,—which, under some circumstances, may be considered as lower still than the former,—might be so supplemented that if there be
not " equality," these things, which should at least
approximate, may not be at the antipodes ?

Surely, up to a certain point at least, it is not

merely those subtle things called *talents* that have to be weighed when young men enter our ministry; but also the pressing and imperative claims of our common humanity. If, indeed, *talents* were weighed, and the matters referred to rigorously adjusted thereby, it is possible that the scales, in some instances, would be turned.

We feel assured that this inequality in the salaries of junior Ministers,—and not in these only,—is a painful sore, a great evil, which it is in the power of our respected laity to remedy; and what they do should be done quickly. We wonder much that they who have *written* so often and so well on these subjects, have not put forth some *practical effort* to lessen an unseemly disparity.

A difference of from twenty to twenty-five pounds, or more, in the small salary of young men on entering our ministry, is too severe a test of their loyalty to Methodism, when, as in the present day, there are many and mighty allurements into other folds. If they are not altogether estranged, yet impressions are often made, innuendoes given, and statements hazarded, tending to shake rather than strengthen the bonds of brotherhood, just when they are first being formed.

Some of these young men are tempted to think, and do not scruple to say, that it is not always superior talents, but often adventitious circumstances, that secure favour. Yea, they are far more disposed to ascribe the difference to human frailty and partiality, than to a Divine Providence; whilst, on the other hand, there are doubtless some of the more privileged who have candour and humility enough to say,—

"Not more than others we deserve."

If to abstain from the appearance of evil is incumbent on individual Christians, it cannot be less imperative on collective Churches, such as are comprised in our Connexion.

That which *appears* to be partiality, may or may not be in reality such in the eyes of Him who walketh in the midst of the golden candlesticks. But the less there is in *appearance*, the less there is likely to be in *reality*; and the less there is in reality, the more pleasing it must be to the Great Head of the Church, who is " no respecter of persons."

Lay deputations might be appointed, public meetings held, hidden resources explored, and the Connexion roused, as on the Centenary and Jubilee occasions; and there could be tales of want and woe unfolded, which would stir the noble hearts of the Methodist people. The *minimum* might be fixed, the scales of justice poised, evil speaking on these points silenced, and a great reproach rolled away. Why not?

CHAPTER XI.

METHODISM, in its origin and triumphant march for more than a century, in its vitality amidst the decline of ancient systems, its stability amid the tossing waves of time and the surging billows of strife, its elasticity and adaptation to the varied circumstances and conditions of men,—extending itself to every point of the compass, sailing over almost every sea, planting its standard on almost every shore, teaching its simple and saving lessons of truth to almost every tribe, and kindred, and people of the earth,—and effecting all this in.little more than a hundred years,—is one of not the least wonders of the world, or marvels, we may rather say, of God's mercy.

Scarcely can even blinded bigotry deny that, during the last century, Methodism has been an almost world-wide blessing. And whatever would change the character of Methodism, whatever would check its onward career, whatever would paralyse its power, whatever would clog its chariot wheels, and make them drag heavily; whatever would sap the vitals of its constitution; whatever would snap or relax the mighty ligaments which bind Methodists together, and make Methodism all over the world one wondrous Connexion; whatever would undermine its manly and muscular Christianity; whatever would enfeeble and effeminate its Samson-like strength; whatever would seduce and steal away the great secret of its marvellous might, so that Methodism in days to come should be the shame of its friends, and the sport of its foes; might be justly mourned over as a *world-wide woe.*

Every member of the Catholic Church might mourn over its doom as a universal calamity. Every true patriot and philanthropist might weep over the decline and fall of Methodism, as an untold loss to his country and to the world. Yea, every *man* might mourn, as belonging to its mighty parish. For, whilst all error and all evil, in their vast variety of forms, may see in Methodism a declared and an undisguised foe, all *men* may see in Methodism an undissembling and a faithful friend.

These are not "great swelling words of vanity," but "words of truth and soberness." We may point to many practical proofs. Methodism wages war not against men nor against Churches; but against error and sin its forces are "in mighty phalanx joined."

Methodism will hold out its hand of cordial fellowship, of compassion, and co-operation, to those who may differ in creed, in Church forms and Church order, if they will but mind their own, and be "about their Master's, business," and allow others to do the same; although there may be more than "five points" on which they cannot concur with them. These things she would rather softly say to some of her "small friends," who are somewhat disposed to carp at and complain of Methodism as being narrow and exclusive. Have these complainers correctly taken the compass of their own Christian charity? How much wider is the region in which their compassions move? Are they not, they themselves who thus speak, a little straitened in this respect?

Was Methodism narrow when it opened its arms to welcome, and its hands to aid, its brethren of the Scottish Free Church in their noble struggle, although on some points of doctrine they were almost as far apart from it as the poles? Both preach Christ, and acknowledge Him as the Head of the Church and as King in Zion; and therefore the Methodists could and did, without any compromise, aid their Scottish brethren, in one of the most magnanimous contests which modern Church history records.

This fraternal charity has been well appreciated by their noble-hearted brethren of the Scottish Church, with some few exceptions. ·Is Methodism narrow, because to those who are prone to strife and "doubtful disputations," and who say, "Come, let us meet together in one of the villages in the plain of Ono," she replies, "I am doing a great work, so that I cannot come down? Why should the work cease, whilst I leave it and come down to you?" *

Is Methodism narrow? Look at its multiplied and multiplying Circuits, now numbering nearly six hundred in Great Britain alone, with all their chapels and congregations, ramifying through the cities, villages, and hamlets of this country, and permeating as leaven the masses of the people. Is Methodism narrow? Look at its Mission Stations, and its vast Mission Report, recording the subscriptions, because it has secured the sympathies, of almost all ranks and conditions of men, in almost all climes, and amongst the most varied creeds. Open this Report, take the trouble to look over this mighty catalogue of contributors, in minute print, which needs microscopic eyes to read. Are these the countless names of sympathizers with, and subscribers to, a narrow, straitened sect? Surely candour and common-sense would reply, ''Not so."

Look, we say, at these things, ye who seldom cast a loving glance beyond your own limited sphere and little selves; and tell us, whether Methodism does not belong to the world, and a good lion's share of the world to Methodism. Look at these things, and tell us whether, if you could, you *would dare* to smite Methodism to the earth. Look at these

* Nehem. vi. 2, 3.

O

things, and tell us whether you have correctly
counted the cost of its downfall, which some seem so
earnestly, but, we trow, so "ignorantly," to desire.
Tell us, if the day of its death and doom had surely
come,—tell us, if this favoured tree, which has
brought forth so much fruit for the healing of the
nations, had now become utterly fruitless,—if it were
covered over only with large leaves, under which no
fig could be found,—whether you could rejoice at the
sentence, "Cut it down: why cumbereth it the
ground?"

If Methodism were registered among the dead,
then over its grave heaven and earth might join in
a funeral dirge, and all lands echo and re-echo,
"How are the mighty fallen!"

But no: Methodism will never fall by the might
and malice of its foes. Methodism will never be
smitten to the earth by the sword of its assailants,
or destroyed by any darts of its enemies,—if it be
not first seduced on the lap of some subtle Delilah.

Methodism will not faint in the day of adversity.
She may possibly fall from the pinnacle of her prosperity. She may at least grow giddy and dizzy amid
the glitter and grandeur of worldly elevation. On the
high mountain of material prosperity she is exposed
to many subtle seductions from her primitive purity
and simplicity, and to many fatal shafts, from which
she was safely sheltered when in the low valley of
her humiliation.

Methodism was mighty, when, in the name and strength of her great Captain, she unfurled her banners in rustic cottages, in rude barns, and on rough horse-blocks. *Then* "she came, she saw, she conquered:" then the prey was taken out of the hand of the mighty, and many, on every hand, were the slain of the Lord; and many and glorious were the spoils and trophies, which were led in her triumphal train, whilst her song was, "This is the Lord's doing, and it is marvellous in our eyes!" " God forbid that I should glory, save in the cross of Christ Jesus my Lord." If now, in the time and on the summit of her temporal prosperity, she should begin proudly to wave her banners beneath vaulted roofs, and metal crosses, and glittering pinnacles, as though the might of her own arm had gotten her the victory, then let some future Gibbon, in the forthcoming days of rampant infidel scorn, rebuke, and blasphemy, dip his pen in the darkest ink, to date "the decline and fall" of a power which had won far wider and mightier conquests than those of which proud Rome could ever boast, or than " carnal weapons" could ever win; a power which had gained trophies that had never been sullied with an orphan's sigh or dimmed with a widow's tear; a power which had attracted and gathered in myriads of outcasts and those who were ready to perish; which had been as eyes to the blind and feet to the lame, health to the sick and life to the dying; which had made many mourning hearts in the land to rejoice, and the desolate wastes of heathendom to be glad !

Methodism has quitted herself valiantly in the evil days, the days of her adversity, and in the times of trouble through which she has passed ; but good soldiers, who, with marvellous might and almost supernatural heroism, have endured " hardness " on small rations in the trenches, in fields of blood, or within sight of the enemy's camp, have often become effeminate in times of peace and plenty. They have "wasted their substance with riotous living." So also that system which was mighty in its growth amid privations and struggles,—which was not nursed like a hot-house plant, but more like the hardy heath of the desert, exposed to the wintry blast, or as the sturdy shrub on the sea shore, washed by the wild waves,—may become enfeebled and delicate on the lap of affluence, and in luxurious repose. Times of degeneracy may come, in which the solemn and startling language addressed to the daughters of Zion may be too applicable to some of the children of our people, and to modern Methodists : " Because the daughters of Zion are haughty, walking and mincing as they go, and making a tinkling with their feet, the Lord will smite the crown of the head of the daughters of Zion :...in

that day the Lord will take away the bravery of
their tinkling ornaments, and their networks, and
their round tires like the moon, the chains, and the
bracelets, and the mufflers, the bonnets, and the ornaments of the legs, and the head-bands, and the tablets,
and the ear-rings, the changeable suits of apparel, and
the mantles, and the wimples, and the crisping pins,
the glasses, the fine linen, and the hoods, and the
veils;" and even in her sanctuaries, and in her holy
places, instead of a fragrant sacrifice and a sweet-
smelling odour, there may be vain oblations and that
incense which is an abomination unto the Lord.
"Instead of a girdle" there may "be a rent;...
instead of a stomacher a girding of sackcloth; and
burning instead of beauty....And her gates shall
lament and mourn; and she being desolate shall
sit upon the ground."* "Be not high-minded, but
fear." "Let him that thinketh he standeth take heed
lest he fall."

To the Methodism of the past we may append
"Tried;" and we may add "Triumphant." The
Goliaths of the past have been slain not by dint
of splendid armour, but with simple slings and
stones. "Not many wise men after the flesh, not
many mighty, not many noble, have been called." †
The fancies of men may change; the circumstances

* Isaiah iii. 16–26.   † 1 Cor. i. 27, 28.

and creeds of Churches may vary; but the purposes of God, the principles of His government as King in Zion, can never change.

Whatever, therefore, tends to flatter human vanity, of which the world is so full that it largely overflows into the professing Church of the meek and lowly Saviour; whatever tends, and especially in the solemn service of the sanctuary, to magnify vainglorious man, instead of bringing to Almighty God the glory due to His name, for which purpose the house of God has been erected and dedicated,—must have brooding over it God's dark and withering curse. Call it by what name we may, and in whatsoever guise it may be clad, it must have the consuming frown of a jealous God, rather than the cheering smile of His gracious countenance. Whilst there is very much to admire in the large-hearted benevolence which builds houses on a magnificent scale for God, yet Satan can, and if possible will, pervert the best purposes of men. The cloven foot may leave its dark imprint in the courts of God's house, in the cloister, and even in the sacred seclusion of the closet. Some defiling demon-touch may smite as with leprosy our sacred things. A drop of poison may be infused into the cup of blessing. A canker-worm may be at the root of the fairest flower. "Architecture, symbolism," the well skilled choir, the full-toned organ with all its solemn sounds,.

"will not keep the serpent out of our sanctuaries." *
No; Satan has been too long accustomed to be present
when the sons of God are gathered together, to be
scared away by the mere symbols and shadows of
sacred things.

* WISEMAN's "Christ in the Wilderness," p. 215.

CHAPTER XII.

DRAWING-ROOMS.

PERHAPS we must now have multiplied among us
to some extent those sanctuaries which, for their style
and splendour, as well as on account of the style of
some of those who are most likely to attend them,
may be appropriately, though not offensively, termed
the DRAWING-ROOMS of Methodism, as distinguished
from those habitations of God's house which may for
their humbler style be not less appropriately termed
the *Kitchens* in the "House of God." The kitchen
was the place in the church as a house that was by
common consent assigned to the first Methodists;
whilst our friends, the Quakers, occupied of course
the sitting-room ; and few would dispute the claim of
" the Church " to the drawing-room. Drawing-
rooms, in this sense, were out of question for
Methodism, had they been desired at the early dawn
of "the Great Revival." She thought it well if, on
the banks of those swollen floods which threatened to
overwhelm her, she could find any ark or "nest for
herself," although of as humble and homely a build
as that which was contrived by the ingenuity of
maternal affection to shelter Moses from Pharaoh's

barbarous decree. Distinctions must necessarily exist between the rich and the poor, and we are not disposed to deride them ; but the less those distinctions are *made to appear* in the places where both " rich and poor" should " meet together" to worship the God and Father of both, and the less the poor are made to feel that they belong to another class in that family which " in earth and heaven are one," the better. Very often, it must be admitted, where distinctions do really exist, arising from rank, wealth, and position, there is less ostentatious display than where such distinctions exist only, or chiefly, in the imagination and fancy of self-assumed superiority. It is refreshing to see those who are really respectable stooping, with Christian grace and dignity, without seeming to stoop, in order to converse and to commune with those of whom worldly pride would whisper, " They are beneath your notice : don't associate with them." It is not a little repulsive, on the other hand, to see some stretching forth " a haughty neck," as though far above those who, at least, are on a par with them, and in many respects above them, except in the loftiness of their " vain imaginations," and the dizzy altitude of their " own conceit." But it is never more repulsive than when such vanity is found in the courts of God's house, or within the borders of that Zion which is " the mother of us all." We have heard of a Christian nobleman who would not be called "Lord" in God's house: *there*, he said, he was a brother.

There are, it is true, too many of those who, with a boastful and boorish plainness, speak of Fraternity and Equality too much after the revolutionary style of the French, as though they had the warranty of Heaven to trample with an iron hoof on all distinctions save of their own self-importance. Such persons, though they may often speak of lowliness and simplicity, are seldom seen in that lowliness of mind which leads them to "esteem others better than themselves." Feigned simplicity is little, if any, better than a feigned superiority.

Often in the drawing-room there is great and excessive expenditure; and that sometimes where there is a well-nigh exhausted exchequer, and where the motive is only to gratify "the lust of the eye," and indulge "the pride of life." There may be "pleasant pictures," elaborate adornments, superb furniture, to make or to "keep up appearances," elbowing away those claims which are pressing and imperative. Such superfluities may, to some extent, be lawful : but if at the shrine of worldly splendour costly offerings be presented, whilst at the same time just claims are neglected, the needy saint is overlooked, and the "neighbour" left stripped and wounded on the other side, what account shall the steward of God's bounties give ?

The heart of king Hezekiah, when he had "exceeding much riches and honour," was lifted up; and he showed the Babylonish messengers "all the house of his precious things, the silver, and the gold, and all that was found in his treasures : there was nothing in his house, nor in all his dominion, that Hezekiah showed them not." Then came the prophet's inquiry in the form of a solemn rebuke, "What have they seen in thine house? And Hezekiah answered, All the things that are in mine house have they seen : there is nothing among my treasures that I have not showed them." Then came the Lord's threatening : "Hear the word of the Lord. Behold, the days come, that all that is in thine house, and that which thy fathers have laid up in store unto this day, shall be carried into Babylon : nothing shall be left, saith the Lord." * The sumptuous apartments, and the rich treasuries of silver and of gold, which had fostered the pride of the heart of even a good king, were soon to be left utterly desolate.

It would be sad if, within the proper sphere and amid all the solemn and inseparable responsibilities of that wealth and influence which can adorn in surpassing splendour a material temple, either the bodies or the souls of the people should be left to starve, from a lack of those *needful* supplies which

* 2 Chron. xxxii. 25, 27 ; 2 Kings xx. 13-17.

have gone off in the *superfluous*. Wherever there is a lofty, and consequently a costly, spire affixed, especially to a Nonconformist, and most especially to a Wesleyan chapel, we can scarcely avoid associating in our ideas that spire with one of the very useless, but very expensive, ornaments of a drawing-room in a house where *claims* can hardly be met, and where some members of the family are in actual want. We have thought of a head arrayed in the costliest feathers, whilst the body has been badly clad. We have thought of a series of solemn services in connexion with the opening of that sanctuary,—not fewer perhaps than six or seven; and yet the aggregate amount of the liberal donations from the whole of these services, as "an exhaustive final effort," may scarcely suffice to rear up one superfluous spire. We have thought of members of the same family with us who want the bread of life, and of men wanted to proclaim "the Gospel of peace." And though that costly ornament be the liberal gift of one person, yet does this come within the sphere of "systematic" giving? Is this large outlay, we respectfully ask, within the scope of a well-considered and enlightened charity? Is it the "more excellent way?" Does wealth here meet "want?" Does this "liberality" supply "that which" is "*lacking*" among the brethren in the same "house?" "Them will I send to bring your liberality," the apostle said, "to Jerusalem." There was want there.* And may we not as truly say of the steepled sanctuary of the Wesleyans, There is *superfluity* there. If, in those things which in the eyes of many seem to be extravagance and excess, it could be shown that as Wesleyans we were doing "a good work," as our Lord said the woman did who poured the costly and fragrant perfume upon His head; then the plea for "plainness" would lose a little of its point. But to affirm this, except in some solitary cases, would be an assumption, not argument. Pretty or paltry ornaments which may please the eyes of some, must not be confounded with that precious perfume which the woman poured on a Divine head, and which a Divine Person pronounced to be "a good work."

We were surprised at the statement of a Minister whom we much respect, with regard to these spiral structures and their *imaginary* use among us. After having stated that he "approved of the new chapel being so *near* to the new church; 't was well to have *two* good things together;" he added, "Some might object to the new edifice having *a spire;* he saw no objection to that *ornament;* on the contrary, he considered it an advantage; it acted as a guide to point out to the wayfarer the locality to which he might direct his steps, in seeking for the house of God." †

Generally this esteemed Minister is conclusive in

* 1 Cor. xvi. 3, 17.   † "Watchman," April 2nd, 1865.

argument; and we have perused with interest and profit what has proceeded from his prolific pen. But to us the above statement seems but like a day dream, when compared with his generally well weighed words.

In the first place, we can hardly see any special reason for approval in the circumstance that a new Wesleyan chapel should be *near* a new church. This may, in some cases, be unavoidable; but both as to site and style we think it is better to have a due and proper distance and distinctiveness. In both respects, if we proceed onward for a few years in the same ratio of approximation towards the Church as we seem to have been doing in the past, we may possibly have some reason to regret that we have got "so near." The Church we wish God speed; we have many friends among the Clergy whom we highly esteem : yet we think it a grave reflection on Wesley's wisdom to suppose that had he lived to this day he would have wished his people to get very near the Church ; or that they should be close copyists of her, any more than he would have wished the Church to copy the ways of the older "Mother."

In the second place, the spire is referred to as an *ornament;* and then it is considered that some *advantage* is attached to it. In that case it would combine the twofold quality which it is thought so desirable for articles in a Bazaar to possess,—the ornamental and the useful. The *use* of the spire is then definitely described. It acted as a *guide* to point out to the wayfarer the locality to which he might direct his steps in seeking for the house of God. This may be partly correct as it respects the spire of the new *church;* (it is not, we suppose, our purpose to build spires to point people to the church;) but for a spire to act as a guide to point a wayfarer to a *Methodist chapel,* which was the edifice of which our friend was speaking, is rather a novel office for a spire to perform, and one into which, if we may so speak, it has rather stealthily crept in these modern times of startling change; an office which does not appear as yet to have received the formal sanction of the Conference, or of the Legal Hundred, although it has gained the expressed approval of the able author of " Modern Anglican Theology."

Cannot the wayfarer, with an English tongue in his head, find his way to City Road, or Bow, or the beautiful chapel at Mildmay Park, without a spire acting as his guide ?

In proof how far some of our spires are likely to guide Wesleyan wayfarers, at least, to a Wesleyan chapel, we may refer to a recent fact. About a mile from one of our chapels lately built in the Church style, a lady, accustomed to attend a Wesleyan chapel, and having pupils under her care, wished to conduct them to the chapel, which she had heard had been opened a week or two before. After wending their way hither and thither, without seeing any structure which bore any resemblance to the style of Wesleyan chapels which she had aforetime attended, almost wearied out with their long search and their circuitous march round what they supposed to be a church having a lofty spire, one of the young ladies, who had been accustomed to attend the Church of England, said, " Well, if we can't find the chapel, let us go into this church; perhaps this is the chapel." " Ridiculous," replied the lady; " *that* a Methodist chapel !" They, however, went in, but would still have been in doubt—as the Prayers were being read —but for the happy circumstance of seeing the familiar countenance of a Wesleyan Minister in the pulpit, who was conducting the devotions.

Not long after, we were in the same locality, and wished to worship in a Wesleyan chapel. It was a lovely Sabbath morning in the early spring. It was pleasing to see so goodly a number, in that quiet part of the great city, going up with various preferences to the different temples of the living God. We were not exactly wayfarers, nor were we far from the newly erected edifice. Had we, however, been favoured with no better " guide " to this Wesleyan chapel than the summit of its steeple, the service would not only have been far spent, but quite over, before we had found it. The edifice is in the Gothic style; and although this style, for sound, for comfort, and for general appearance as a place of worship, is not, in the opinion of many, comparable to either the Grecian or the Italian, yet, compared with some, it is modest and unpretending. The pews and free seats are similar in style, and no special signs of class or caste appear where God only should be worshipped, and where all, whether plebeian or prince, whether they wear a pauper's badge or have a glittering coronet on their brow, have one Father, and one common centre of attraction for the true worshipper in the cross of Christ; and the nearer they draw to that cross, the nearer they must draw to each other. We had prompt and polite attention; books were soon handed to us; a kindness which is gratefully appreciated by strangers, and in which Wesleyans have been lamentably lacking. Much improvement appears in these matters in many of the modern sanctuaries; and we no longer are pained by seeing blind people left to stumble up the aisle, and strangers treated as aliens.

Prayers were being read. If there be any poor there, it is a pity no proper provision is made for the becoming posture of *kneeling*. Scarcely any in the free seats, and but *few* in the body of the chapel, *knelt* during prayer. Surely those who are able to raise a lofty spire cannot plead their inability to provide kneeling-boards or hassocks for the poor. Yet

P

there seems to be a great lack, in these respects, in some of those chapels which are now rising up among us. The Minister read the Prayers devoutly and earnestly, but few responded. One respectable person did so fervently, and was a pattern to the rest; but few seemed disposed to imitate his example. There was no *joint* supplication audible, no volume of voice in the response to the prayer; and to many the service seemed to be as " some strange thing ; " indicating the truth of the remark made in one of our papers, to the effect that " the use of the Church Service does not suit the *general taste of our people.*" *

In the Prayers and Collects for the day, we thought the Minister and a few of the people seemed to throw their souls into the inspiration of this form of sound words; whilst in the prayer and the deeply earnest ejaculations of the Minister after the " prayers," the inspiration seemed to be in the *soul*, and " out of the abundance of the heart the mouth spake." Yet, strange and, as we think, sad to say, even the one solitary audible response which we heard during the form of prayers, died away during the fervent prayer presented by the Minister, whose soul breathed forth its deep desires, and seemed to be stirred within him, whilst he prayed for the Church in its coldness, and the world in its wickedness.

Had not the time been so far spent in the *prayers,*

* " Methodist Recorder."

and had but a little more time been left for the
prayer of the Minister, it would, we doubt not, have
comprehended all that was necessary for saints and
sinners, for the Church and the world, and " for all
ranks and conditions of men." Yet, devout and
" God-breathed " as was that prayer, no mouth testi-
fied, so far as we could hear, in the way of response,
by even a solitary " Amen," that the. hearts of any
were warmed within them, and in unison with that of
the Minister who led the devotions. All lips seemed
to be strangely sealed. How is this? Is it right
that " the people " should say " Amen " to the
prayers as they appear in print and are read ; and is
it indecorous and unbecoming to say " Amen "
during the prayer of the Minister? Where is
the Christian spirit or even the common sense of
this ?

As to a spire being really " an ornament," that,
we suppose, depends much upon the taste of those
who look at it. It interferes too much, some think,
with the uniformity of the appearance to be truly
ornamental. The front of the Mildmay Park, the
Liverpool Road, and such-like chapels, is uniform in
its appearance, and quite as beautiful to look upon
as some we have seen with their lofty and church-
like spires. The majestic *façade* of the mother chapel
in City Road, and the unmistakable Methodist
chapel at Bow, with " Wesleyan " on its front, are

quite as sightly as many of the elaborately ornamented structures which are now rising up.

The spire, then, we regard to be quite unsafe as a
guide at present to *Methodist chapels;* doubtful and
disputed as an ornament; useless as to practical purposes among us; and therefore a great and *costly*
superfluity. If every stone placed one upon another
in its construction during the day, were to be
removed in the night, by the fairies or some such
subtle creatures, to a suitable site, in which a Home
Mission Chapel for a poor neighbourhood was wanted,
a great gain would arise to those needy neighbours,
without any one having to mourn over a great loss
being sustained. No one should mourn over a great
superfluity being dissolved to meet a great *necessity.*
It would be better to sell the ornaments, the jewellery, the trinkets, and even to melt down the plate,
than for any of the family to lack bread. So the
philanthropic Howard thought. The Israelites parted
with their jewels, and sold their possessions, for
bread. There may be a due and proper distance
between the different inmates of a mansion, without
the drawing-room and the kitchen being removed to
the antipodes of prodigality and poverty, superfluity
and starvation; and this simply to keep up appearances.

It would seem passing strange if we found, written
all over the drawing-room of the house, "Super-

,fluous! Superfluous!" and over the kitchen and its empty shelves, "Wanted! Wanted!" If these two words could be emblazoned in juxtaposition, as ex-pressing the extremes of the House of God, then there might also be discerned,—except by those who are in part blinded by the god of this world,—traced by a firm but gentle and gracious hand, that strange sentence: "Sell all that thou hast, and give to the poor." If this precept be not in spirit and substance heeded, may there not sooner or later be beheld, flaming in mystic characters, "Thou art weighed in the balances, and found wanting?"

We should not for a moment scruple to subscribe, under many of the flourishing Reports of Chapel proceedings of modern times, "Superfluous! Super-fluous!"—not as regards their multiplication, but their excessive ornamentation. Whilst the super-fluity of splendour has been raising its steepled head, where there is certainly undisputed room for it to rise higher still in the immensity of space, we have heard, or fancied we have heard, around the base thereof, cries from afar, "Come over and help us!" We have heard the ominous sound of Mission debt,— Institution debt: we have heard the claims of Italy, eager for the bread of life. We have heard of married Ministers striving to subsist on about £80; junior Ministers in England on the sum of £50 or £60; junior Ministers in Wales on about £33. 10s.;

including, as we were told, "*every thing.*" We have
heard of one servant of Christ having only one suit
of clothes in every fifteen years. We have heard of
a devoted Missionary at his wits' end both for clothes
and bread for himself and family, and feeding on
chestnuts. We have heard of Methodist Preachers
in France, without sufficient to eat, and unable to buy
clothing enough to preserve the health and comfort
of their wives and children. We have heard of these
"*starving brethren,*" * who belong to that very house
in which there is "bread enough," and "money
enough," and "to spare." And yet we sing,

"One family we dwell in Him."

"As to that practice of the apostolic Church, the
having all things in common, the early Methodists
had no rule nor any formal design concerning it. But
it was so in effect, and it could not be otherwise; for
none could *want* any thing that *another* could *spare.*
This was the infancy of the work. They had no
conception of any thing that would follow."†

We sing our incomparable Society Hymns :—

"By word and by deed, The bodies in need,
The souls to relieve,
And freely as Jesus hath given to give.

"Then let us attend Our heavenly Friend,
In His members distrest,
By want, or affliction, or sickness opprest :

* "Methodist Recorder," August 4th, 1865, p. 270.
† Wesley.

" Supply all their wants,
And spend and be spent in assisting His saints." *

Some of these suffering members sing also,

"The rougher our way, The shorter our stay ;
The troubles that come
Shall come to our rescue, and hasten us home."

Let not, however, their souls be *in*-gloriously hurried
"away to the skies." They are needed on earth !
The only time we find in the New Testament the
word " superfluity," there is added, " of naughtiness ; "
and it seems to some strange, if not naughty, that
spires should be starting up here and there by the
side of Wesleyan sanctuaries, not only as liberal gifts,
but where it is found hard to beg enough for the
cost. Any matters which, taken in *their association*,
assume the aspect of a grave change, should, we
imagine, not only have the sanction of a few individuals, or even of the Chapel Committee, but be
fairly mooted in the Conference. The tastes and
opinions of a thousand Ministers, and of many
thousands of people, in our great Connexion, should
neither be too largely taken for granted, nor too
quietly ignored. Matters not more significant than
spires, which seem so to connect and confound us
with the churches of the land, have been discussed
in full Conference. We well remember that when

* Hymn 495.

the kind feelings and refined taste of the ladies would have arrayed Ministers in gowns, the subject was well ventilated; eloquent orations were delivered *pro* and *con.*; and, with almost the fire of a Demosthenes, the gown was pronounced to be "a rag of Popery." The able discussion on this question proved for the time fatal to the gown, as far as its general use is concerned. Yet the gown might not only have been a little ornamental, but also useful, if the ladies would kindly have presented all the gowns that would be required as a covering for the coat in the winter, and as a cool and slender substitute in the summer, —in such cases especially as those which have been reported, where new coats come so few and so far between, that two or three coats would be likely to serve the time of one generation.

It can also be remembered how the question, as to whether two or four lines of our hymns should be given out at a time, was discussed with an ability and eloquence which perhaps only Ministers among us who had the tastes of so many people to consult could have brought to bear on so seemingly trivial a topic. Possibly cogent arguments could be given to show that as spires had acted as guides to the churches of this country for centuries past, now they may act as guides for Wesleyan chapels. We con-fess we can see some reason for a spire or a tower containing a bell or bells to summon the people to church in due time; yet no Minister could desire more bells to be ringing on a Sabbath evening, when he seeks to be quiet; and, as far as we know, the spires of Methodism lack the bells. We have not therefore even this show of reason for our spires. Possibly the bells, with some other " sounding brass and tinkling cymbals," may, without care, shortly come.

Some say, spires guide to the Church below; some, they point to the heavens above. But, as it was sagely said in favour of the two lines of our hymns, " Cannot they see how the sense runs ? " so it may be asked, Do we need a finger of stone to point us either to the Church militant or to the Church triumphant ? Do we not, or may we not, " know the way " to both without such a guide? Had the spire no firmer foundation ou which to rest than has the argument which has been adduced for its support, it would, we think, soon come toppling down.

Of course, where towers and spires are liberally presented, persons may please themselves ; yet even then it may be respectfully asked, Would not the " well done " be more surely secured by doing something for the general good ? If there were to be a large Society Meeting, and a great connexional gathering, and it were to be asked, " Shall the wants of ' the body ' be supplied, and all debts paid ; or shall costly towers be built first ? " the good sense and prin-

ciple of the laity, we doubt not, would lead them to
say, "Let us pay our debts first, and then see if there
be any thing to spare for spires." They would hardly
say, "Let us have another collection, which seems
now to be needed." Much less would they say,
"Let us have, as a body, the costliest feathers flying
about our head, although the feet be frost-bitten."
Our skilful architects may think differently, and bring
forth strong arguments another way. The cry has
long been, "Come back to the Church." Our
towers, our spires, our increasing forms seem to say,
"We are coming as near as we can."

We see of how sublime a use is a spire in the esti-
mation of some of high Anglican views. We read of
that church built by the large liberality of Miss
Burdett Coutts at St. Stephen's, Westminster, at a
cost of thirty thousand pounds, whilst many poor
curates have to strive to subsist on sixty pounds *per
annum*. Here, again, are the antipodes of superfluity
and starvation, extravagance and exhaustion, prodigality and privation, Dives and Lazarus! "The
spire is two hundred feet from the ground. See how
its noble spire rises heaven-ward two hundred feet,
and how the 'Day-spring from on high' sheds its
holy light upon tower, turret, upon porch and buttress, setting off the elaborate beauty of their en-
richments in moulding and tracery, in canopy, crocket,
and finial, and the beautiful varieties of sculpture

and architectonic art. A dim religious light har-
monizes the ornamentation throughout this truly
beautiful house of God."* The force of the "architectonic art," we should think, can "no farther go."
When there are breakers a-head, it is well to keep a
strict look-out. The kindness of friends in their
contributions to the cause of God, like that of parents
in the family, needs prudent direction ; or there may
be a cruel and killing fondness. They may poison
while they feed. They may, practically at least,
instead of a fish, give a stone. We sincerely wish
that those modern Methodists, whose tendencies are
to a spire,—especially in localities where there is
nothing to compensate for the expense of the giddy
elevation,—would not only count the cost, but pause
a little, ponder solemnly the principle of stewardship,
and also the principle of proportionate and con-
scientious giving, as taught by the Systematic
Beneficence Society. If, after other claims have
been well considered, they can clearly and confidently
say, with Nehemiah, "The God of heaven, He will
prosper us," let them then arise and build : but let
not the superabounding adornments and superfluous
splendour of the drawing-rooms monopolize the
means for supplying the humble kitchens and the
faithful servants with the necessary provisions.†

* "The Book of Wonders."

† "Do not waste so precious a talent (as money) in gratifying

Again, strict *etiquette,* and often mere empty *form*
and *ceremony,* distinguish the fashionable drawing-
room party. Later lessons than those which Lord
Chesterfield gave to his son, may be deemed
proper for the fashionable of modern times. Guests
are often expected to come in what is curiously
enough called "full dress." They must enter, they
must sit and rise, in due form, they must interchange
compliments; they must bow and retire with all that
politeness and proper punctiliousness which charac-
terize good society. And if there were no feigned
lips there, no vain words, no arts of dissimulation,
no fulsome compliments,—false as the flattering
epitaph on the cold marble,—then how much more

the desire of the eye by superfluous or expensive apparel, or by needless ornaments. Waste no part of it in curiously adorning your
houses; in superfluous or expensive furniture; in costly pictures,
painting, gilding, books; in elegant rather than useful gardens.
Let your neighbours, who know nothing better, do this: 'Let the
dead bury their dead; but what is that to thee?' says our Lord:
'Follow thou Me.' Are you willing? Then you are able so to do.
Why should you throw away your money in superfluities of any
kind? Whenever you expend anything to please your taste, you pay
so much for sensuality. When you lay out money to please your
eye, you give so much for an increase of curiosity. While you are
purchasing anything which men use to applaud, you are purchasing
mere vanity. Had you then not enough vanity, sensuality, and
curiosity before? Was there need of any addition? And would
you pay for it too? What manner of wisdom is this? Would not
the literally throwing your money into the sea be a less mischievous
folly?"—WESLEY's Sermon "On the Use of Money."

to be desired is the true and real refinement of polished society than that rustic rudeness and boast-ful boorishness in which some seem to glory ! But, if we must be between the horns of such a dilemma, we should greatly prefer even Johnsonian bluntness, which disclosed both a *head* and a *heart*, to that sickly sentimentality which betrays the absence of both ; and that deep dissimulation which is so often and so artfully disguised beneath the glittering tinsel, the strict proprieties and punctilios, of those who live and move only in the " world of fashion." There is often masked, beneath the flattering mien which is no index to the contents of the heart, much mental reservation ; and the true meaning of the vain words which fall from the feigned lips may be generally taken as directly the opposite—the very antipodes—of what it seems, on the surface of things, to be. " Let love be without dissimulation," was the apostle's admonitory advice. Let there be no sham : let there be nothing hollow and pretentious; no seeming to be what you really are not. That searching scrutiny which is so often spoken of, as exercised by the great Head of the Church over the heart, admonishes us of its deep deceitfulness. " And all the churches shall know that I am He which searcheth the reins and hearts." * So deceitful is that heart,

* Rev. ii. 23.

that man not only deceives others, but, most fully and most fatally, deceives himself.

Decency, due form, proper decorum, become the house of God, in all its departments. In these respects, there has been, doubtless, much improvement among Wesleyans in modern days; as was, indeed, greatly needed. A slovenliness of style in the sanctuary was associated, too generally, with a shameful slovenliness of manner in the worshippers. Both have been, of late, "under correction." A meed of praise is due to Dr. Jobson, whose acknowledged architectural skill stirred up the Connexion from its slovenliness in this department. Extremes, however, beset us on every hand; and from the one we run, with amazing and almost imperceptible rapidity, to the other. So, from the careless, the negligent, and the slovenly, we may proceed to the

" Icily regular and the splendidly null."

That we are doing so on too large a scale, here and there, is no matter of question in the minds of many good-hearted Methodists. "I don't know what we Methodists are coming to," is the unshaped sentence which, in some form or other, is frequently falling from the lips of many of our people, who are not disposed to complain, or to seek any bone of contention, and who make no more of their sundry misgivings than quietly lamenting over the strange things they see and hear. The subject on which we now speak has been already in part anticipated. How is it that in so many of our modern chapels, whilst the "Church Service," so termed, is *reviving*, the scriptural and hearty responses, the fervent "Amens" of old Methodist times, are fast *dying out?* We seem to be living in times which, in the future history of Methodism, may be marked by a revival of *forms*, rather than, as was wont, by a revival of the *work of God.*

We have heard prayers, at the dedication of some of our sanctuaries, such as could scarcely be put into print,—prayers as from tongues of fire,—prayers as of the Spirit's immediate inspiration, "while they were yet speaking,"—prayers of unutterable fervour and importunity, and as suitable and comprehensive as Solomon's dedicatory prayer; and we could not but think at such times, that had there been the manifestly joint and earnest supplication of the people, accompanied by a general and audible response of intelligent but hearty "Amens," such as seem to be implied in, "Let all the people say, Amen," and such as were wont to be heard in our Methodist sanctuaries, the flame of devotion would have been fanned, the windows of heaven would have been opened, Pentecostal power, floods of heavenly influence, would have descended; so that at the close of the service something else would have had to be done besides counting a good collection, and telling how many pounds were added to the building funds. Most Methodists would admit that it would be much better to have to tell the number of the saved, and how many, on the very day of the temple's dedication, the Lord added to the Church.

"It will be cold," said a Christian lady, as she was going to one of the dedicatory services of a costly chapel, eminently in the Church style, "It will be cold for the penitents to kneel round that communion;"—for it seems there was cold stone even there;—"but, O, I fear we shall not have many penitents to kneel there." "It was," as we were informed one of the Ministers at the opening services stated, "more like an *altar* in a Romish chapel than a *communion*." The cold stone,—the variegated colours on the crimson communion cloth,—the large Gothic-looking chairs, with their crimson cushions, —in short, the general appearance, as that prudent Minister pronounced it to be, was "positively Popish." The kind and liberal-hearted friends who largely contributed, and those who made their different offerings, according to their different tastes, had not, we believe, even a distant idea of anything that savoured of the Popish. Yet these undesigned Popish appearances and misguided contributions show how easy it is to *slide* without intending it, when we wilfully get into *slippery* places.

These Popish appearances seem likely, in some cases, to furnish a bone of contention in the Church. In more than one place we have heard of the steeple being a subject of strife. In another the communion cloth seems likely to be a cause of contention. Some say, it looks Popish, and must be taken out of the way. This, of course, may be more easily removed than the spire. Such occurrences seem to mark the propriety and grave necessity of some *general plan* being prescribed, which, while avoiding absolute uniformity, as to the style and garniture of our chapels or "churches," as some now incline to call them, would nevertheless put an end to these endless diversities and clashing anomalies of appearance among us. For that which may please the tastes of a few, may offend the tastes of many. Thus the seeds of discord may be unwittingly sown; strife, evil surmising, and evil-speaking may be engendered. A large powder-magazine may be preparing, which, though silently slumbering for a season, may at length startle the "men" who "slept" by a tremendous explosion. However wide extremes may do in isolated Congregational Churches, it would surely be prudent policy, as far as possible, to avoid them in a Connexion like ours, which is one body, and which so many of its members call "*our* body." It would be vain to think that these clashing opinions, even on these minor matters, which, to judge from our weekly papers, are stirring the minds of many of our people, can long co-exist among us without endangering our Connexional unity and harmony. It would be worse than vain, by any dogmatic deliverances about " morbid views " and " gloomy notions," and such like, to suppress the upheavings of those minds whose jealous fears cannot be worse than a carnal security, or the mere dream of peace and safety.

We would therefore respectfully, but earnestly, call upon the Conference, and especially the members of the Legal Hundred, to turn formal attention to these matters of style in our Church, which in time may become matters of strife. The House of Lords sits on very small matters. Can it be beneath the dignity or design of such a grave and glorious gathering as the Conference, to speak decisively on the *style* of things, to speak on the *fashions* in our church, as well as on the fashion of the world, and to tell us how near akin they are? Surely some of these things are as important in their aspect and bearing as the question whether two or four lines of our hymns should be given out at a time,—a question which has been ably and eloquently discussed. We call on the Conference, instead of consigning and confining these matters of style to the careful consideration of the Chapel Committee, and then receiving the report of its noble doings, and meekly hear-

ing its reproofs as to irregular cases, to take into its
own calm and collective consideration the general
style of our chapel-building in these modern days,
and to tell us whether our esteemed Chapel Committee has not, in the very midst of its glorious
march, given its sanction to as great and grave
irregularities in the style of our churches, as any it
has recorded and reproved in its own excellent and
beautiful Chapel Report.   We call on the Conference to tell us where the old and noble ship is steering.   Is she in some narrow straits, with rocks close
on either hand?   Is she getting near the sands or
shoals?   Is the compass correct?   Any slight
variations may endanger the vessel.   Are we getting
out of our latitude, or are we steering by the same
old rules, and minding the same thing?   Have so
many of " the people called Methodists " only the
nightmare, or are they troubled by the hauntings of
a morbid imagination?   And may they still say,
" Give to the winds thy fears? "   What counsel
would some of the old men and the fathers give, as
to the fashion of things here and there appearing?
Would not Wesley, if among us, make an unmis-
takeable onslaught on some of these innovations?
Should we not have another masterly " Appeal to
Men of Reason and Religion ? "   We need not wish
for his " ghost."   In his faithful Sermons, with their
peculiar point and power, and in the bright pattern

of a pure and practical life, which he has left us as a legacy, he " being dead yet speaketh."

The world is so full of style and fashion, that it would be strange if the wondrous wand of that mighty enchantress were not waved over the Church, so as to ensnare with its witchery, if possible, even the very elect.

Reverence, of course, becomes the house of the Lord; but what is "the *dignity* of worship," but its true spirituality, sincerity, and *simplicity?* What is dignity in the eyes of that God who looketh not at the outward appearance, but pondereth the heart? The word, so applied, seems to us a little novel and misleading, and to have a strong smatch of the worldly in it.

It is not thought unseemly, or even undignified, for tens of thousands, in the churches of this land, in due and proper form, and with cold ceremonialism, as they pray, to *say* that they are " miserable sinners;" but if only a few poor penitent publicans were so to *feel* that they were miserable sinners as to cry mightily for mercy, and especially if each were to smite upon his breast, as he cried, "God be merciful to me, a sinner!" this would doubtless be deemed as unbecoming to "the dignity of public worship," as would the crying of a child be considered beneath the propriety of the drawing-room. Some penitents, we have heard, who have thus been stricken with a sense of sin, have cried aloud for mercy; but it was not at the proper time or in the proper way; and lest the infection should spread, and the decorum of devotion should be further disturbed, they have been taken out, and some medical man has been called to them, as the most proper person to prescribe for them, and to check the disorder. What is such dignity or decorum to the Deity? It is beneath "the Lofty One." "But a broken and a contrite heart God will not despise."

We had penned the substance of the preceding pages, when we incidentally met with an article full of important and suggestive sentences in the "London Quarterly Review," on "the Recent Methodist Conference." Two aptly chosen words in that able article, we found, contained the substance of what, in other words, we had just before written. The two extremes to which we have referred in connexion with the sanctuary, are in that article well put, as the "reaction from *carelessness* towards *ceremonialism.*" * That, it is added, would be a "deadly danger." We felt grateful to the writer for these remarks, so tersely and so strongly put. The views embodied in that article seem to be cautiously balanced. The writer, we apprehend, is not in danger on the side of carelessness, if he do not err on

---

* " London Quarterly Review," October, 1864, p. 231.

the side of the ceremonial. There are words wise and weighty enough to be expanded into a volume.

In the minds, then, both of the scrupulous and of the sanguine, there seems to be a prevailing idea of danger in the position and aspects of modern Methodism; danger lest we should strive to be satisfied with the semblance and the shadow of good things rather than with their substance; danger lest, whilst we retain the form, we should deny the power. And with regard even to the *appearance* and the *posture* of devotion in several of our modern sanctuaries, we have too little reason to congratulate ourselves as to improvement. Are not many of the worshippers among us less reverential in these respects than the Puseyite and the Papist? There is less of the dignity of public devotion, unless it be considered dignified to *sit* during prayers. Could we find Romish chapels, in this country or on the Continent, in which, during prayers or the mass, the generality of the worshippers would be seen comfortably seated? We trow not. Are they not to be found kneeling during their many and long prayers in their chapels and cathedrals, and, on the Continent, kneeling long before their *croix* on the cold ground? Yet we have seen, and that, too, at the dedication of the chapel, and during most fervent and importunate prayers, scarcely any besides a few children kneeling; a sight which forcibly reminded us of our Lord's language,

"Except ye be converted, and become as little children." About four or five men were standing, and, as far as we could possibly perceive, all the rest were sitting.

In chapels of very moderate pretensions as to style, we often find the poor sufficiently repelled and restrained, especially where the worshippers have a style of worldly conformity and worldly bearing about them, and where, although many of them are professing Christians, they seem to forget that they are strangers and pilgrims on the earth, and to forget, too, that the fashion of this world passeth away. A devoted Christian gentleman had adjoining his own house a plain humble-looking room, in which there was Methodist preaching, and Prayer Meetings and Class Meetings were held, and where a goodly number of the poor were accustomed to gather week after week. "We built," he said, "a chapel; and although it was a plain building, yet we lost the poor, and could never gather them again. I don't now how it is, except that they thought the chapel was too fine for them, and they felt more cozy in the room, where all seemed to be on a level, as they ought to be in the house of God."

If there be great splendour in the style of the building, great outward show in the attendants, accompanied with a haughty bearing, then, if the pious poor be not repelled altogether from the chapel,

they are likely to feel under such restraint when they
are there, that it will hardly be to them as their
Father's house,—hardly a home of the soul. They,
it is evident, will not, cannot, under such restraining influences, feel at home, as all God's children
ought to feel, how humble and poor soever they may
be. Though the chapel be like a magnificent
drawing-room, when compared with the humble cottage which they call their home, yet the pious poor
should, somehow or other, be made to feel that that
beautiful house of God is not for the rich people and
the fine folks merely, but that it is their Father's
house, and that they are always welcome, and
expected there.

If this free, happy, home-feeling be first lessened
and then lost, whatever material grandeur may be
gained in God's house, it will be a poor and pitiful
exchange ; it will be as the barter of the heavenly
birthright of God's children for a mess of pottage.
There can be nothing in the material finery of the
habitation of God's house, or of its attendants, that
can supply the lack of the home feeling which should
subsist among those who, whether rich or poor, are
alike the needy and dependent children of the one
Father in heaven, and who form part of one family
upon earth. There can be nothing in the mere
material grandeur of God's house to carry them in
sweet constraint from the poverty of their own dwell-

ings to a holy atmosphere where they shall forget for a
time all their cares and trials; nothing to create in
them, when absent, that longing of spirit for the communion of the sanctuary which the Psalmist so
strongly and beautifully expresses : " My soul longeth,
yea, even fainteth for the courts of the Lord."* The
worshippers there must not be stiff, stern, statue-
like isolations, like so many dignitaries, seeming, at
least, to say, " Stand thou at a distance ; for I am
greater—if not holier—than thou." When the
children come, not to adore or worship each other,
but to worship the Father, and to beg for a Father's
blessing, there should be family meetings, spiritually
social gatherings. " Yea, the sparrow hath found an
house,"—or, " As the sparrow findeth an house, and
the swallow a nest for herself, so findeth my soul
Thine altars, O Lord of hosts, my King, and my
God. Blessed are they that dwell in Thy house :
they will be still praising thee." " They go from
strength to strength," " from company to company,"
gathering happy associations as they go. " Every
one of them in Zion appeareth before God." †

We know many large and beautiful sanctuaries in
our Zion, where the chief adornment is that beauty of
holiness in which the Lord is worshipped there.
These sanctuaries comprise several of the leading and
most influential laymen among us. They may be

* Psalm lxxxiv. 2. † Psalm lxxxiv. 3–7.

truly called "great men," but not less truly may they be called "good men." These chief men, without abating one jot of their greatness, by divers acts of kindness during the week, as well as by sundry attentions on the Sabbath, dispel from the minds of the worthy poor the dread idea of there being any great gulf between them. If they are distinguished as the chief men there, they are not less so by their acts of charity. They have a willing ear to listen to the tale of woe, a tender heart to sympathize with the poor in their struggles and sorrows, and, as the almoners of Christ, a liberal hand to help them in their great distresses. Thus the poor are made, not to envy, but to share the wealth and greatness of their richer brethren. They cheerfully render the honour which is due to them, and gladly give them, without their asking, the well-deserved title of "gentlemen." How greatly do those who have the ornament of a Christ-like spirit beautify and adorn the house of the Lord! There the rich and the poor meet together; they pray together, they sing together, they commune together. There the rich recognise in the poor the grandeur of a deathless soul,—a soul that will live as long as their own,—a soul that cost as much and as precious a price to redeem it,—a soul that may possess as glorious a mansion, as rich an inheritance, and blaze forth as brightly with cherubim and seraphim in the presence of God, where the distinctions of earth shall have passed away, and where character alone shall be honoured.

Where the rich and the poor thus meet together, there is to be found the perfection of that order which "becometh the house of the Lord." Where there is such a happy combination of the two classes, mutual dependence is recognised, and both, as brethren and as members of Christ's body, dwell together in unity, thus constituting, not a select gathering, not a class, but a complete "house," a "whole assembly," one family and household of faith, having Christ as their Head. In this body the head does not despise the feet, nor do the feet envy the higher position of the head. In this "great house" the weightier vessels do not clash against and crush the weaker ones. "The vessels of gold and of silver," although they may belong to the more ornamental part of the house, are not more useful nor more prized than the vessels of wood and of earth,—the potter's vessels. The latter will have often to be used in the Master's service; whilst the former may be more admired, as having a higher and more honourable department of service. Both should have their proper place in the great house.

There may, however, be the greater glitter where there is the less gold. There may be the mimicry and mockery of what is good where there is no part or lot in the matter. There may be the haughty head, the strut of significance, the air of importance; there may be great swelling words of vanity, and the walking in a vain show, where there is little or nothing "lovely and of good report." Grandees of this kind, instead of radiating religious heat, and bringing live coals with them, cast a chilling influence round them from their centre to their circumference, and are likely to think much more of the dignity than of the devotion that becomes the house of the Lord. They are much more for the ornamental than for the useful part of the great house; and may find it hard to say, "I had rather be a *door-keeper* in the house of God than dwell in the tents of wickedness." If the influence of such predominates in the Church of which they are the nominal members, then most things will be after their mould, and bear their impress. Things even within the house of the living God will be after a worldly fashion, after the fashion of things within their own house. There will be a worldly sanctuary. Under such influences, the sacred things, yea, the sacred services of the sanctuary, may savour more of the spirit of the world than of the things which be of God; and the living word itself may prove the "savour of death unto death." There may thus be in the holy place the style and spirit of the fashionable party rather than the worship in spirit and in truth. Style, style, style, may reign supreme there; the outward appearance,—that on which God looks least, but man looks most.

Under such influences, spirits that should be free indeed may be so straitened as to become like religious statuary, soulless, lifeless. They may appear before the Lord, and tune their " formal songs ; " but

> " Hosannahs languish on their tongues,
> And their devotion dies."

They may be more like blocks of marble or of ice than living souls or flames of fire. This splendid semblance may pass for the dignity of public devotion, but such public devotion may be as that of the Pharisee,—a devotion to that which is public and may be seen of men, rather than the worship of the Invisible, and a supreme regard to things not seen. The order of God's house may be much after the order of our own. The decorum of the sanctuary may draw too near in its spirit to the cold formalities of the drawing-room. There may be carnal ordinances and a worldly sanctuary. Little may be seen and realized except that which is visible to mortal eye, and tangible to mortal touch. It may not be inward spiritual worship, but sensuous externalism ; and amid the sensuous, the spiritual outflowings of souls that taste the powers of the world to come are likely to be repressed and restrained. The enemy may thus lift up a standard against the Spirit, when He comes as a mighty rushing wind, or as floods on the dry ground.

Is there no danger, amid this stiffening style of

things among us, of there being a compression, instead of an expansion, of the chest, and of souls being so straitened that they can hardly breathe freely up to God, when God breathes most fully into the soul the breath of life?—a danger of putting bonds around the bounding heart which the Son has made free?—a danger of making mute those tongues which should sing, and sometimes shout aloud, their great Redeemer's praise, loud enough for others to "hear thereof and be glad?"—a danger of making strait paths for the feet of those who may be well excused, if, after having long been lame, they leap for joy as soon as they have found their feet?—a danger, after the fashion of these modern times, of getting on our souls a yoke of stiff forms and ceremonies, rather than getting our souls into glorious liberty?—a danger lest the once proverbially free-speaking Methodists should "basely fear," even in their Father's house, to speak of a Father's love, and should become so silent in His praise that even the comparatively dumb of other denominations will be constrained to admonish us?

The house of God may thus be narrowed and circumscribed, where it is not designed nor desired, till the Sabbath gathering be more after the manner of a select stylish party than one which comprises all the different members of one great household and parts of a "general assembly." That house, with its splendid style of architecture, its style of singing, its style of service, its style of attendants, may be but part of a house for God: a part may be kept back by so much style. The service rendered there may be as proper and punctilious as though decreed by the law of the land, or by the law of Moses, rather than by the law of love. There may be more of cold ceremony than of the warm glow of Christian communion. There may be more of the servility of superstition than of the simplicity and spirituality of true worship. There may be more of the stern restraint of the servant or the slave than of the unrestrained filial freedom of a child. We may thus be brought into bondage again; yea, even the Father's house may be felt to be a house of bondage, where there is more of the etiquette that governs the drawing-room than of the ease of children at home.

The once warm-hearted Methodist may possibly become, by as stealthy a process as that of petrifaction, almost as much hedged in by prescription as the punctilious Puseyite,—as ceremonial as the Church, and as cold as the Church vestry. There may be in the sanctuaries among us that style displayed in various forms, which places the poor in as painful restraint as if, with their humble apparel, their conscious provincialisms, their unpolished manners, they were to be ushered into the midst of a full-dress drawing-room party. That which pleases the eyes of some so much may dazzle, to a painful degree, and then drive away the poor, who were to be always with us, and without whom we have not a full family, nor a complete circle of the household of faith.

Moreover, if the poor were to come in those numbers in which it is desirable they should come to the house of God, and in that manner in which they must come, if they come at all, and gather, as penitents once did, around the communion rail, there may be fears that the varnish may be injured, and that some damage may be done to the decorative parts of the sanctuary. Such fears, we have heard, are cherished by some, and not, we suppose, without just ground. We would have no damage done to those splendid sanctuaries which have been built by the large offerings of Christian benevolence; and which serve at least to show what even the Methodists can do in the way of architecture. In many places, indeed, they are not a whit behind the churches of the land, and in some localities are much before them. But these grand buildings also show that whilst a house of God can be built in which " nothing has been spent in the way of mere ornament, but the whole of which is a perfect ornament, chaste, beautiful, and pleasing, in its arrangements, every way becoming the house of God, with sitting accommodation for four hundred and sixty-three persons, with vestries, and a good school-room; the cost of the whole being only £1,500; " another, which will hold perhaps scarcely double the number, may be so expensively built, and so elaborately adorned, that it may cost three, four, or five times as much money,* —nine or ten thousand pounds.

But by all means let there be, not a small cramped up vestry, but a good, simple, commodious room, which, for its plainness, its warmth, and suitable provisions, may be likened to the kitchen in the house; a room in which the rich need not be ashamed to meet the poor, nor the poor afraid to meet the rich.

Many of the poor would prefer an humble room with plain provisions, where they could have freedom and social enjoyment, and could "eat their meat with gladness," to even a rich repast under painful restraint. "Better is a dinner of herbs where love is, than a stalled ox and hatred therewith."† The poor must have something suited to their tastes, as well as the rich. "Plain things for plain people." Better to them would be the simple breaking of bread, as in the upper room, where they had all things common, where they could enjoy the fellowship of saints, and where they could all with one accord give glory to their common Lord, than the

---

* "Chapel Report, 1864," p. 106.   † Proverbs xv. 17.

R

richest intellectual repast, the choicest flowers of rhetoric, and the most imposing forms and ceremonies, where the whole fashion of things placed them under religious restraint. The general family feeling pervading the Methodist people has made them one, from whatever point of the compass they came. They have felt, though from the antipodes, that they were of the same kith and kin. Though of different languages, one could ejaculate, "Hallelujah!" and another could respond, "Amen!" This fraternal feeling has been fostered by their meetings for Christian fellowship, by the weekly Class, by their feasts of love, their ἀγάπαι. Whatever would weaken these family bonds would weaken the great body of Methodists. Splendour of style and of service would be a sad substitute for this family feeling.

For this social element good provision must be made, somehow or somewhere, in connexion with God's house. In Mechanics' Institutes, club-rooms, and such like, it is not forgotten that man is a social being. Christian Churches are not isolations, but social gatherings: they form a household, a family, a flock. And in these gatherings there should be a sacred warmth, so that Christians should not be like pillars of stone, or as cold as moonlight, but should rather resemble glowing sunbeams, that those who are afar off may see their light, and feel the sun, and that those who come from a cold bleak world may have no just cause to complain that it is colder still in the church, which is the house of the living God, and where there should be provisions always ready, ever burning fires, with the warmest welcomes to all who may come.

Let there be rooms to which rude rustics and sluggish swains from the highways and hedges may be compelled to come; a room to which the poor, the maimed, the halt, the blind, and the work-people may come and be welcome; where there shall be no mystic sign, which the poor so soon and so sensitively interpret, that seems to say that they are not wanted there; where the aged and infirm who yet linger among us, still retaining the old Methodist stamp, but who are so fast dying out, may freely speak, in "thoughts that breathe and words that burn," of the great things which God has done for them. What matter though Murray's rules and the Queen's English be a little marred there, if there be loyalty to the Queen, and love and honour to the King of Kings?

Let there be a room in which good service shall be done for a good Master; where dull scholars shall find a fashion of teaching as free as it is wonderful; where perishing prodigals shall meet with bread enough; where the ragged may be clad; and where not only the soul may find manna, but the body may, in special cases, be supplied with the necessaries of life. Let there be there, too, a good staff of willing and humble servants, who do not stand upon terms, who are ready to hew wood, or to draw water, or to wash the disciples' feet; ready to catch the Master's least command; and who are always about the Master's business. Let rooms be multiplied in which and around which a good deal of *Home Mission work* shall be done; for this seems now especially to be the salt of Methodism, without which, whatever may be the march of its magnificence, it will lose the freshness of its vitality, and see corruption. Without such works of faith and labour of love, chapels may be multiplied and magnified, but their magnificence will be but the mockery of her departed glory. Even the boasted uncorruptness of her faith without these works will be dead.

If there be felt by our simple-minded people, amid the splendours of style, more of the restraining than of the constraining influences, we must have, as Methodists and as members of the household of faith, social and family gatherings somewhere, where all may not only freely partake of the provisions of the Gospel, but where it shall not be deemed impolite and out of place freely to descant on the quality of the provisions; where the rich and poor may frankly declare what they have felt and seen, and say that they have tasted that the Lord is good; and sing as in the ancient days,—

" The King Himself comes near,
And feasts His saints to-day:
Here we may sit, and see him here,
And love, and praise, and pray."

We hardly know which to admire most, the prudence or the piety of the esteemed President of the
Jubilee year, in the plan proposed of having a kind
of lovefeast associated with the Jubilee offerings.
That which Missionaries had felt and seen was told
us; hearts were moved and warmed, hands were
opened, many of the people freely cast into the
treasury. We want a revival of this heartfelt old-
fashioned Methodism among us. This would adorn
with the beauty of holiness our humblest rooms,
make even our most beautiful sanctuaries more
beautiful still, and give a dignity to our worship on
which the Lofty One Himself would look with
delight. We want a revival of this old lovefeast
spirit; a revival of the old family feeling throughout
all our drawing-rooms and kitchens; a revival of the
old fashion of things in some of these respects among
us, before all the venerable old men of Methodism
quite die out; before old Methodism gets altogether
into new hands, and takes a new and strange,
though not a softer, not a more spiritual mould;
before all our chapels become churches, our preachers
clergymen, our sacred psalmody a skilled performance; before our life-inspiring, heaven-moving

prayers shall be lost in lifeless forms, liturgical services, and vain repetitions; and before the people once known as "those who turned the world upside down," shall be no longer to be recognised as "the people called Methodists."

CHAPTER XIII.

May not lay agency be employed among us to a much greater extent than it now is? We have doubtless a vast number of laymen who are well able, if they were willing, not only to give their gold to God's cause,—one sovereign per year to our various funds,—but also to watch and work one hour for God during some of the days of the week. It would be a sad and strange thing if, while some of the Churches of the land are waking up to the claims of the world around them, and to the importance of lay agency in order to overtake those claims, the Methodists, who have startled the slumbering Churches, should now fold their arms, and begin to slumber themselves. It would be a pity if, while others are rapidly advancing in this respect, there should be a retrograde movement with Wesleyans. It would be a shame if, while others are evoking the long latent talents of their laity, ours should become dormant. It would be a disgrace if, while others now begin to confess that it is really better " that souls should be uncanonically saved than that they should be canonically damned," * we Wesleyans, who were once said to be

* Dr. Cumming.

" all at it, and always at it," should begin to contract our soul-saving agency to any class or order of men.

Surely, any man saved by the grace of God himself should strive to save others. Surely those who have tasted the good word of God will not want to eat their morsel alone. Surely those who have been saved from the burning gulf themselves will try to pluck others as brands from the burning. Surely the wrecked one, now safe in the lifeboat, will hold out his hand to save another from the wreck. "There is another man on board," was the sepulchral whisper that came from a shrivelled skeleton of a man who had long lain under the canvass of part of a wrecked vessel, and had been taken by brave British tars on board their own frigate. As they were bending over the lifeless-looking form, this was the first utterance of lips which till then seemed to be sealed in death, —" There is another man on board."* You, brethren, have been rescued from death ; will you not come to the rescue of others? Myriads of other men there are, in this " world that lieth in wickedness," who are in danger of being drowned in perdition. We want you not only to help by your money those who seek in order to save the lost, but also, as much as you can, to try *yourselves* to save souls from death, and thus to hide multitudes of sins. Go and help those

---

* Dr. Guthrie's Ezekiel.

whose mission it is to save men. Go, too, alone; and yet not alone, for the Father will be with you. Go when and where you can. Go in season and out of season. Souls are wrecked and perishing; man the lifeboat; haste to their help; save the lost.

The labours from which the dead in Christ shall rest, and the works which follow them, cannot be labour only for the bread that perisheth, and for riches that corrupt. There must be *working*, as well as *giving*, for God. Many of our laity do both work and give, and some seem to be "servants of all work." They are ready to do any work that is wanted to be done in the vineyard of the Lord. Some we know who lead classes, preach, visit the sick, give their counsel in committees, often sit many tedious hours at a magistrates' meeting during the day, preside at a Missionary Meeting in the evening, and in various ways abound in the work of the Lord. Yet, though attentive to their Master's business, they do not neglect their own, nor suffer their servants to neglect it; and they have upon it that blessing of God which maketh rich. Such men make the best of both worlds; and prove the truth of the old maxim that "to live well is to have two lives,"— "the promise of the life that now is, and of that which is to come."

Such persons seem to have a kind of ubiquity and omnipotence. They have arrived at the "all things possible ; " and hardly is a work allotted them before they are ready to say, " It shall be done." They put forth not an officious hand in " a lordly" way, but the hand of kind co-operation in every good work, both in the world around them, and in the Church of which they are members. They aid the counsels, share the cares, and bear the burdens of those who are over them in the Lord. Like the sun, they are " beautiful, blessing, and blest." " I do not wish," was the remark of one of these zealous servants of God to the writer, " that it should be said at my death, ' I am glad he is gone.' "

We would not say too hard things of the opposite class; yet are there not many sad drones in the Methodist hive? Are there not many who rest on their lees,—many loiterers in the vineyard? Whilst there are some who are ever ready to do whatever is wanted to be done, are there not many others who have next to nothing to do, and who have hardly time to do that? What is worse, they stand in the way of the well-doings of others; they are a constant check to the workers,—dead weights and heavy drags on the wheels of the chariots. There are some who can hardly be said, though in the vineyard, to work at all : they are idle all the day, nor do they live or give except to themselves. They " sleep as do others." They say, " Lord, Lord ; " but their meat is not " to do the will of" their " Father." They know not the sublime luxury of doing good, of ministering unto others, of serving the Lord. Every body and every thing must wait on and minister unto them. They seem to be surrounded by a sort of revolving machinery, which marvellously adapts itself to their wants, their wishes, and their whims. Scarcely have they arisen from their slumbers before their table is spread before them. They take their morning drive, survey the smiling landscape, and are fanned by the sea-breeze. They beguile the time, and drive away dull care, by reading, it may be, the religious novels; then, after the fatigues of the day, they again seek "nature's sweet restorer, balmy sleep." Thus day after day is spent, and no duty is done, no service performed for Christ. There is no sowing to the Spirit.

It is possible to be liberal, and yet listless and lazy. Some give who will not work for God. Nay, they give in order that they may not be expected to work. They "commute with their gold;" they perform their duty by proxy. Are there not many among us who, when they are wanted to work, do nothing but make excuse? Who can hear our gifted and godly laymen speak in our committees and elsewhere, and not be impressed with the solemn fact that Methodism has vast and as yet unexplored resources, besides those of a mere monetary nature, in her laity? Here is a deep and unfathomed mine, from which much precious ore may be extracted, and many "a gem may be brought up, flashing with the light of intellect, and glowing with the hues of Christian graces!"* A host of men might be called out, not to the regular ministry only, but to work for God; "called," in some sense, to the "home work" in the varied spheres in which they live and move.

Can you not, dear brethren, in your cities, towns, villages, hamlets, if not in a pulpit, in a room in a house, preach the Gospel behind a chair, hold forth the world of life? or, if not *preach*, can you not *speak* words of truth and soberness for Christ, words that may win souls to Christ? "A word spoken in season, how good it is!" "A verse may find him who a sermon flies." † Could you not, if baptized with the Holy Ghost, go into the city, and say to the men of the city, "Come and see a man that told me all things that ever I did? Is not this the Christ?" Cannot you, as lovers of Christ, by your influence, by your example, by your prayers, by your earnest efforts, be Missionaries to the heathen at home? You may erect the cross in your own house; preach Christ to your own family, and friends, and neighbours; form a Church in your own dwelling; establish a Mission station in the midst of the masses who are perishing around you. You may instruct the ignorant, warn the wicked, win the wanderer, save the

* Rev. R. Watson.   † Herbert's "Church Porch."

lost. Let the laity in their different localities itine-rate a little, as they have time; go now and then on missions of mercy; follow more fully in the steps of the Great Pattern; go about doing good; and thus leave some footprints on the sands of time, and leave the world better for their having been in it. Take a few tracts with you, when you seek a change of air; these will speak when you cannot. Sow thus the seeds of truth; sow beside all waters; sow in righteousness; sow as you expect a harvest; and you shall reap in mercy. " And let us not be weary in well doing; for in due season we *shall* reap, if we faintnot."

It has been said, that in the day of final account the first subject of inquiry, next to our own personal salvation, will be, " How came thy wife, thy child, thy servant, thy neighbour, to perish ? " * O ! were dormant energies roused, were the sinners in Zion startled from their slumbers, were buried talents called up from their graves; were our Zion to arise and shake herself from the dust; then, instead of about seventy Home Missionaries, we might have some seventy thousand or more rising up, who as burning luminaries might " chase the gloom of hellish night."

In Methodism there are fine opportunities for all kinds of talents to be employed. There is a post for

* Dr. Harris.

every man ; would that every man were at his post ! At the " poor dying rate " at which we are going, we can never overtake the wants and woes of the rapidly multiplying world which is our parish.   Our spiritual state, as individuals and as Churches, would be revived by earnest godly exercise.   The man ready to perish in the snow-storm, who sees one who is prostrate and perishing, wrapped in his winding-sheet of snow, and begins to rub the frozen limbs of his fellow traveller, invigorates his own, circulates his own blood, and saves himself from the dreadful death-chill by saving another.   When Wesley was dull and low on board ship, he did not read a novel to dispel the dulness, but spoke to the poor cabin-boy; and that did both the boy and himself good.   When Andrew Fuller's Church was low, he preached comfortably to them; he largely administered cordials; yet still they languished.   At length they began to pray for the perishing heathen, and then they began to revive themselves.

Go and work in God's vineyard, and you will have God's smile; and that smile will be far better to you than reading religious fiction, or whiling away time in religious dissipation.   Go and water others, and you shall be watered ; bless others, and you shall be blessed in your deed.

" Wilt thou dine with the boys to-day ?" said the late Joseph Sturge to his friend Mr. Bowley.   Those

boys were very bad boys, whom the benevolent
Sturge was trying to make better in a Reformatory
School. "I have no objection," replied his friend.
He did so, and in doing so his heart was glad that
he had grace to imitate that Saviour who stooped
Himself to lift up the fallen from their low and lost
estate. This, we are persuaded, is the *style* of thing
which, as modern Methodists, we want on a much
larger scale than we have at present. "The
iron Duke," who, as a soldier, had to steel his
heart when wading through fields of blood, showed
his sympathy for a poor boy, who moaned over a pet
toad which he had to leave for a little time. The
hero, it is said, took the toad under his own care, and
issued a bulletin that it was alive and doing well.
The Earl of Shaftesbury seems to perform the part of
a moral scavenger, in seeking to rid the streets of
rude and ragged boys, and placing some of them in
posts of trust and honour. In aiding also in the
moonlight mission of mercy, the noble Earl seeks to
transform the foulest and vilest of human kind into
bright gems to adorn the diadem of Christ, whilst he
is adding lustre to his own coronet. Our noble
Queen will visit the poor and the sick, read and kneel
by the bedside of the bedridden and the dying, and
strew flowers on the grave of her own poor servant
whom she had prized. And is she less a lady, or
less a Queen, for doing these things? Meanwhile,

what are many modern Methodists doing? Are they not, in an excess of style in various ways, like Baruch, seeking "great things," whilst they sing "adieu" to these "glittering snares?" Yet our Lord did not seek such vanities: He sought, that He might save, the lost. The King of Kings did not pursue the world's fading pomp. He was not allured by "the kingdoms of this world or the glory of them." Why should those be thus ensnared who are joint heirs with Him, and who can claim, in virtue of their birth, a never-fading crown? He did not confine Himself to select society; He mingled with the common people, and sat down with publicans and sinners, that He might teach them lessons, and do them good.

Let the rising laity, then, as well as the rising ministry, strive to soar by stooping first to lift up the fallen; let them get to perfection's height, and to the mountain top, through the low vale of humble love. Let us pursue the path of our great Pattern, and we shall rise with Christ.

"Human nature is the same in all ranks and ages also. The heart, whether it beat under fustian or under the star of the peer, goes the same as do the works of a watch, whether the case is gold or only pinchbeck. I don't believe in a religion that expends itself in praying and preaching; and still less do I believe in a religion that lies in costly temples and gorgeous ceremonials. The genius of Christianity is love; and her highest worship lies in such works as spring from loving God with all our heart, and loving our neighbour as we do ourselves. Mercy is better than sacrifice. Our religion is one of love, and counts the soul of the poorest cotton-worker to be as precious as the soul of the wealthiest cotton-lord. A diamond is a diamond, whether it lie sparkling on a dust-heap, or shine in a royal crown." *

* Guthrie's "Address on Practical Sympathy."

CHAPTER XIV.

EVER and anon something is being said or written with reference to the rising Ministry amongst us. We do not presume to supply any lack, but wish that those who have written a little on this subject would themselves supply what may be wanting, and would set forth as clearly and as fully as possible that standard to which the Ministry should rise in these days, and what should be the qualification of its candidates. We know that many wise heads have had anxious thoughts on these subjects, and have not scrupled to express them both in private and in public.

Of late, considerable change has been made in the current coin of the realm. The large pennies, the massive old crowns, the hard-gotten old guineas, are now and then to be seen and felt, yet—the last especially—but few and far between. Some time ago we received a long letter making bitter complaints of the manner in which the public had been mulcted by a moulding process, which, while it had brought gain to the Government, had been a loss to the people, who were said not to have now so much for their money. Moreover the change, to simple minds, was a little confounding, as some of the new coin had to be called by a new name and counted in a different way. The old is bigger, and some say better, than the new, having less alloy. We do not wish too much to be made of the above in the way of illustration. The Great Head of the Church has raised up a noble army of young Ministers, " workmen who need not to be ashamed;" nor have the Methodist Churches any reason to be ashamed of them. There are amongst them men eminently adapted to these modern days of scepticism and scorn, of rebuke and blasphemy. As a Connexion, we cannot be too grateful to that God who has called them, and endued them with power from on high. Gold may be had for the claims of the Church; but who, except God Himself, can give the men, the Ministers, whom the Church and the world so greatly need?

Yet we think too much may be made of what these times are said to require. The times, sin, the world, the flesh, and the foes of truth, have been much the same in most ages, and are likely still to be. The laws of God, too, which govern the Church, and the conditions of the Gospel, are the same; and they require that man's pride should be abased, and his lofty looks brought low. Often what has been

said as to the men needed, to say the least, has looked
a little bold : it has seemed like telling the only wise
God not only what we wish, but what we think is the
best for Him to do, rather than letting Him do what
seemeth Him good in sending men " after His own
heart," although they may not therefore be after " the
hearts of men."

Much learning is thought by many to be absolutely
necessary for the Ministry. Here again, on this subject as on most others, we find wide extremes, and
rocks on either hand. Some decry learning altogether; whilst by others it is too much magnified.
Learning with some is next to, or less than, nothing ;
whilst with others it is almost everything. Some
scorn and snarl at learning as though it were a subtle serpent, or a demon ; others worship it as though
it were a god. With the man who was brought
up at Gamaliel's feet before us, and a long list of
men of learning and piety, who have been burning
and shining lights in the Church, and able and successful Ministers of Christ, it would be folly to
regard learning as a paralysis of pulpit power.
Learning need not make divines or doctors of divi-
nity dry. We have men of well-earned honours
meekly borne, whose ministry is marked with much
power and unction. If with learning the freshness
of the life of God and the fervour of the love of
Christ must needs decline, this would be too serious a

spiritual loss to risk for any mere mental gain. To seem, by any words not well weighed or fitly spoken, to set learning above the life and power of religion, is a grand delusion. Many who would not do this in theory, do it in reality; they do it practically. The one is high, the other is submerged, in their esteem. The goodly pearls and precious stones lie hidden in the sand; the lighter material, the wood, the hay, and the stubble, float on the surface. Such persons reverse the Apostle's estimate of things; they count all loss, not for the excellency of the knowledge of Christ, but for the excellency of human learning. This is as foolish as it may be fatal to the true interests of the Church of Christ. It is in effect leading men from the living fountain to broken cisterns. To assert that there could not be able Ministers of the New Testament, or power in the pulpit, without great erudition or much learning, would be greatly to ignore the past, and to overlook some of the brightest names that have adorned the Church, those whom God has delighted to honour, who, though among the "weak" of the world, have had power to move masses of men, have skilfully and successfully wielded the Spirit's sword, and have confounded the mighty.

There may be idolatry of learning and of intellect, as well as of wood and of stone, of silver and of gold. By many who do not themselves lack mind, idolatry of intellect is thought to be one of the many idolatries of the age. There is with some a great craving for what is often falsely called "intellectual" preaching. This has been enumerated among the causes of the present deficiency of Methodism by Dr. Rigg; and admonition has been administered on this subject by our venerable father, the Rev. Thomas Jackson. Some doubt being expressed, a few years ago, as to the spiritual state of a candidate for the ministry, it was remarked that he was well skilled in mathematics; and one of the fathers replied, " I hope we shall not substitute mathematics for religion." Suspicion in this case was far from groundless, as an awful subsequent apostasy too fully proved.

If fine chapels are built, and if these should be filled with fine congregations, and fine rather than faithful preachers should be required to fill the pulpits, the last of these fine things would be far worse than the first. Nothing, we believe, will preserve Methodism, with all her material prosperity, from spiritual decline, but faithful preaching, sustained by fervent prayer; whether the chapels be filled or by some forsaken, and whether men will hear or whether they will forbear. Without these, there will be a withering worm at the root; without these, there may be a kind of prosperity which will be but as blooming roses on the cheek of death.

There may be flash where there is little fire; there may be much glitter where there is no gold; propriety, where there is no pathos or power; tinsel, where there is no solid truth. Of the many adulterations practised by the "seed of evil-doers" in this country, the adulteration of bread, the staff of life, is one of the vilest and worst. To grind up plaster of Paris with flour is an outrage which should be punished by the judges. But, bad as this is, it is innocent when compared with the adulteration of the bread of life, and seeking to satisfy souls with that which is not bread, "nor can their hungry souls sustain;" especially when this is practised by those to whom the Saviour, as the good Shepherd, has given the solemn charge, "Feed my sheep."

Mere finery may flow into the Church with wealth, like a mighty stream; and Ministers, who should stem the torrent, and lift up a standard against it, may be in danger of getting into the swollen waters, and of being carried downward by the flood. Some of us, we believe, are guilty, together with our brethren the laity, in these matters of mere pomp and show. Amongst those who thus think, there are hearers of the word who "take heed how" they "hear." In the splendid sanctuaries, have there not been some "splendid sermons?" Besides the painted window, has there not been painting here and there in the pulpit,—a stained sermon as well as stained glass? There may have been "gay tulips and useless daffodils, instead of medicinal plants from the margin of the fountain of salvation." Instead of wielding the naked two-edged sword, there may have been the brandishing of a mere gilded scabbard.

Is there no danger lest those "potent evils" which are said to exist with regard to preaching should yet more fully prevail? Is there no danger lest, with the increasing splendour of our chapels, the showy and splendid should be substituted in the pulpit for that which is solid and sterling? Is there no danger lest in the course of time there may be a change in preachers and preaching too much like the change in the current coin of the realm? There may be something small and pretty where there is no weighty matter. Is there not much danger lest we beguile ourselves and others with the "wisdom of words," and thus "the cross of Christ be made of none effect?"* The Apostle wrote to a people of polished manners, and of literary tastes and pursuits,—a people who studied science as set before them by philosophers who were well skilled in the subtleties of speech, and the meretricious charms of a gaudy rhetoric. It was natural, therefore, for these Corinthians to desire that the system of truth which the Apostle had to make known should be invested with the same attractive charms and fascinating style of address, —with an imposing array of high-sounding words, with similar embellishments of language, with splendid tropes and figures, and the harmony of well-formed periods. And did not the Apostle possess, in an

* 1 Cor. i. 17.

eminent degree, the power to gratify these intellectual
tastes?—he who had been brought up at the feet of
Gamaliel; he who had at command all the resources
of a vigorous, highly gifted, and amply furnished
mind; he who was quick in perception, profound in
judgment, mighty in argument, irresistible in pathos;
whose forceful appeals, when even a prisoner, made
his judge tremble, and almost won a king to his
cause? But the Apostle went forth, not as an orator,
to attract the applause of mortals to himself; but as
a herald, to proclaim the Prince of Peace. The
Apostle went forth, not to win fading laurels, where-
with to adorn his own brow; but to gem, with souls
saved from death, the diadem of the King Eternal.
He went forth as an ambassador to allure the rebel to
that reconciling cross in which alone he gloried. He
went forth to preach not himself, but Christ Jesus
the Lord.

There is a marvellous power in the simple story of
the cross, which the Apostle scorned to adulterate
with the enticing words of man's wisdom, or any of
the world's witcheries. There is a terrible keen-
ness in the naked two-edged sword of the Spirit,
flashing its sin-reproving light through the guilty
conscience, and down to the depths of the deceitful
heart; and the Apostle was too valiant a soldier to
brandish, in its place, a mere glittering sheath. The
pearls of truth were too radiant and precious in the
Apostle's eyes to need any paint or pencilling which

man's art or device could give them. The torch of truth blazes too brightly to require the aid of the twinkling taper of human wisdom. Heaven-inspired truth has charms which are only concealed or disfigured by the gaudy drapery or artificial flowers in which human vanity may seek to array her. It is true there may be the sublimest eloquence in dispensing the word of life,—an eloquence which does not darken, but the more faithfully declares the "counsel of God," more fully displays "the unsearchable riches of Christ," and unfolds "the truth as it is in Jesus," rather than hides it under the shadowing wings of its own imagination, or conceals it amid the immense foliage of the trees of its own garden;— an eloquence which so declares the truth that God, and not man, is glorified. "We use," the Apostle says, "great plainness of speech."

If there be a restless craving among the people for pulpit display, that craving is likely to create and call forth a supply of glittering tinsel. If the mere filling of the chapel—a point by no means unimportant—be the first and chief thing sought, there are ways and means akin to those by which some of the popular penny entertainments are got up and sustained, which may, and do in some places, call crowds to the chapel. But we have known even young people, among the more discerning, turn aside with disgust from what they have considered mere display, which, though it might be a little tolerated in a lecture-room, was loathsome in the pulpit, where Christ crucified should alone be set forth.

There is often the loudest call for the intellectual where there is the least claim to that quality. We remember a respectable farmer who attended a country chapel in a large circuit, in which many eminent Ministers who have passed away have preached the word of life. In that congregation he was considered the chief complainant and critic; one on whom it is so trying to the nerves of a junior Minister to look. Few could fully please his taste, or gratify his "itching ears." The preaching was not scientific and intellectual enough for him. This farmer had, according to the custom of modern times, applied science to agriculture. As in the cultivation of his fields, and the sowing of his seed, so in listening in God's house, he expected science from the pulpit; desiring his smattering of science in the vegetable kingdom to be met by a corresponding *quantum* in the spiritual. He would hardly suffer the fallow ground of human hearts to be broken up, except in a scientific way; nor stony hearts to be smitten, except as by a geological hammer. Nay, strange as it may seem, he carried his scientific notions not only into the habitation of God's house, but into the inner sanctuary of religion; for he was a member of Society. His Leader was an eminent Christian gentleman, who had been an officer in the army, but had learned the lessons of truth, as Mary, at the Master's feet, and had the lowly and lovely simplicity of a child in Christ Jesus. But he was not, on that account, any the more suited to our scientific friend the farmer. "Why, I respect him; he is a *good* man;"—a compliment often paid to what is considered extreme simplicity;—"but he is not up to *my* mark. *I* like a *scientific* Leader."

Wesley had a frequent and familiar correspondent, who much perplexed his own mind on the decrees, and on other doubtful points; to whom he administered a characteristic rebuke, well merited in such cases:—

"DEAR SAMMY,—I shall expect to hear that you are confined in Bedlam soon. You say you cannot understand.—'Understand!' we can understand nothing. But, however little we may understand, we can understand this,—God is wise, and I am foolish; and that He wills all men to be saved. I am

"Yours,

"J. WESLEY."

Many seem to listen to sermons in the same spirit of cold criticism as if they were listening to lectures on the different stones or strata of the earth, or on those fossil remains on which geology, in *some* instances, has shed just light enough to make darkness visible. The sacred seed does indeed in such cases fall "on stony ground." Let hearers take heed how they hear; whilst Ministers should take heed to themselves and to their doctrine, and beware of pandering to vain and vitiated tastes, miscalled "the spirit of the times."

Men, it has again and again been urged, are wanted for the ministry. "Men," said Napoleon, "are scarce things." The more clearly the qualifications of candidates for the ministry are defined, the fewer mistakes are likely to be made; and the less frequent will be the anomalous rejection by some wise men in council, of those whom other wise men have recommended, and who, as some have not scrupled to hold and say, have given as great promise of usefulness as those who have been received. From cases we have known, we apprehend that there is danger of allowing the choice of candidates, especially in Quarterly Meetings, to be influenced by worldly wisdom, so as to suit the tastes of men by exalting mere human learning and position above purely spiritual gifts and graces; thus grieving the Spirit of God, whose "ways are not as" our "ways."

Men may be pleased because human pride is not mortified; but one object of God's order of choice is to abase human vanity. Those whom Christ chose at the first were not from among learned doctors of the temple, or from Herod's court, or from the schools of philosophers: they were "just opposite" to what the old Jewish divines and Grecian philosophers would have selected. They were not

the wise and mighty in man's esteem, but the
"foolish," the "weak," and the "things that are
not,"—to shame the wise, and to shame the things
that are mighty, and to bring to nought the things
that are.*

Human pride needs abasing now as much as it
ever did. There are, alas! too many proofs to show
that the wise and mighty after the flesh are often
proportionately foolish and powerless for the grand,
the spiritual, the sublime, the soul-saving purposes
of the Christian ministry. There are, on the other
hand, those who scarcely know the tongue wherein
they were born, but blunder in their own vernacular,
who yet are blest in showing men the way of salvation, because that which they are called to teach,
they know, being taught of God, and therein having
the advantage of those who speak "with the tongues
of men," and "have all knowledge," except that
which they profess to be moved to teach.

Are not many of these to be found in the Churches
and pulpits of the land,—as cold as they are clever,
as powerless as they are polished, as dry as they are
dignified, as pointless as they are punctilious, as
soulless as they are systematic, as lifeless as they are
learned? Their much learning, if it has not made
them "exceedingly mad against" those who are about
their Master's business, has not made them wise to
win souls.

* Wesley's "Notes," 1 Cor. ii. 27.

"Who can wonder that in vain
  Scores of dullards preach for years;
  Lulling conscience to its bane,
  Fast asleep in hopes and fears?"*

We remember hearing a truly apostolic Clergy-man, who had the signs, without the empty boast, of apostleship, say that he hoped the time was past when a fine church would be built at one end of the town, next to the squire's house, in which a drawing-room parson would do duty, who knew little besides Latin and Greek, and would declare that if the people were not saved it was their own fault. We would not even appear to offer any apology for needless blunders or wilful ignorance, any more than we would for that strange design of God in adopting such simple means and agencies as to man's wisdom seem to be foolishness.

See a simple but sincere man, who can scarcely form a sentence without a breach of some rule of syntax, yet so speaking that a multitude of men hang on his lips, and are mightily moved by his word. Eyes sparkle with interest; stout hearts tremble; slumberers start from their deadly sleep; the careless are roused to anxious concern; gentle and simple alike feel the force of truth; penitents fall at the foot of the cross; souls are saved from death: and that simple man, scorned though he be by those who are far more simple,—call him a blunderer, or a babbler, or what you please,—yet

* Tupper.

has given good proof and clear credentials of his
mission, and has shown that he has not run before
he was sent. And though he may not be wise
enough in man's wisdom to shine on earth, he will,
if faithful, shine in a brighter and better sphere.
There is

> "*Living* truth, that bubbles hot
> Like a geyser in the soul."

See another, as correct and proper as learning and
logic, rules and rhetoric, can make him. He seems
to speak, for his lips move; but there is scarcely
any sign of breath or symptom of spiritual life.
He is no more the means of movement among
the dry bones than if he himself were a dry bone,
or a cold marble monument, reared up at vast expense
in the midst of the valley, or some mighty fossil
remain. Great he may be; so, too, the congregation
may be great; but the vast assemblage of stones at
Stonehenge is highly symbolic of such greatness,—
it is a greatness that seems to belong to a "stone
age." The Minister, who should be the means of
life to others, seems to be most devoid of life; the
great arch-stone, like the largest fossil, remains
" deepest imbedded." There—

> " All is *death:* each fossil thought,
> Word-imbedded, lies in clay ;
> And no heart is touched or taught
> To feel, to tremble, or to pray."

Do we not see, in such a contrast as this, a demonstration of the Divine axiom?—"Not by might, nor by power, but by My Spirit, saith the Lord."

These are solemn truths, which men amid worldly power and pride and pomp scorn to learn. These are stern truths, which, even in the place where God's honour dwelleth, those who have professed, either themselves or by proxy, to renounce the world's pleasing pomps, the flesh, and the devil, do but slowly learn. These are sacred truths, which should greatly moderate dogmatic deliverances as to the style and type of men which the times require.

It may be thought that the rapid march of modern scepticism can be checked only by much learning in those who minister the truth. The more learning is sanctified in setting forth the truth the better; but to depend too much on learning in the Christian contest would be as grave an error as many of those errors against which Christianity is waging war.

The times do doubtless require men of sound mind and sanctified scholarship; but to overtake the spiritual claims of the multiplying masses of the people that swarm around us on every hand, spiritual, earnest, godly men, men of burning charity, men of Christlike compassion and self-consuming zeal, men who know, have seen and felt, *that* which they have a mission to teach to others, and who can fully prove their mission by signs following,—these

T

are the men for whom the times make their longest and loudest call.

Clear heads may be needed; but among the most "wanted" are *warm hearts.* There may be clear heads where there are very cold hearts. Lore and logic may do much; the life and love of God constraining the soul may do much more towards converting the masses of the people. The college course may be good, compassion for souls is better, for those whom God calls to save the lost by preaching the Gospel to the poor.

> "Then seek a living *warmth* within,
> To work with vital force without."

If "the pair so long disjoined,—Knowledge and vital Piety,"—can be found in union to as wide an extent, and in as many cases, as the claims of this country require; then let them, as good yoke-fellows, work together in God's vineyard, and win this wandering world to Christ. But if they cannot,— and surely as yet they cannot,—then let not such instruments as God in His wisdom in times past has been wont to wield, scorned though they be by simple ones, be cast aside by the Church in its worldliness.

Nor "should the work cease" or wait too long for the counsels of men, whilst a sin-stricken world is lying bleeding at our feet, and the death-wails of souls are sounding in our ears. A man may be as correct and as clever in his calculations as Colenso, and yet meanwhile in matters which most concern that mission to which he professes to be moved, he may make such grievous and glaring blunders as to kindle the blush of shame in the Church, and cause the world to wonder and blaspheme. A man who is clever at anything, except that which he professes to teach others, and which too he is largely paid for teaching, should scorn no simplicity or subtlety but his own. A man may be too clever simply to believe for himself, and simply to preach to others the Gospel of Christ. He may be too wise in man's wisdom to become wise unto salvation. His cleverness may end in his own confusion.

A traveller, in the old coach times, is said to have put numerous questions to the coachman, as to the names of places and the owners of mansions which they passed on their journey; but could get little or no answer, except, " I don't know." Wearied at length with the monotony of such a reply, the disappointed traveller said,—" Know ! you know nothing." The roused coachman smartly replied, " I know how to drive you from Bristol to Bath." This, after all, was the knowledge which the traveller, as such, most needed,—the knowledge for which he had paid his fare, was perched on the top of the coach, and had consigned himself to the care of the coachman. But let it be supposed that this coach- man could have well descanted on the surrounding scenery, could have given a detailed account of the owners of mansions, and had been well informed and interesting as to persons and places in general, but had been quite ignorant of the way to the place towards which he was professedly driving. Suppose he had been so "blind" or besotted as to have driven both himself and the inquiring traveller by his side into the mire of "a ditch:" would not that traveller have had far greater reason to complain of the coachman who was so well informed on all things but the one thing most needful for him as a coachman to know,—to wit, the way the traveller wished to go? Could such a coachman be found, would it not be a strange thing in the earth? It would be stranger still if he were to be long continued in the post for which he had given such proof that he was altogether unfit. It would be strangest of all if an enlightened public were delighted with such a deception, and pleased to have it so.

Men, however, who are sound and sane on things seen and temporal, are crazed on those things which most concern them. Prophets may "prophesy falsely;" teachers "in Israel" may know much, but may not know that which they profess to be called to teach, and which they are paid to teach; they may be "blind leaders of the blind." Yet men delight in the "smooth things," in the false rather than the faithful and the true prophesyings, and in being blindly led, and so beguiled as not to discern any danger, or to know that there is a ditch into which both may fall, until the sense of feeling rather than sight too late and too sadly demonstrates the terrible reality.

That man who himself knows Christ, and can so "preach Christ" to his fellow men as to lead them to the Lamb of God, whether he be literate or illiterate, refined or rustic, a lord or a livery servant, whether in fine cloth or in fustian, whether under a crimson robe or a "coat of camel's hair,"—whether under the vaulted roof or the canopy of heaven,—whether behind the glittering screen amid the gorgeous pomp of the cathedral, or behind the chair-back of the humble cottage,—whether he preach to choristers or to cabmen, to princes, to peasants, or to paupers,—has the best of all knowledge, and turns that knowledge to the best account. "He that winneth souls is wise."

"Human things may be too perfect for the adoption and use of the Spirit of God. A Minister may be too wise, too clever, too eloquent. He is too great for his Master's glory. He stands before his Master, and conceals Him from the people. He fails in nothing but that human souls are not converted under his ministry and by his agency. Again, human means may be too clever, too well arranged, too exact, too perfect for the service of God." *

* See "Wesleyan Magazine," 1853.

The Pharisee was too pure and perfect to be penitent like the publican. He was too good for the operations of grace. He was too just in himself to be justified of God. Such righteousness needs as much to be renounced and removed as the greatest sin, and is often a far greater barrier to an entrance into the kingdom of God. The sin-laden rather than the self-righteous, publicans and harlots rather than Pharisees, enter in. The prostrate rather than the puffed up, the bowed down, those who bend with broken hearts beneath a mountain of sin and misery, rather than those who in their vain imaginations are on the mountain top of merit, first find the foot of the cross. The sovereign balm is applied to the sin-stricken, not to the self-sufficient ; to the broken, not to the boasting, heart.

With consummate ignorance there is often consummate vanity and self-confidence. There is often, and especially in the ministry, much vain confidence in mere human learning,—a confidence which it is God's pleasure to abase and confound. That vain confidence is man's " might," which is in God's way, as a barrier to the work of His Spirit : just as man's " righteousness," as much as man's " sin," " obstructs " God's " pardoning love," and must be removed, His " glory to display."

Faith toward God is full of paradoxes, which experience in the things of God alone can well teach. We must be guilty to be justified, poor to be made rich, weak to be made strong, humbled to be exalted, fools to become wise. Vain confidence in anything is as hateful to God as a heathen deity. Human learning, right and proper in itself, if there be vain confidence in it, may be as great an evil as ignorance in the Church and Ministry. The evil is not in the learning, but in the vain confidence which centres in it, just as the root of all evil is not in money, but in the idolatrous love of it. Learning, like money, is a great good, if it be rightly used, and not abused. Man's dependence on learning reverses that truth which concerns the glory of God, of which He is so jealous. It is " not by might nor by power; " vain confidence says it is. Those who are thus defiant of God's word, because they are self-reliant, who in this respect lie to God and lie to the Holy Ghost, may go on and be given up to " speak lies in hypocrisy; " and with the best means in their power of rightly interpreting the word of God, they may wrest that word to their own destruction, and to the destruction of those who are blindly beguiled by their seducing words.

There may be " spiritual wickedness in high places." Scholarship and scepticism may go hand in hand; and Satan may have his throne among the seats of learning, and the son of perdition may sit in the temple of God. Even Bishops, if they are not simple enough to believe, may become bold enough to blaspheme. Polished Essayists in their profanity may scarcely be a whit behind the sneering Voltaire, or the pestiferous Tom Paine; and if their boasted apostleship be taken into the account, they must be regarded as among the chief of sinners. One of the great dangers of the day is that of depending too much on human learning, and deifying human intellect; and it must not be thought that either the pews or the pulpits in Methodist sanctuaries are entirely exempt from the wide-spreading infection.

Those who would represent the writer as undervaluing learning much mistake his meaning. Let none despise or decry learning; let none, on the other hand, deify it, especially in the temple of God, by representing it as absolutely necessary in order to " speak," with power and profit, " in the temple to the people all the words of this life."

" The educated ears of the scribes of Jerusalem at once recognised, in the workers of miracles and the teachers of an increasing Church, unlearned and ignorant men. But their want of learning related only to matters of polite education, not to the deep things of the word of God, the doctrines, facts, and promises of which they were commissioned to expound to the world. It is plain that even the Apostles, in the height and glory of their apostolical preaching, were not gifted with any power which would cover the provincial peculiarities of their speech, or enable them to conciliate the refined by graceful enunciation." *

Minds, on the other hand, may be so full of Murray's Grammar and mathematics, of arithmetic, accidence, and algebra, of Cicero and conic sections, of philosophy and problems, that it may become quite a problem whether such can preach in simplicity and power, and in the wisdom which the Holy Ghost teacheth. That pulpit power need not be lacking where there is much erudition, that knowledge and piety may be combined in the highest order, is evident from the examples of many whose holy lives have adorned the Church, and whose works of learning enrich our libraries. It is evident from the examples of many who still live and labour in the Church of Christ, whose eminent gifts are consecrated to the great Giver; on whose minds there seems to be deeply engraven, "Holiness to the Lord;" and in whose works profound homage is paid to the Parent Mind, "the only wise God." And this reverential homage to the Infinite Understanding is the salt which seasons and sanctifies their scholarship, and which saves it from seeing corruption, which that of the Colenso school, and of all such as do not bring human reason to the bar of revelation, rather than revelation to the bar of reason, is des-

* Arthur's "Tongue of Fire."

tined to see. Those who will put nothing but queries and quibbles at the end of every sentence on the sacred page, must not be much surprised if they find their own self-confident productions turned into a doubtful domain by the questions and queries of others.

> "Learning's redundant part and vain
> Be here cut off and cast aside."

Learning and holiness were seen beautifully blended in our late beloved President, the Rev. W. L. Thornton, M.A. In him were joined, in a high degree, a cultivated mind, lofty scholarship, with profound piety, and the unction of the Holy One. Do we not see a similar union in those gifted and godly men who yet linger with us, to whom has been wisely committed the work of tuition in our excellent Institutions? Under such training and influence, none, we think, need fear the mere "knowledge which puffeth up."

Many have gone forth from those Institutions earnest, self-denying Ministers and Missionaries, distinguished by gifts and grace. Their lamps have been trimmed; the flame of their devotion has been fanned; they have given good proof that with increasing light there has been advancing spiritual life; "no abatement of the" sacred "fire," but a kindling to a higher intensity. And the more those Ministers are known and heard, who have been favoured with such a training, the more, in general, (exceptions of course there may be,) will they be esteemed; the more liberally, it is likely, those noble Institutions will have the support they justly deserve; and the less will be the fears of the simple, the sincere, and the scrupulous as to the tendency of that training.

But many may be called to preach who cannot enjoy these advantages,—who may not be able to enter any school of the prophets. Yet these may be not the less called of God, nor the less, in some "wonderful fashion," taught of God, and therefore not the less able to teach that which they are specifically called to teach, and that which above all things lost men most need to know, namely, the simple way of Gospel salvation.

Let not such messengers be despised in fine chapels and by fine congregations; nor can they be, without greatly grieving that Spirit by whom they have been moved, and that God from whom they have received their solemn commission. He that despiseth them, despiseth Him that sent them.

It is as perilous as it is presumptuous for vain mortals to put forth their puny hands to check or contract the general commission which God has given to His servants, to "go into the temple, and speak to the people all the words of this life;" and to "go into all the world, and preach the Gospel to every

creature." It is true, these legates of the skies may
lack those qualities which men may think most needful ; yet their being "chosen of God" may be not
only for the special purpose of comforting those who
are of an humble and contrite spirit, but also to confound those who are wise in their own conceit. You
cannot laud their learning, or eloquence, or anything
in them which is merely of man ; but if they show
you the way of salvation, you may esteem them very
highly for their work's sake, and glorify the grace of
God in them. The Church that should reject and
reprobate those who are thus called of God may
well expect reprobation itself. First dearth, then
death may ensue in those Churches ; yet worldly
wealth and Pharisaic sanctity may "*garnish* the
sepulchres" still.

God is greater than the temple, and greater than
its worshippers. These must not receive homage
instead of Him to whom that temple has been dedicated, and who has the first right to say who shall
speak in His own house, and make known His
message to the sons of men. Where "man's wisdom" and human learning are too much magnified,
God may see fit, as signally as He has done aforetime,
to abase them. It ought to be humbling enough to
any Minister to have few, if any, seals to his ministry.
But the greater the learning and the more refined the
training, the greater the ground for shame if there be

no seals, no success, no sanction given by God. It should be to seals, and not to scholarship, that the Minister should be able to point in proof that he has not run in vain, nor before he was sent. The man who points to honours at the end of his name, rather than to signs following his ministry, as the proofs of apostleship, makes a serious mistake, or practises a solemn cheat.

What is it to the point, for those who so loudly boast of their claims, that they have honourably passed through their collegiate course, and can say, "These are the degrees we have gained; these are the honours we have won," if there be no living souls whom they have saved from death, and of whom they can say, "These are our epistles?" We must ask for some stronger proof, some clearer credentials, some surer signs that they are not quite mistaken as to their call to the ministry, than any mere scholarship, however lofty, can afford. If the great part of a life be spent in the ministry without such, it would surely be much more befitting to blush than to boast. Boasting, one may suppose, would be the last thing a man of sound mind would think of doing in so humbling a position. Yet how many are there who do so "boast" of themselves, and "against" those whom God deigns and delights to honour, that their boasting borders on profanity and blasphemy!

Preaching from heart to heart, and "from house

to house," in those strong but simple words which the Saxon language supplies, may, by the Spirit's help, do more to move the masses of men who, in this land of light, are in darkness, and sleeping the sleep of death, than the most "elaborate lessons" drawn from the stores of learning and intellect.

The heart sways the intellect. The heart commands the man. "The heart is the greatest thing below the sky."* The appeals of God's love are from His own heart to the hearts of men. The heart of Christ bled, that by His precious blood He might buy back and win men's hearts from the love of sin to the love of Himself. God deigns to ask for the heart. "My son, give Me thy heart." The heart is the surest, safest way to the head. The wish of the heart will win the thoughts, change the creed, sway a subtle sceptre over the sentiments. It is as the waving wand of an enchantress over the mind. The fool first says "in his heart," rather than his head, "No God;" then forms his godless creed; then tries to believe it, because he wishes it; and he wishes it because he loves darkness rather than light; and he loves darkness because his deeds are evil. Paine, as the foe of truth, fought in the dark; without the Book, blindfolded, he sought to overturn it; without a copy of the New Testament, he wrote virulently against it.†

* Rev. W. Arthur, M.A. † Barnes's Notes on Acts.

" 'T is health that chiefly keeps an atheist in the dark ;
A fever argues better than a Clarke."

Move the heart, and you move the man ; change
the heart, and you change the man. A changed heart
is a changed love. Constraining love can therefore
do more to change human hearts than the most conclusive logic. " A sound heart is the best casuist." *
Love is the grand power which God Himself
wields to win back a rebel world to Himself. If,
whilst light waxes stronger, love shall wane, the loss
of love will be the greatest loss which the Church can
sustain. Love is the greatest in the trinity of graces.
The moon is right in her own sphere and season, but
a moon instead of a sun to rule the day would be a
sad exchange. Cold though clear moonlight, instead
of genial, glowing sunbeams, would make another, or
rather a perpetual, night. Then, indeed, should we
be moon-smitten, and the world death-stricken ;
for the light of the sun is the life of the natural
world. Yet this would not be worse for the world
than to have creeping over the warm heart of the
Church the cold death-chill of a clever and scholarly
scepticism.

That light is increasing, there can be little doubt :
that at the same time the love of many is waxing
cold, is perhaps little less certain. We lately heard

* Cecil.

of a congregation, comprising a large Church, long favoured with the preaching of one of the most eminent Ministers of our day, and still privileged with what may be called in some respects the perfection of preaching, such as may please most ears, and ought to profit many hearts : yet that large congregation and Church can scarcely now keep up a small week-evening prayer-meeting! The hearers of the word are not minished, nor the interest in hearing lessened; the soil on which the precious seed is sown is as spacious as ever ; yet it would seem much more stony, more choked with worldly care, more chilled with cold ceremony, frigid formalism; and the light that shines on it may be as that of the cold pale planet, the moon, rather than that of the glowing sun.

We heard but recently a bitter lament over this cold and apathetic state of things from the lips of a venerable Minister and valiant champion for the truth, now retiring from a life of learned labour, and from the fatigues of a long campaign, in which he has often wielded a glittering sword with so firm and faithful a hand as to excite the fears both of friends and of foes; sometimes, it is true, seeming somewhat Ishmael-like ; though most men, we believe, will give the redoubtable champion, Dr. C., credit for true conscientiousness, as well as dauntless courage, in a life of almost continual conflict. May his sun set, as it seems likely to do, in a cloudless sky, and at eventide may there be light ! ·

There are loud calls for men of such a class and calibre in these times of cowardly compromise. Mistakes they may make ; they may take out their keen sword when it had better be in its sheath ; they may sometimes strike off an ear which had better have been spared : but that valour which, although it may be a little lacking in prudence, will quit itself well in the day of battle, is better than that prudence which is but another word for pusillanimity,—a prudence which has no valour, and which in the soldier of Christ has spared reputation from the altar of sacrifice, and follows the Captain " afar off," and only " in honour " and in " good report."

With complaints in other Churches as to growing coldness our own have been in too perfect and plaintive harmony. Full many cases could be adduced by most Ministers amongst us who have had any length and breadth of observation, to prove that under the shadow of sanctuaries well attended, under faithful preaching which stirs slumberers and startles sinners in Zion, there are many of those who hear the word of God with attention, and feel its truth and power, who evince an interest in the cause of Christ, who will liberally aid its funds, and with whom there is much that is lovely and of good report : yet at the same time there is a prevailing worldliness, a lingering

U

indecision, a deep-rooted and most melancholy aversion to that old-fashioned Methodism which was wont to luxuriate in Christian communion in the weekly Class, in the Lovefeast, and the blessed fellowship of saints. They like a good chapel to worship in; they like a good choir, good singing; they like good preaching; they like an intellectual treat : but they do not like to "witness a good confession." "They find it easier to walk many miles to hear a good sermon than to pray one hour that it may prove the power of God to salvation."

In times past some of "the least in the kingdom of God," "the simplest believers," "an impotent throng," have been raised up, "to baffle the wise, and mighty, and strong." "Such was the attractive influence of the cross that by the mouth of a few simple unlettered men its pure, self-denying, world-opposing principles had been first promulgated, and had triumphed over Paganism hoary with ages."*

As the power of the cross in the ages past has won such glorious trophies, so in the times present, and in times to come till the end of time, it can win similar trophies by similar means ; and, if God shall see fit, by the mouths of as "simple men," so that there shall be no possible ground for man to

* Rev. Canon Miller.

glory in man; no more ground than if God did not speak by the mouth of man at all, but by the mouth of as senseless a creature as that by which He rebuked a mad prophet, or simply by the "blasts of rams' horns." Surely the shameless scepticism now rising up in halls of science and seats of learning is enough to provoke a jealous God to anger. God has taken, and He will yet "take, the wise in their own craftiness." *

Whatever would weaken the *peculiar* preaching power, which many who do not belong to the Wesleyan Body have candidly considered it to possess, would be a great and grave Connexional loss and calamity, for which no material gain could compensate. There may be prevailing, to a wider extent than aforetime, among Preachers, an attempt, by a popular style, to please rather than to profit. Some, with no such ambitious aim, can scarcely avoid popularity. Voice, manner, style, all conspire to please : these things are to the hearers as a "very lovely song." †   But that which is so very "pleasant" may not be so very profitable. The precepts and patterns of the New Testament would lead us to conclude that the preaching which pleases all, and offends none, may justly be regarded with solemn jealousy. So plain, so pointed, so personal, and pungent are the denuncia-

* 1 Cor. iii. 19.   † Ezek. xxxiii. 32.

tions against sin and appeals to the sinner, that, as
well-aimed arrows, they reach and prick the heart;
they pierce through the soul as the Spirit's sword,
wielded by no weak or wavering hand. They hardly
allow a way of escape, or the possibility of a mistake
as to the sinner meant, or the sin to be slain. They
lay "the axe unto the root of the tree." "*Thou* art
the man." "Who hath warned you?" "I say
unto you." "Thou hypocrite!" "Thou blind
Pharisee!" "Him *ye* have taken, and by wicked
hands have crucified and slain." "Repent therefore
of this thy wickedness." It seems hard to conceive
how similar conscience-thrusts should end in mere
compliment on the style of preaching. It is hard to
think that those who are thus conscience-smitten should
rise from their knees, retire from the chapel, whilst
the arrow is rankling in the heart, with a compliment
on their lips as to the sermon preached. We may
long beat the air; long flash the sword before the
eyes, and wield it around the head, without wounding
any heart.

We believe the idea is greatly gaining ground,
both in pews and pulpits, that people's ears must be
pleased by preaching, rather than their hearts pierced
by the sword of the Spirit. The temptations to aim
at popularity, to be "men-pleasers," amid increasing
worldliness and material splendour, are many and
mighty; so many, that if Ministers do not yield to

them in one seducing guise and form, they may in another, yet "more subtle;" so mighty, that nothing short of almighty grace can give them courage to preach so pointedly as to be able to say at the close of their career, "I am pure from the blood of all men. For I have not shunned to declare unto you all the counsel of God." *

Not long ago we heard of a rich man, a "chief captain," a hearer of the word in a country church, who, when the word preached was a little too pointed, was wont, in the winter, to take up the poker, and briskly poke the fire,—although he did not like others to take the same liberty with the poker. A faithful Minister who did duty for some time at that church, dared, on one occasion, to take his text from the stern Epistle of the faithful James: "Go to now, ye rich men, weep and howl for your miseries that shall come upon you."† The poker for the fire was soon in request, and a passport too for the Minister: though *that* John was not decapitated, he soon departed; "His travelling ticket," the narrator stated, "was soon given him." That rich man had power to detain the man who pleased, and to dismiss the one who warned.

The popular Preacher may be proposed by the youthful aspirant for fame as his pattern for the

* Acts xx. 26, 27. † James v. 1.

pulpit, when he possesses little or no power to copy that part of the pattern which is most prominently placed before him. By vainly attempting that which is Utopian, and quite above his mark, he may get out of "his own" natural and proper "order," and thus make himself, as a slender stripling in Saul's massive armour, useless and ridiculous; whilst, had he gone forth trusting in God, with a simple sling and stone, he might possibly have laid some giant low, and put the Philistines to flight.

The futile and fatal attempt of the fabled frog to rise by a process of inflation to the grand proportions of the ox, is too well known to need more than a reference. The scanty stream, the gently flowing rivulet, may refresh the meadow, gladden the garden, fill the pitcher, slake the thirst of the scorched traveller; but if that shallow stream were to strive to splash itself into a foaming flood or a mighty cataract, its little depth would be sprinkled and lost on a surface too wide for its source, so that it would be of small use for fruit or flower, would fail to quench the thirst of man or beast, and would do far less good by its pretentious drops than the gentle, noiseless, unostentatious dew. Every running streamlet cannot be a majestic river; every gentle waterfall cannot be a grand Niagara; every gem cannot be a great Koh-i-noor. Every man cannot be a Goliath;

every speaker cannot be a Demosthenes; every preacher cannot be a Spurgeon or a Punshon. And even if these things could be, men might marvel the more, yet not be born again; they might " wonder and perish."

If Ministers could be saved by the kind aid of lay friends from devoting so much absorbing attention to multifarious monetary matters, they would not only have so much the more *time* for their true, their proper and supreme work, but they would doubtless have also more *spiritual power*, as Preachers and Pastors, in the performance of that work.

Poring over from period to period the dry details of subscription lists and schedules, which revolve, like the seasons, in quick and ceaseless succession, bringing with them winter in their train, with clouds and " rainy days; " and, like Job's messengers, treading close one upon the heels of another; whilst the former is yet speaking, its successor steps up with its tale of trouble;—giving that continued and earnest attention to these matters of mere finance, which must be given by those on whom the duty devolves,—seriously defrauds Ministers of that time which should be devoted to an infinitely higher work, and lessens, if it do not in some instances almost paralyse, their influence in that work. Monetary claims are too much mixed up with pastoral

calls. Do not the long subscription lists for divers
funds in our large Circuits testify this ?

If, as our great and glorious Connexion shall
extend and grow, there shall be a greater and growing multiplicity and complexity of funds and finances,
to which it shall be deemed necessary for *Ministers*
to give increased attention, such a necessity will be a
necessary evil. That which, materially considered,
would be our Connexional strength, religiously and
ministerially viewed would be a great Connexional
weakness. Ministers might possibly, by giving
increased time and attention to mere finances, promote the *temporal prosperity* of the Body ; but it
would be at the serious risk of *spiritual decline.*
We have heard grave questions proposed by thoughtful persons on this subject, as to how far the finances
in the Methodism of the future, judging from past
progression, may engross the attention of its Ministers, and thereby endanger its becoming, to a greater
extent than would comport with its purely spiritual
interests, a great "financial system."

A devoted Minister whom we know, and who
combines in a pre-eminent degree preaching talent
with " business tact," ability, and despatch, has
bitterly bemoaned the serious absorption of his time
in looking over subscription lists, schedules, and
statistics. " We are almost scheduled to death."
None, we apprehend, could hear him without hav-

ing such proofs of the pulpit power he possesses as
would afford sufficient reason for regret that weeks of
his precious time should be absorbed in discharging
duties for which a clerk in a counting-house might
be considered competent. "Our time," another
Minister of profound thought and of great pulpit
talent, and having the charge of an important Circuit
in a large town, has remarked, "is taken up in doing
that which many other men may do; whilst we are
drawn away from those solemn duties which none
else can discharge for us."

If it were possible that the ministry could be so
merged in that which is merely monetary,—however
important the objects for which appeals are made,—
that Ministers should find their element and delight
in these semi-secularities, and become adapted for
these things rather than the sacred duties of preaching and of the pastorate, for which they have been
solemnly set apart, then the matter would assume a
more serious and melancholy aspect still, and the
stronger and graver would be the reason that lay
agency to a greater extent should step in to relieve
Ministers so burdened and secularized, in order that
they might give themselves *wholly* to the ministry.

Whilst Ministers in general would lament that the
time which should be devoted to the sacred office of
the ministry should be infringed upon by serving
tables to any extent, there may be some cases in

which attention to these temporalities, to funds and finances, has so absorbed the time, and seemed to drink and dry up the spirit, that little pastoral visitation, little preaching from house to house, and but little power in the pulpit, are expected from them. Nor can it be a matter of surprise if much attention to mere dry details of subscription lists, schedules, and statistics, when these are in any degree a divergence from proper and professed duties, should tend to spiritual dearth and dryness.

Nay, it seems to be conceded, to a great and grievous extent, that some, in attending chiefly to what are called "matters of business," are, though Ministers, moving in their proper province; and these, by a sort of common and "carnal" consent, are consigned over to mere routine,—a perfunctory performance of sacred duty. Power in preaching, the grand means which God has ordained to save men, and which should therefore be supreme, seems in such cases to be made secondary and subordinate. To supply in some measure this lack some one must be "mixed up with these," as it is said, who is fresh and fervent in those duties of the pastorate which form the first if not the "sole concern," and the chief if not the "single care." This, we suppose, many besides ourselves have heard from the lips of those who are not disposed to be harsh or censorious in judgment.

That cumbrous "carefulness" about many things which so sorely taxes many of our Ministers, especially Superintendents and our worthy officials, is the more to be lamented in its burdensome growth when it is considered that some of these Ministers who are thus heavily laden with cares are labouring in the word and doctrine in the same large towns, and side by side, with popular Dissenting Ministers, whose large salaries may be supposed to free them from the entanglements of care as to material support, and whose *deacons*, by attending to *temporalities*, properly dissever these Ministers from any carking concern about funds, such as harasses our Ministers and overtaxed officials from Conference to Conference, in one ceaseless circle.

Enlightened and reflecting Wesleyans may see how it is that Methodist Ministers and monetary appeals seem as closely connected as " publicans and sinners ;" and in such cases these appeals may not present any serious obstacle to the success of their spiritual work. Yet even their best friends would be glad to see the two now so closely joined together a little divorced.

But our Ministers have or ought to come into close contact with those who are neither able nor disposed to appreciate their peculiar position in these pecuniary matters ; those who are scared by even the distant sound of an appeal for money, (because they love it,) and are ready to fly from the appliant as they would from the face of a serpent. Ministers ought to be in a position to make frequent and fervent appeals from house to house, to those who have not given themselves to God, in order to turn them from their worship of silver and gold to the living God; and their pastoral visits should be paid without a liability of being neutralized and paralysed by pecuniary applications, or by the latent suspicion that a monetary appeal will come off in some form or other at the end. Ministers ought to be able to make these appeals for the purpose of winning souls to Christ, the great and solemn work to which they are dedicated,—and to make them with " cries and entreaties," and freedom to declare, unsuspected and unchallenged, " We seek not *yours*, but *you*." May we not, as Ministers, ask, What shall it profit if we could gain a world of gold, though for good objects, if meanwhile souls are lost that might have been saved, had we been more faithfully, more fully and exclusively in our great work ? Are we not often begging *money* for our funds, when we should be begging *men* in Christ's stead to be reconciled to God ?

Surely there are many who might beg money, yet who could not so well beseech men to present themselves a sacrifice to God. It is full well known that so urgent are the claims of our several funds, so pathetic the pleadings of those whose peculiar pro-

vince it is to promote the interests of the funds, such
the emulation to advance them, such the unseemly
and painful pressure often brought to bear upon
Ministers when deficient in the average to be collected by the end of the year, that they are glad
to get them up and keep them up in the best way
they can, and from whom they can, be they saints
or sinners. All this, we solemnly believe, is, in a
spiritual sense, mischievous in manifold ways
and to a melancholy degree. We may thus make
a monetary and temporal advance; but it is at the
risk of spiritual decline, in some form or other.

Let any one of our liberal-minded lay friends look
over the long lists of collections and subscriptions in
some of the large Circuits, as they successively appear
in the varied and manifold Reports. Private subscriptions and public collections for our Schools;
subscriptions, and now a public collection, for our
Theological Institutions; public collections and subscriptions for our General Chapel Fund; public collections and private subscriptions for our Education
Fund; private subscriptions and public collections
for our Foreign Mission Fund; private subscriptions
for the Auxiliary Fund; subscriptions and collections
for our Home Mission Fund;—let him look on these
long lists, and he will, we think, be struck, not so
much with the largeness of the individual givings of
lay friends, as with the endless, ceaseless continuity

of appeals which must necessarily, as matters now stand, have to be made to the people by their Ministers.

Add to these *connexional* Funds a nameless host of appeals which have sometimes to be made by Ministers for *local* and other charities; when the poor are in pinching poverty, and are perishing around them; when chapels have to be built or enlarged, and the work of God extended in their own Circuits; when fallow ground is to be broken up; when dependent Societies look up like hungry sheep; when Lancashire's deep distress calls loudly from a distance for help; when the new-made wants of "Freedmen" have to be met. Add to these the several calls which often have to be made for the same subscriptions; and the *twofold* appeal which *twice* in the year Ministers have to make in the Class. There are the ticket monies and the sixpences for Worn-out Ministers and Widows; and surely sixpence per year, one halfpenny per month, (less than most give monthly, we suppose, to impostors,) can hardly be too much to give to those who have been "in labours more abundant," but are now in premature "age and feebleness extreme." If they want but sixpence from you in the year, they "want but little,—nor want that little long." Friends are not asked, in general, for too much at a time, but are asked too frequently for littles. It is the continual dropping that wears away the stone.

Add to these again the *twofold* appeal which
Ministers have to make for the ticket and the Yearly
Collection in the Class.   And surely little enough is
asked and given for dependent Circuits,—" a shilling,
a sixpence, a mite," a penny, a farthing !   The little
given had better be doubled than dispensed with.
But why should Ministers have ever and anon to ask,
ask, ask, for these mites ?   Why should laymen be
almost mute on these subjects ?   Why may not laymen manage, more than they do at present, these
monetary matters ?   Are laymen so unused to have to
do with money ?   Are laymen indisposed to bear these
burdens, when they are respectfully laid upon them ?
Or are these things more the concern of Ministers
than of our lay friends ?   We trow not.   Why, then,
should that which is so monetary be made to appear
so ministerial ?   This idea is as pernicious as it is
prevalent ; and this delusive appearance of things is
injurious to Ministers in their spiritual duties and
influence, inasmuch as money is too much mixed up
with their sacred work.

It is made to appear that it is more the duty and
interest of Ministers to look after these things than
it is of laymen.   But, when rightly viewed, it is
really no such thing.   Ministers, in the eyes of many,
seem to be, if they are not, somewhat *" secularized "*
by these matters, and by " meetings of mere business,
when   such   business   refers   only   to   the   *temporal*

affairs of the Church of God." *   If Ministers, by mixing so much with these secular things, should become adapted and inclined to them, rather than to the sacred duties of that ministry to which they have been specially set apart, then they have become so far secularized. This may, perhaps, be regarded as the natural result of having much to do with the temporalities even of the Church. Ministers may in this way get so far materialized that they may mind these things rather than " the things of the Spirit." And those who come into close and frequent contact with them in matters of " mere business," though pertaining to the Church, may, in course of time, get to think and speak of them as " shrewd business and clever commercial men," rather than to " esteem them very highly for their work's sake," as Ministers of Christ, and as their Pastors and shepherds. Has not this been the case in some instances?

But, surely, secularity in spirit, if it exist at all among Ministers, must be only in some solitary cases; solitary indeed, compared with the great majority of Ministers, who would most gladly be freed from " these bonds," who long to escape these beggarly elements, and the thraldom of these temporal trammels.

If strict attention to " business," and peculiar tact in mere temporalities and the management of Funds,

---

* Grindrod's "Compendium," p. 97.

should be made a self-sought stepping-stone to prominent posts of trust and honour, that might be a
seducing snare to Ministers to divert and draw them
away from their proper province as Preachers and
Pastors, and from the prize of their high calling. That
stepping-stone might be a stumbling-stone in the way
of their winning souls to Christ, and turning sinners
to righteousness, and would, we think, be a Connexional infirmity. We hardly know whether it
should be called, in the medical, if not mystical,
language of Dr. Rigg, a "chronic ailment" of the
body.

We respectfully submit to the candid and con-
siderate, whether there is not reason to fear that
these frequent appeals from Ministers are a fatal
barrier to the union of many with us, who are just
on the threshold of the Church. These are, perhaps,
present in the Class for the first time; they are feeling after God; the vision is not clear, they see men
as trees walking; and when two appeals are made by
the Minister to the members for money at the close
of the one Class-meeting, it need not much surprise
us if those who see men as walking trees should see
Ministers as money-changers, and should make yet
another mistake in seeing money, if not as the *alpha*,
as the *omega* of the meeting. This, at the very
entrance of the Church, may be made to many " a
stone of stumbling and a snare of the devil."

That this twofold tribute, not to say tax, twice in the year, together with other appeals, does tend to check the increase of members, is, we know, the opinion of many of our devoted Leaders and loyal friends among the laity; and this view, it is notorious, has been held by some eminent Ministers of the body. Dr. Osborn, years ago, " in the debate on the new regulation for the support of the Schools' Fund," expressed a just and jealous anxiety lest any of these economical arrangements should tend to check that natural increase which ought to spring through the country from the continued successful preaching of the Gospel.* " Many of the Ministers feel it a burden to have to make a twofold application for money on the occasion of the quarterly visitation, and a great relief when no such application is to be made." And is it any wonder that they should feel it a burden? Is it not burden enough that they should have, first, in the midst of their toil, to beg for themselves; and then to beg for their brethren, who, in the same ministry, have laboured, and have not fainted, but are now worn out; begging again for themselves prospectively, as those who beneath these burdens are fast wearing out? Why may not our laity more fully take this honour? We believe they have a heart to do it, and would, if it were more

---

* Hessel on Our Financial Economy, pp. 14, 15.

fully consigned to them, put their shoulders to the work. Could not our loyal and loving lay friends speak with more freedom and greater grace on the toils and travels of Ministers than Ministers themselves can do? Let the laity be well and judiciously tried : why should they not?

We ask, whether these finances, with all that appertains to them in the shape of endless schedules, the pressing and pathetic appeals of the secretaries of the various funds, and so forth, do not form a heavy addition to the burdens of our Ministers, and a serious infringement on their solemn duties as the ambassadors of Christ, as those who must watch for souls, as those who have daily coming upon them the care of the Churches,—Churches comprising from ten to thirty Societies, in the circumference of wide Circuits, and numbering from three hundred to two thousand scattered sheep that have to be guided, guarded, and fed, with thousands of little lambs, that have need to be cared for and carried tenderly. Take into consideration the pastoral visits, besides visits to prodigals, Pharisees, publicans, and sinners; visits also to the fatherless and the widow, to the sick, the aged, and the dying;—with congregations varying from a dozen to fifteen hundred or more, to whom they have, Sabbath after Sabbath, and night after night, to preach the word of life; bringing out of the treasury things new and old; with fallow ground

here and there to break up; with frequent calls from
their flock; with perplexities to unravel, and problems
to solve; demands for counsel, caution, or comfort,
according to their several states; and chapel cases to
control, with a long tale of other things, which the
experience of years only can unfold; and add to
these what belongs to Ministers, as to other human
beings,—often anxious domestic solicitude awakened
by affliction: and may it not well be asked, " Who,
then, is sufficient for these things? "

Is it any wonder that, thus surcharged and overtaxed, the average duration of the lives of Ministers
should be short, and that grey hairs should soon be
seen upon them? Is it any wonder that some should
soon be placed on the list of Supernumeraries? that
brains should soften, and heart-strings should snap?
that, while they sing, and pray, and preach, the silver
cord should be loosed, and the golden bowl broken?
that princes in the prime of life should fall in our
Israel, and that their sun should go down while it is
yet day? Is it any wonder that sometimes they suddenly bow beneath these burdens; and that the song
they began on earth, mixed, it may be, with sighs
and tears, should in a moment be exchanged for the
sighless songs of the spirits of the just in heaven?
There is a solemn pause in the pulpit, and a panic in
the pews; the spirit of their Pastor, whose voice is yet
sounding in their ears, has passed away to the rest of

heaven. He has finished his course; his warfare is
accomplished; his wish is realized :—

> " My body with my charge lay down,
> And cease at once to work and live."

At their graves fatherless children and widows have
wept and wailed, though not without hope; and still
they water their couch with their tears. Are there
not wealthy and worthy laity among us who have
leisure enough and love enough to remind the people
of the debt to be discharged on account of those
Pastors whose loss these widows mourn ; and thus, if
not to wipe away the widows' tears, to lighten their
burden, soothe their sorrows, and supply their need ?

Meanwhile, let Ministers be at their own peculiar
post, and wait as wholly as they can on their ministry. How can they do this as they ought, as they
are pledged and set apart to do, thus encumbered
and entangled with finances? How can they, as they
ought, open new places and be Home Missionaries ?
How can they enlarge and extend, as well as keep,
the Circuit ? or be unremitting in pastoral visits to
the sick, the careless, and the lukewarm ? * With
the crowding cares and circumstantialities of business
and finance, and those "trivialities," as some sage
men have termed them, which take up so much of
the time of Ministers, and which have to be formally

* Grindrod's " Compendium," p. 97.

reported, reviewed, and descanted upon at the Annual
District Meeting, is it surprising that whole days
should pass in rigid routine, and scarcely an hour be
left at the close for the calm consideration of the spiritual work of God in the several Circuits, scarcely time
left for the Superintendents to deliberate on the best
means for promoting the *un*secular prosperity of our
Zion ?   Nay, how often has the time in these annual
gatherings been so far spent in these things, which
assume the aspect of hurrying business dispatch, that
there has been time only for a rapid, rather than a
reverent, reading of the " Liverpool Minutes," and no
time at the close for deep, deliberate thought upon
the weighty words, the solemn counsels, the golden
maxims, which those Minutes contain ; and but little
time with many during the livelong year to turn
them in any worthy degree to a good practical
account, or to make much more of them, on some
solemn points, than dead letters !

Nothing but dire necessity should thus overtax the
time and overload the energies of Ministers.   We
doubt much whether such necessity exists.   Are there
not hosts of honest laymen among us, of good report,
whom Ministers might look out, and who would
come up more fully to the apostolic idea and design
in the office of a deacon, " amply providing for the
support of the Pastor, supplying the wants of the
poor of the Church, and becoming the CHANNELS of

contributions to every form of Christian activity ? " *
And is it not more seemly that those who are specially
engaged in secular matters should be, at least, the
chief, if not the sole, channels of contributions for
the cause of God, rather than merely conduct the
streams of charity through those earthen vessels which
have besides to bear the untold weight of the heavenly
treasure; and which, by the continuous flow and
friction of the one, and the heavy pressure of the
other, are too soon, as we well know, worn out or
broken down?

If the Funds must be continued as separate and as
numerous as they are, which some prudent men have
thought, and which we think, poor and not profound
policy,—if we must so proceed until the Funds shall
be, for the *one* Connexion, the *one* great Church, and
the *one* cause of the living God, more than as many
as the months in the year; then may not suitable
men be found to interest themselves in, and be the
lay representative each of, one Fund, and to collect
monies, receive reports, correspond with committees,
and have the year before them for this one Church
business, if needs be, under the general guidance
of the Superintendent? One lay friend having the
charge of one Fund in a Circuit could devote a
little of his leisure to its interest throughout the

* "Watchman," November, 1865, p. 358.

year; might bring his influence, his eloquence, and his affluence in happy unison to promote its prosperity; and by showing its claims, circulating information, answering objections, might enlist the sympathies and obtain the subscriptions of others on a wider scale of success than has yet attended some of the Funds which at present are chiefly under ministerial management.

Appeals from a *lay* friend on behalf of connexional funds would seem to be, although they may not really be, more disinterested than from a Minister, and may not be so often pooh-poohed privately or publicly, as though these pecuniary matters were truly the chief business of Ministers, and as if therefore they were "mercenary men." Lay influence—in which lie rich resources, and which, like a wealthy mine, in the Methodist Connexion, is comparatively unexplored—may be enlisted to a wider extent; the bonds of brotherhood between Ministers and laity be strengthened; a stronger fortification thrown around our Connexion against times of factious trouble, by identifying the laity on a larger scale with the interests of Methodism; a safety-valve provided for surplus steam arising from selfish and over-scrupulous objections to our system; a longer list of subscribers possibly obtained, arising from a more general interest awakened in our funds; and last, though not least, Ministers, especially Superintendents,

may be mightily relieved from those financial burdens which, piled upon the top of those which they
bear as the Ministers of Christ and the messengers of
the Churches, are, as many confess and complain, too
great for them to bear.

Or, if the above be thought to be a risk by any
members of the great and slowly-moving body, may
not several of our funds which have a close affinity
" be joined together ? " and instead of these petty
and perennial appeals, let there be one or two good
earnest meetings held in the year for the *Home Work
in general,* on a similar scale, throughout the Connexion, with those held on behalf of our Foreign
Missions ; and let one or two good long lists of subscriptions for these combined and amalgamated funds
for the *General Home Work* be obtained from among
those, and as many more as possible, whose charity
begins, where it should *begin,* at home, although it
must not end there.

In a pamphlet penned ten years ago, by one who,
though now dead, yet speaketh, it is forcibly shown
that the financial result of the gradually growing
number of annual applications (from four to eleven
for six funds) falls far below what was raised for our
Foreign Missions. For these important funds the
sum of £34,023. 2s. 9d. was raised ; " not nearly
half the amount realized in that year for our Missions." How, it may be asked, is this strange

anomaly to be accounted for? Is the old home-loving Charity now so fond of the far off as to forget her family, her nearest neighbours, the heathen at home, and the just claims of that Church which is the mother of us all?

It is true that besides the above aggregate amount the Ministry at home had to be sustained. Yet how many who give little indeed for any other object will cheerfully contribute liberally to the *Foreign* Missions! Some we have known who would freely give five pounds for the Foreign Missions, who yet would hardly give five shillings to all the funds; and "those gentlemen who give from two to five pounds to all our funds, will freely and joyfully give £10, or £20, or £50, to the Missions, a local charity, or a favourite political object." * We believe the beggars are chiefly to be blamed, and not the givers. Let our funds for the *Home Work* have as fair a field as that for the foreign work; and let them have as earnest appeals, as eloquent advocates, in one or two meetings every year, for their *combined objects,* as our Missions have. The mischief is in the multiplicity of our appeals for things that are essentially *one.* Cannot the major part, if not all, be comprehended in one or two words,—our *Connexional claims?*

---

* Hessel, p. 17.

Many are wearied, not by the magnitude, but by the *multiplicity* of the applications they have for the *same objects*. If a poor family were destitute and perishing, would not kind-hearted neighbours rather combine in one charitable effort to relieve them, than have constant comers craving for charity,—now for food, then for fuel, to-day for meat, and to-morrow for money,—and this week after week through the year? Who would not rather have now and then a good thunder-peal, than a *continual knocking* at the door, keeping the servants in constant attendance? Who would not prefer occasional showers, with fine days, and breaks of cheering sunshine, to continued drizzly weather through a long and dreary season, with dark days filling people's minds with gloom rather than their cisterns with water, and scarcely supplying rain enough to wash the streets or to keep the mills a-going?

May not our endless little appeals throughout the year, with their small consequences, be compared to the long gloomy weather, yielding scanty supplies of water? whilst our public meetings for Foreign Missions, with their interesting information, electrifying speeches, and startling appeals, as from sons of thunder, bring forth both showers and sunshine, giving a fresh impetus to the working machinery, and calling forth sympathies and subscriptions that could not otherwise have been secured, and talents and energies that have long lain dormant. Almost simultaneously tithes are brought into the store-house, and the Spirit is poured out from on high.

Some members of our Society recently read speeches in a local paper on behalf of the " Freedmen " of the South : their sympathies were excited, and a sum was placed unasked in the Minister's hands, many times exceeding the amount which they give in response to the annual appeal on behalf of the Worn-out Minis-ters' and Widows' Fund. Yet there are among these widows "in the land" those who have been in deep want, who have wept in secret and "pined unseen." Why may there not be other and better seasons to plead the cause of the fatherless and widow than at the end of a Class-meeting or at the end of Sabbath sermons, when often there is little time or patience left to listen, and as little power to plead? Would it not be meet to make the interest of this Fund and others a ground of earnest appeal to our Connexion at a general meeting, merging several funds into one, and thus increasing the aggregate annual amount by lessening the number of annual appeals? If unity be strength, this *continued division and sub-division of One great whole* seems to be a great weakness, tending to make our body halt. Why may there not be fourfold raised for combined objects to meet our *Connexional claims,* if properly put, as other things have been, before our willing people?

If, however, good general public meetings which have served so successfully for our Missions, for our Centenary, for our Jubilee, and for most other matters of much moment, should be thought by prudent but perhaps too slow and cautious minds to be a risk as a substitute for the many appeals, then let our lay friends *lay by them in store, as God hath prospered them, upon the first day of the week;* and, as before said, by *their systematic giving* supersede *our systematic begging.*

Our financial system seems, in some way or other, to need revision and reform. There are yet places where the old lumbering waggon may be seen dragging its weary way along the rough roads, having a horn blown at every little village station it passes, picking up a parcel here and another parcel there, piling up a box from this house and a bag from that, travelling from midday until midnight at the rate of two miles or so per hour, greatly taxing the patience of all parties concerned, coming up at the close of the wearisome journey with its cumbrous load, with creaking wheels sadly wanting oil. The old stage-coach now and then to be seen is a great improvement doubtless on the old stage-van; but the swift train drawn by steam-power, with the long line of laden carriages behind, gliding along the prepared way, taking up the passengers and parcels awaiting it at the several stations in the route of its rapid flight, though a modern mode of travelling, is greatly preferred by those to whom time and comfort are matters of consideration.

It was the old eastern custom for the ox, which by the Jewish law might not be muzzled, to tread out the corn. It has been the English custom, up to our own time, by the continuous thresh, thresh, thresh of the old wooden flail, to beat out, day by day and week by week, as was wanted, the precious grain : yet this almost ceaseless stroke produced but slow and scanty supplies compared with those that are produced by the well-skilled threshing machine with its wondrous steam-power, which on most large farms supersedes the old wooden flail, which served its time, and is now a respected relic of the past. Our present continuous and cumbrous begging machinery may not be inaptly compared to some of these old customs, except that in its complex construction it cannot claim so great antiquity, and does not go quite so far back into apostolic times.

If, after having been first laid by in store for the Lord, *willing offerings* were to be *presented*, as claims appeared, would it not be better than having grudging ones *petitioned* for funds, when they have fallen down to freezing-point? If our lay friends, those who have greatly prospered and to whom God has given liberally, would more generally ask themselves, as a goodly number do,—" How much owest thou my Lord ? " and faithfully answer this question, can it be supposed that our *Connexional contributions* would not be found equal to our *Connexional claims*, or that the *resources* in our section of Christ's Church would not be equal to the *requirements?* Is there not sufficient *wealth* somewhere in that Church, equal to its *wants?* If so, may there not, if properly called out, be found " liberality " to supply all that is " lacking ? "

It may be but just to remark that whilst there are Ministers who secretly sigh that time, which should be devoted to more sacred duties, is so much absorbed by the " quasi-secular," as one terms them, and by those monetary appeals which should be forestalled by free-will offerings, and by the advancing aid, in some form or other, of lay friends, they at the same time strive to attend to these things with the cares of large Circuits comprising from one to two thousand members, and not only to keep up but to advance the funds, as, it is but fair to add, the writer himself has done. And Ministers must and will yet attend to these " multifarious extras," as the venerable Entwisle terms them, so long as such duties are imposed upon them, although, as Dr. Rigg has remarked, " Ministers of the present day are" thus " sadly over-weighted." Nevertheless they do not the less earnestly long for the day of emancipation from these bonds, when, in this sense, they may become as fully as possible "Freedmen." Mr. Entwisle wrote, about thirty years ago, "Amidst the multifarious extras, Committees, &c., which occupy the time of the Preachers *in these days,* and often leave the mind barren, I look backward with regret to the times when *all our work* was *spiritual* work,—reading, study, prayer, preaching, and visiting the sick." * "And how have the engagements of Preachers increased even since that sentence was penned! Tea-meetings, the visitation of Day Schools, Cate-chumen Classes, now make further and continually recurring demands upon the time of the Ministers. Then, again, how much closer and more various and extensive is the study now absolutely necessary for Wesleyan Ministers, if they would meet the demands of the age, and guide the expanding intelligence of their flocks, than it was fifty or even twenty years ago!" †

Ministers wish, then, to be freed, as much as pos-sible, by their lay friends from the burden and entanglements of these temporalities, because they feel that these cumbrous cares, together with "the labour and hardship of propagating the Gospel," ‡ are too heavy for them. Ministers wish thus to be freed, that they may give themselves more fully to their "agonistical work and warfare, throwing aside

---

* Entwisle's Life, p. 441.   † Dr. Rigg.

‡ Bloomfield's Greek Testament, 2 Tim. ii. 3–5.

every encumbrance, giving their opponent no advantage over them whilst they war and wrestle together."
They wish to give themselves so fully to the ministry, that they may bring out of the sacred treasury
things new and old. They wish to be thus freed,
not only that they may preach more freshly and fervently in the temple to the people, but also more
frequently and fully from house to house, and thus
win souls to Christ. In this probably many of us
have been greatly, and some necessarily, lacking,
whilst attending to duties of a less sacred character,
which, had they been distributed a little more among
the laity, might have been discharged by them.
Let not any gruffly or carelessly say, " Ministers
have time enough : what else have they to do ? "
By so saying you would hazard a serious reflection on
your own judgment and intellect. Ministers have
not sufficient time to attend to all these pecuniary
matters, and to the work of preaching and of the
pastorate, as faithfully and as fully as the manifold
claims of these varied works demand. They may
subtract from the one to supply the other, and thus
too lamely do a little at each, so that both the
spiritual and the financial may be imperfectly
attended to. And this seems to some extent to have
been the case : for neither just now seems to be in so
sound and prosperous a state—considering the number of Ministers, and the means employed—as

Y

might reasonably be expected. There seems to be somewhere, and not without a cause, a "chronic ailment" in the body.*

Moreover, many Ministers have had pleasing proofs that pastoral visits may be as useful as pulpit discourses. "A word spoken in season,"—"a word on the wheel," denoting the peculiar facility with which it finds its way to the heart,—"how good it is!" Yea, hundreds of names could be adduced from pastoral visiting books, of those who have been gained to the Church, and gathered into the fold of Christ, not simply or chiefly by sermons, but by visitation and personal appeals. One of these, among many, is well remembered, who, after having sat under the ministry thirty years, an attentive hearer, accepted the *first* invitation she ever had during that long period to join the Church of Christ. She came to the Class, chided the neglect which in this respect she had experienced, but above all chided and condemned herself; was in a week converted to God, and became the most regular attendant on the means of grace, and one of the most consistent and earnest members of our Society; grateful to God, that, though late, she had heard the invitation, "Come thou with us, and we will do thee good." How many thousands might in like manner be gathered

---

* Dr. Rigg.

with Christ, and added to the Church, had Methodist Pastors the time and opportunity !

This is the kind of service which our extensive Connexion and scattered members especially need on an immeasurably wider scale. This is the kind of service which most Ministers would be glad, if they could, to perform, as some of their epistles would testify. Ye men of Israel, help ! Help so far as your time, your talent, your influence and substance will allow. Help well and truly to discharge such duties as the temporalities of the Church require, and as deacons and lay-members of the Church may and ought to discharge. Help that our sadly overweighted Ministers may give their time, their talents, and energies more fully to that ministry, whose solemn work and weighty responsibilities made even the gifted and godly Apostle exclaim, " Who then is sufficient for these things ? " and in which an arch-angel's powers might find full and constant employ.

CHAPTER XV.

RESUSCITATION OF DISCIPLINE.

SUCH is the significant sentence we find in a recent paper written by a powerful pen. The article has reference to the present position of Methodism, and takes a faithful and an impartial view of its more modern aspects and claims; a view not slight and superficial, but sound and searching; not so sanguine as to take it for granted that Methodism is not only all right, but is marching rapidly onward in her might, with no weight to clog her chariot wheels, no sin which easily besets her; nor yet so morbid and melancholy as to see every thing wrong. Each extreme should be guarded against. The sky may not be so black, nor the sea so billowy, as to put the pilot to his wits' end, and the passengers into a panic; and yet the sky may not be so sunny, nor the sea so still, that the pilot should sleep at the helm, and the sailors rest on their oars. When as yet there is no cloud surcharged with thunder, and no surging billow, there may be such signs in the sky, and such a swell in the sea, that skill may be required at the helm, and the service of the sailors needed on deck.

The old coach-guard, after soporific draughts at each successive stage, did not scruple to say, " All right ! " when by the superincumbent weight the coach was well nigh toppling over, when the wheels dragged heavily, or were ready to fly off, or to take fire, or, left too long without the drag, were in danger of running violently down the steep hill. Too late, perhaps, the bluff old guard awoke to the peril of his position, when the passenger—it may be, the preacher, who was on his way to the Conference—was hurled headlong from his seat, and the wife in a moment was made a mourning widow.

There was the signal, " all clear ; " and so it continued till the collision came. There was an old truck in the way, or lumber in the dark tunnel, which was not seen till it was felt, and by the terrible shock scores of lives were perilled, scores of limbs were bruised and bones broken, and families and friends plunged into sorrow. " It might have been prevented," said a sharp little boy to the servant, just as he was snatched from the fire with a burning coal in his bosom, which discovered itself by burning within, until the breast and the clothes that covered it were burning without. This was a literal and painful illustration of the moral and spiritual significance of Solomon's inquiry : "Can a man take fire in his bosom, and his clothes not be burned?"* Had Christians and Churches no dangerous enemies without, they might carry deadly elements within their own bosom. If Satan slept, and sought no longer to destroy or devour, yet by secretly cherished sins Christians and Churches, like the chosen people of old, may become suicidal. "O Israel, *thou* hast destroyed *thyself!*"† It is the traitors, the Achans within the camp, that we have all the most need to dread. The worst foes of Turkey may be the Turks themselves. Self-consuming lusts may make flaming bolts from the foe quite superfluous : a little longer, and Turkey may die for want of Turks, and the Euphrates may be dried up like rotten wood.

Charming serpents, with sleek skins and secret stings, may coil around our body, and creep close to our heart. The baneful is most so when it is bound up with the beautiful. There may be harps in well-skilled hands, which may charm us with the melody of their music, like King Alfred's in the Danish camp; but those harpings may smite us more surely and sorely than the open hate of Saul's evil spirit, or than Saul's javelin, could do. If there be unworthy or inconsistent members within the pale of the professing Church, and if there be also a lack of discipline to deal with them, or if that discipline, from a lack

---

* Proverbs vi. 27. † Hosea xiii. 9.

of fidelity, lie dormant, so that these are still counted as Church members, numerical strength for the time may be gained ; but with such gain there will be a loss of moral power, and a tendency to spiritual languor and decline.

Discipline is the great safeguard and bulwark of the Church, her tower of strength. A Church without discipline would be as a field without a fence, as a garden without an enclosure. Nay, it could scarcely, in any worthy sense, be called a Church, as there would be no clear line of demarcation to distinguish it from the world. Whatever may be the glory and grandeur of the Church of England in other respects, as it regards discipline she has, of late especially, presented a most pitiable spectacle; and whilst some of her sons have indulged in vain and empty boasting, she has been the shame and sorrow of her friends, and the scorn and sport of her foes. A Church that is so tied and bound by legal trammels that she cannot move her hand to shake off the venomous viper that fastens on it, must soon lose the little life she has. What support can she derive from such a carnal union with the state, to compensate the loss of that spiritual life which is fast ebbing out of her very soul, or to charm the fatal poison that is flowing into her veins? She may not, any more than other Churches, be able to detect subtle deceivers, or to discern spirits ; but if she really can-

not silence the tongue of a bold Popish or infidel
blasphemy, when it dares to make itself heard in her
borders, to profane her pulpits, and to parade its
pernicious publications throughout the land; if she
should thus become more than heretofore the mere
machinery of the state, having lawyers to explain and
declare what shall be her " grace and truth," and the
law to decide what is her Gospel, having her springs
moved and managed by worldly hands; then would
she be but little better than a whited wall and a
painted sepulchre, and the fewer would be the
mourners at her grave. Her best friends would
sorrow the less, should she—whose bigotry, whilst it
so tenderly spares her own sceptical sons, is ever and
anon smiting so-called " sects " and " schismatics "—
be smitten of God for that blasphemy which she is
too frail or too faithless effectually to rebuke.

Any Church which has nothing but censures for
the ailments of others, and no check but complacent
smiles for her own corruptions,—which has a microscopic vision to detect the motes in the eyes of others,
but is too blinded by bigotry to perceive the beams
in her own eye,—that has charity enough to commit
the most " desecrated dust " of her own to the most
dishonoured graves, in consecrated ground, " in sure
and certain hope of a resurrection to eternal life," but
that has scarcely compassion enough to find a few feet
of earth for innocent infants who have not been

sprinkled at *her* fonts, and made anew by *her* hands, although " of such is the kingdom of heaven : "— such a Church, if she improve not her space for repentance, must expect little lamentation at her grave, except from those who enjoy a large share of her temporal goods.

Any Church which has nought but strife and bitterness for those whom she need not blush to call her brethren, but, Ishmael-like, is ever lifting up her hand against them, whilst she has no standard to lift up against the floods of ungodly men, no barrier to raise against the overflowings of blasphemy within her own borders,—any Church which shall become so utterly bereft of power as to be unable to purify herself from her pollutions, as much so as the world that lieth in wickedness, must needs die, because not fit to live; and may well, having lost her power to *bless*, pass away unmourned by earth and heaven. Our heart-felt prayer is, that such may not be the doom of the Established Church of these realms ; yet she now seems—in the haughtiness and heresy of some of her sons, " howbeit, not all "—to have as much need of the apostolic caution as even the harlot Church of Rome herself : " Be not high-minded, but fear : for if God spare not the natural branches, take heed lest He spare not thee."

If men are bold enough to blaspheme, even though Bishops, let them have honesty enough to do it on their own account; let them at least be as English as Bolingbroke, as Tom Paine, or Voltaire. Let them not obtain the sanction and supplies of a professedly Protestant Church to sustain them in their career of profanity and blasphemy. Let them not ask the Church of England for board and lodging, or tax the national purse. Let them set up for themselves. Let them "come out of her." Let them, if they can, get their "own hired room" to form the traitorous plot, and forge the missiles, for the ruin of her on whose lap and at whose bosom they have been nourished and brought up. If men are weak enough to play at Popish tricks, or wicked enough to practise profane juggling, let them get what patronage they can from the prince of darkness and his emissaries; but let them show their colours like men. Let them not, in their subtle spiritual spheres, play pranks behind the scene like the Davenport Brothers. Let us look into their mysterious "cabinet," and see whether their strange "knots" cannot be untied, and know what manner of men they are, and whether they have a just claim on public sympathy and support. Let them at any rate not bring their wares and witcheries into the Protestant temples of the land, and turn the house of God into a market for their merchandise, and make it a den of thieves. Let them form themselves into a distinct company: let the character of their commodities be considered, and let those who are pleased with them *pay* for them. Let not Popery, Profanity, and Protestantism, enter into a secret triple alliance, form a family compact, bearing the same name on their front, and dipping their hands into the same dish.

If poison must be sold, let it all be, according to the prudent proviso of the Government, labelled in plain bold English type, so that a child that knows the alphabet may read, and that people may know what they purchase and pay for, and whether that poison as a specific is worth their money. If we must have Popery, let us have it as pure and as perfect as possible from the fountain-head,—from Pope and Priests and Cardinals,—and not through the serpentine windings of Puseyite streams, which almost defy us to tell what they really are, whence they flow, and where they will empty themselves. If wolves must come, let them not be supplied with sheep's clothing from the wardrobes of Protestantism.

It would have been well, had the Clergy of the Church of England, instead of displaying so censorious a spirit towards Dissenters, and so ill requiting the favour and forbearance of Wesleyans, betaken themselves to the work of reforming her Rubric, amending her Liturgy, and lowering the tone of her own haughty and exclusive claims and proud pretensions; instead of echoing the " cry of Bishops,

'Touch not, meddle not,' till indeed it will be too late to do either." * But they may be assured that in this age of advancing liberalism the free-born and indomitable spirit of Protestant Nonconformists will not suffer them long to bow their necks under feet which are no longer beautiful because of the glad tidings they bring, but which rudely trample down, so far as they are able, all that is beautiful in every garden which they have not planted, and ignore the claims of every Church of Christ, except that which is by law established. The time and zeal of some we know are chiefly expended in endeavouring to prove that the sheep of other folds are being misled, whilst they give no signs of their own superior wisdom, but that of empty boasting; and there are Nonconformists who think it is hardly fair they should be taxed for this kind of thing,—hardly fair they should have to pay those who make such lofty claims, chiefly to smite them. If some of the Clergy must wage this warfare with Nonconformists, let them not have the hardihood to ask those against whom they fight to supply the sinews of war. It would be far better that they should employ all their energies in seeking to obtain a divorce from the man of sin and of blasphemy. For "what communion hath light with darkness? and what concord hath Christ with

* Dr. Arnold.

Belial? or what part hath he that believeth with an infidel?" *

The power and promptitude of Wesleyan discipline have been displayed in the past, to a degree that has made Methodism look despotic in the eyes of some, and terrible to most "as an army with banners." When power and position, talent and wealth, have all combined to excite dismay; when foes have quibbled, and friends have quailed; when editors have stepped out of their political province to protest against they hardly knew what; when the minds not only of those within the Church, but of masses of them which are without, have been much moved; when the Church herself has been more like a storm-tossed sea than a quiet haven; stern discipline has seemed to look down, dauntless and defiant, on the upheaving and swelling floods, like the rock of Gibraltar on the restless waves and billows that rage and surge at its mighty base.

Nothing could be more natural than that, with increasing worldly wealth and influence, with "rising respectability" and luxurious living, there should ensue a little laxity of discipline as regards the laity. Discipline with respect to the Ministry seems likely at present to preserve its pristine power: only, as was meet, much more freedom of thought and speech

* 2 Cor. vi. 14, 15.

is allowed than when one or two minds, from their unrivalled talent, their sterling integrity, their indomitable will, and great governing tact, swayed the Conference, and well nigh ruled the body. Now no one occupies so prominent and powerful a post; nor need it be coveted by any.

One who has written in laudatory terms even on the financial economy of Methodism, who never felt with his pastorate the pressure of its practical working, but whose testimony is so far valuable, vindicating as it does the just and righteous claims of our various Funds, says of Methodism, "Its danger at this moment is from the rising respectability of its people." * Now what is the danger to which this able writer refers? Evidently not the danger of the body waning from a stoppage of supplies, but rather the danger that with temporal prosperity there should be spiritual decline.

We suppose some such thought was in the mind of the author who penned the significant sentence which points to a *resuscitation of discipline*. *Resuscitation*—what does it mean? The act of raising up again either from sleep or death. Is then this warning word like a trumpet-blast, to revive old and practically obsolete rules and laws which have long been lying in musty statute-books, and which have

---

* Dr. Campbell, in the "Christian Witness."

well nigh gone to the grave of oblivion? *Resuscitation*—is this as an ominous alarum, to arouse a dormant or drowsy discipline, which is folding its arms
to a little more slumber, and which is now told that
it is high time for it to awake? *Resuscitation*—
" stirring up anew "—is it as a shrill clarion-note
that startles slumbering soldiers, to apprise them that
the garrison is besieged, that the enemy is at the
gates, that a breach has been made in the bulwarks,
that the fortresses are falling fast into the hands of
the foe, that some are on the scaling ladders, that the
city is in danger of being taken by the armies of the
aliens, and that if the sentinels are not at their posts
and the soldiers alert, the standard of a rival sovereign will be planted, and his banners wave, in the
very midst of the citadel?

Resuscitate—" stir up anew ! " The old rules in
the Class-books, and the old Rules of a Helper, and
the old Minutes, so regularly read, (*pro formâ,*) after
long and wearisome business details, and those rules
of Wesley that were to be not mended but kept,—
have they all fallen asleep? are they now a dead
letter? are they as some of the obsolete and almost
forgotten laws on England's statute book, the mere
mention of whose musty rolls makes even legislators
smile?

Resuscitate—" stir up anew ! " Whilst the rules
and regulations of the Chapel Committee have been

all awake, and almost all-pervading, and vigilant eyes
have been kept on the financial and material parts of
our machinery, have weightier matters been suffered
to slumber? Have not the watchmen of Zion been
on their watch-towers? Have slumbering sentinels
to be stirred up, and a sepulchred discipline to be
awoke out of its sleep, and called up from its grave?
Can it be that our own Church, which has been as a
loud alarum to stir up lethargic and slumbering
Churches, and to "provoke them to jealousy," is now
herself falling asleep, and that meanwhile the enemy
is sowing his tares?

Resuscitate—it can hardly mean that the sainted
spirit of Wesley should be evoked; that he, as
Samuel, should re-appear in our Conference and
solemn convocations; or that some Cromwellian
voice should tell us that it is vain for us to seek the
Lord there, unless the wicked forsake his way.

Resuscitate—return from the grave! O, were
there a voice mighty enough to speak this startling
word effectually to the dormant discipline in the
Church of England,—a voice mighty enough to confound and cashier any future Colenso that might
arise, and promptly to rebuke and remove perverse
Puseyites and profane Essayists!

Thank God, Wesleyan discipline would be found
powerful enough to silence at once the tongue of
scepticism, should it ever presume to distil its

poison within our borders, or to preach another gospel.

Some Ministers, when mourning over the spiritual state of our Zion, as not keeping pace with its temporal prosperity, have not scrupled to say, " Anything would be better than stagnation." We have had terrible times of trouble ; and well may any Christian, especially a Minister, tremble to meddle needlessly with that which tends to strife. Bitter indeed are the waters of strife ; and fierce have been religious quarrels, and fiery the contentions among brethren, which have disfigured and disgraced the Church of Christ. But although so bitter are the waters of Meribah that none could desire to drink them, they are hardly so bad as the bituminous waters of the Dead Sea, the stagnant and sulphurous receptacle of the Jordan. It is pleasant to be beside the still waters, but we may luxuriate there too long. Yea, when there are voices loudly calling us to action, to be up and doing, to strive for the faith, and wrestle against spiritual foes, we may sit amid scenes of sordid ease and stillness, and repose in carnal sloth, till we sleep, and we may " sleep on" till we sleep the sleep of death. And yet that may be called " peace," which should be called " Laodicean ease."

Peace, pleasant and precious as it is, may be purchased at too dear a price,—at the cost of purity and Christian principle, and by cowardly and criminal

z

compromise. Let no proper means be left untried to preserve and promote peace, but let not plain precepts be passed by, and rules regularly read be no more to those whom they concern than " a tale that is told." " A burnt child dreads the fire : " and even sturdy sailors, rocked by the raging billows and cradled in the storm, after the terrific tempest will welcome the coming calm. But a dead calm will not do long for the merchant or the mariner; he would rather risk the stormy wind, which, whilst it howls about him, fills the sails of the noble vessel, and is hurrying it away with merchandise and mariners to the destined port and the desired haven. We have seen ships long lying in the roadstead, wearily waiting for a favourable breeze, and which, if they could, would gladly have raised the wind. " I should like," said a loyal layman, who well bore the brunt of the last faction, " to see our Connexion in a ferment; I think it would do us good." This may seem an extreme, yet not more so than that of the judicious Minister who said, " Anything is better than stagnation ; " nor a worse extreme, surely, than that described in Wesley's Hymns on Formal Religion,* so seldom sung now in our sanctuaries, but which, if we may venture to suggest, would be suitable substitutes for some of the chants which

* Hymns 91-94.

it is becoming the fashion to sing, and which remind the hearer of the humdrum ditties he may have heard in an unknown tongue in Romish cathedrals on the Continent, which many of the choristers in this country seem inclined to copy as closely as they can, just as the French fashions of dress are fancied by the ladies of England.

The dreaded extreme of ferment and agitation would not be worse than a flattering but fatal formalism, and a calm corruption, or than any of those evils which are " bred in the stagnant marshes of a corrupted Christianity."*

A ferment in the Church, or an earnest contention "for the faith once delivered to the saints," need not be so much dreaded as that formalism which finds a "flattering peace," or as a deceitful heart, which strives to make its owner

> " A goodly formal saint,
> *   *   *   *
> By self and Satan taught to paint
> My tomb, my nature, white."

The raging tempest, while it severely tests the skill of the pilot, puts the sailors to their wits' end, perils the passengers, and makes shipwreck of many a noble vessel, at the same time purifies the atmosphere, sweeps away noxious exhalations and deadly

* Robert Hall.

malaria, which had gathered in the still air, and under a serene sky, and which were surcharged with disease and death. The wintry blast or the terrific tempest is better than the wasting pestilence or the deadly plague, whose poisoned arrows fall so fast and secretly as scarcely to suffer us to divide the dead from the living.

Storms, however they may scare us, seem to be as unavoidable, if not in the end as salutary, in the spiritual as in the natural world. Sifting seasons must sooner or later come. The greater the gatherings, the greater the mixture of good and bad; the greater, therefore, the need of some purifying process. The intense fire refines the metal from its dross, and separates the base alloy from the precious gold. The wind winnows the chaff from the wheat: The dust flies before the whirlwind; dry leaves are driven hither and thither; dead branches are broken off; slender saplings are proved to need support; hollow trees, and some that seemed sound and firm, are. shattered or torn up by the roots; whilst others become more "firmly rooted and grounded." In the storm creaking timbers and crazy walls may totter to their fall; but the Church need fear no foe, nor stormy wind, nor foaming flood. "Her firm foundations cannot move." "Though the waters roar and be troubled, though the mountains shake with the swelling thereof, God is in the midst of her, she shall not be moved."* The Church will

> " In storms and hurricanes abide
> Firm as the mount of God."

There appears to be apprehension in the minds of many Ministers and laymen, lest our Connexional stillness should subside into spiritual stagnation; a fear lest, to preserve peace, we should be less faithful than our fathers were,—lest we should become " men-pleasers,"—lest, to avert a mortal's frown, and " soothe the unholy throng," we should " soften the truth, and smooth our tongue."

The apostolic exhortation suggests the extreme difficulty of long preserving a pure peace, a peace that lives and dwells with righteousness and truth.† A timorous nature and a time-serving spirit shrink from rebuking sin, " flee the cross," procure a peace " at any price." Their maxim is, " *First* peaceable," whether pure or not; but the order of the wisdom that is from above is, " *First* pure, *then* peaceable."‡ Were men more faithful with their own hearts, they would have less peace in their own consciences. Were men more faithful with each other, were fidelity to take the place of cringing fear or fulsome flattery, then there would be less false peace between man and

---

* Psalm xlvi. † Romans xii. 18. ‡ James iii. 17.

man; fewer complacent smiles and good wishes on the lip, while revenge and jealousy rankle in the heart. Were Ministers more faithful with their flocks, there would be less false peace in Churches; there would be fewer Pharisees within, fewer whited walls and painted tombs. *A fearless fidelity in reproving sin,* "speaking the truth in love," is one of the greatest wants of the Churches of this day. Less of the love which has dissimulation with it, would be no loss over which the Church need mourn. Less of that peace which makes friendship with the world and sin, would bring more of that pure peace which Christ bequeathed, although with it there may be more "tribulation" also. "A just war is a thousand times better than an ill-conditioned peace."* War with the Papacy brought the glorious Reformation of the sixteenth century; and that Reformation needed more than the learning of the timorous Erasmus, and more than the ability of the amiable and accomplished Melancthon; it needed the moral magnanimity and dauntless heroism of a Martin Luther.

What is the special danger dreaded from "the rising respectability of the people?" It cannot consist in a defection in doctrine; that seems to be almost unalterably fixed: it is rather a danger, in the

---

* Dr. Barrow.

midst of temporal prosperity, of declining fidelity
in the exercise of discipline. This may falter, whilst
Model Deeds remain firm. Let any one read the
mighty moral victories won by Old Testament
worthies. Let him read the Acts of the Apostles
and the history of the New Testament Churches.
Let him read those stern words of pointed rebuke
addressed by the faithful John to the crooked generation that came to his baptism. Let him read those
solemn denunciations which fell like words of fire
from the lips of Him who was "meek and lowly of
heart," addressed to dissembling hypocrites. Let
him read the scathing sentence which came like a
lightning-stroke from the now bold and valiant Peter
upon the guilty pair who approached him with a lie
in their right hand, and were consigned to one common grave. Let him read the withering words
which were addressed by the same Apostle to a
"certain man called Simon, which beforetime in the
same city used sorcery, and bewitched the people,
giving out that himself was some great one," and who
now wished to purchase the priceless gift of God
with money : "Thy money perish with thee !"* Let
him read St. Paul's solemn admonition which required
the putting away of those professors that polluted
the Corinthian Church.† Let him read those admoni-

* Acts viii. 9–20.   † 1 Cor. v. 9–13.

tory letters addressed to the Angels of the seven Asiatic Churches, commending the firm and faithful, and condemning the lax and faithless. Let the history of the Church be read from apostolic times down to the present day. Let Wesley's Journals be read, and his plain and pointed Sermons. Let our Rules be read. Let the wide extent of our Connexion be considered: then let it be calmly asked, whether it is likely that the members of our own Church, or of the Churches of Christendom, are more pure and faithful, taking them member for member, than were the Church members of apostolic times. Let it be asked whether these days of Christian profession do not demand as faithful dealing, as sharp and pointed rebukes, as firm and decisive a discipline, as did the days of the early Christian Church or of primitive Methodism.

Are there not now many false professors, many who in effect " lie to the Holy Ghost ? " Have the " unreasonable men," and the " generation of vipers," died out? Are there no false swearers, no perjured persons, no intemperate, no unclean, no dissembling hypocrites within the borders of Zion? Are there no great men who are lepers, who may be surrounded by some seducing charms, some sort of sorcery, by which they have bewitched the people, bribed justice, beguiled, evaded, or disarmed the power of discipline? Are there not some of these, we ask,

enclosed within the pale of the Churches of the land ?
Are there not some of these within our own Church ?
If discipline amongst us has become lax and sluggish, so that those who should have been "tried"
have been too tenderly treated, then can it be any
wonder that Zion should languish and be brought
low, and that she should be seeking, on so large a
scale, to supply her decaying inward life, her languishing vitality, by external forms and empty ceremonies, and supplanting a simple spirituality by the
style of a worldly sanctuary ?

Shall it be supposed that those who are *without*
are able to say to any of them that are *within* the
professing Church ?—" You wish us to unite with you,
but there are some who are chief among you who do
not bear a consistent character ; nay, we should consider ourselves morally degraded by close contact
with them ; we could not commune or meet at the
Lord's Table with them. They are not truthful ; they
are not sober and temperate persons ; they are not
just and honest in their dealings ; they are not
chaste in their conversation and conduct ; they are
sometimes to be seen in the tavern when they should
be in the temple. And this we state, not from
vague and idle reports, but from the mouth of
credible witnesses ; nay, it is commonly reported
among yourselves, and you cannot deny it." Would
not this sadly show that there was great laxity of

discipline? It can hardly be denied that these or similar statements are made with regard to many professed members of the Church of England and other Churches. Are we quite clear ourselves from such imputations?

Often when there is a doubtful or defective character, there is not only a strong desire to retain membership, but unfortunately a *love of office.* Office to doubtful characters is as a wooden prop to frail and falling fabrics. As a tottering tenement is kept up by the buttress or the beam, where the mine has shaken the foundations and sunk and cracked the wall, so office may afford a temporary support to falling professors.

The more prominent such persons are, generally the more pernicious they are to the spiritual interests of the Church whose offices they fill. Whilst some are shy and sensitive, modest and retiring,—men of genius, of talent, and of piety,—there are others, on the contrary, who seem to be sadly smitten with a desire for some official position; and many peace-loving Pastors have often been involved in painful perplexity by those whose love of office has been their chief, if not their only, qualification for it; whilst those whose mental, moral, and religious qualifications fit them for posts of honour in the Church, too readily recede before the officious obtrusion of others. A hankering for office may sometimes smite a society as a plague or a leprosy, for which no specific seems to be found, except that of removal.

It is sad if the purer patterns of moral excellence and loveliness are found among the mere hearers of the word, rather than among the members of the Christian Church: yet we have heard those who have long had the pastoral oversight of Churches say that they have too often had to point to the former, instead of the latter, as examples of a blameless morality, an amiable character, and that which "is lovely and of good report." This state of things would be greatly aggravated, if any who sustain offices in the Church were to lift up their voice in private to accuse and condemn; and yet, when the accused is in court, were, under the influence of a criminal cowardice, either to be silent, or to falsify their own private statements by lifting up their hand in token of confidence and commendation. We have seen complaints recorded in one of our papers on this subject, and that justly. How can the Church be cleansed, and discipline maintained, if there be not an impartial court or jury,—if those who compose the court are false or fearful, instead of firm and faithful?

It is possible that we may be near, if not in, those times in which there was to be a great "falling away." And if so, it may be a time especially for "putting away" from, as well as adding to, the

Church: and the resuscitation of discipline may greatly tend to the real revival of the work of God, although for a time it might lead to a decrease of numbers. It has often been so heretofore, aud may be so again. If one Achan brought defeat upon ancient Israel, can it be any wonder if many of the Churches of modern times are almost powerless and paralysed before the Philistines, shorn of their spiritual strength by some Delilah? The moral might and grandeur of God's witnessing Church are seen in the faithful exercise of her discipline. But this in some cases can hardly be done without peril to a false peace, and exposing those who discharge the unwelcome duty to the "much evil" of some "Alexander." One of our faithful fathers in the Gospel speaks of having put out on one occasion about sixty or seventy professed members. This he regarded as a safe and salutary act,—as the sequel proved it to be. Certainly no such act should be hastily or harshly performed. Ministers surely have not great inducements to "put away," except from a painful conviction of duty. The inducements and dangers are rather on the other side. Although some, in times of thoughtless, reckless strife, have seemed to forget this, what pleasure or profit can there be in putting away? what motive, except "for conscience sake?"

We have heard a thoughtful Minister in times of

peace say with regard to his own Church, " If about six had been removed, we should have been stronger and better." Perhaps somewhat similar were the sober thoughts of the learned Doctor who speaks of " a resuscitation of discipline." Such have been the painful thoughts that have pressed on the minds of many Pastors, who have had strong and sore temptations to shun the irksome cross.

The faithful exercise of discipline among the thousands of our Israel, amid advancing worldliness and religious laxity, may almost preclude the possibility of preserving a pure peace to a very prolonged extent throughout the borders of our Zion. Here lies a great and general danger, lest, after successive seasons of strife, we should, to preserve peace, sacrifice purity, and reverse the Divine order,—" *First* pure,. *then* peaceable."

If but a little garden needs much attention to keep it from being overrun with unsightly and noxious weeds ; if but the small field that smiled with wheat has had a large sprinkling of tares growing up with the precious grain, (which in the *world* must necessarily grow together until the harvest;) if but a narrow net, cast into the wide sea, may bring up a mixture of fish both good and bad ; if the early Churches needed so much searching and sifting ; then what varied elements, what doubtful cases, what conflicting characters must necessarily be comprised together with the eminently devout and godly, among upwards of three hundred thousand, forming a Connexion in which "numbering the people," if it be not one of its sins, is one of its rules; and in which advancing numbers have generally been considered, whether rightly or not, as a great sign of advancing prosperity!

It is pleasing, and may in some respects be profitable, to know our numbers; yet if in this matter we have not erred, as David did, we may be in danger of erring. The practical working of our Connexional system may dispose us to look more at our numerical strength than well comports with that purity and Christian perfection which our doctrines and our discipline call us to maintain. If "righteousness exalteth a nation," especially must it be the guard and glory of the Church of Christ: and although her flock be little, her numbers small, compared with the masses that crowd the broad way of sin and death; although her friends be few, and in this world feeble, her foes many and mighty, yet around this her glory, as around God's throne, there will ever be a defence. It may be well to look less at our *numerical*, and more after our *moral*, strength.

We have great reason to be grateful that at this time so many private members, and so many godly laymen of talent, influence, and substance, are one with Ministers in the great work of our common

Master, and in all that concerns the purity and prosperity of our Zion. Yet, were a thorough sifting to
take place, were there to be that "resuscitation of discipline" which has been so eloquently and urgently
called for, there might be found in our general Connexional quiet as much reason for chiding as for congratulation. Seen in the strict light of the precepts
of the New Testament, and of our Society Rules,
much that has passed for calm and sacred serenity
may be but carnal security. Our general peace may
not be so generally flowing from a pure and practical.
faith. There may be many among us who are killed
by the world's opiates ; there may be a growing Antinomian laxity, and Laodicean ease ; there may be
many who have found "rest," yet not by faith, but
"on their lees ; " their peace may be man-made, not
God-spoken. They "compass" themselves about
with sparks "which they have kindled." * There
may be a peace which is not as a vital stream, which
refreshes, revives, and gladdens the garden of God,
but is as stagnant water, that corrupts rather than
cleanses, and pollutes rather than purifies. Waters
may be tranquil, yet turbid as those of the Dead Sea,
more to be dreaded with their sulphureous breath
than the boisterous billows of the Galilean Lake, as
it bore on its stormy bosom the Prince of Life, whom
winds and waves, and seas and storms, obey.

* Isai. l. 11.

There may be a stillness because the virgins are slumbering with oilless vessels, rather than awake and astir, girding their loins, and trimming their lamps, making ready to meet, at the midnight cry, the heavenly Bridegroom. It is startling to read, " While the Bridegroom tarried, they all slumbered and slept." * Is this the season of spiritual slumber in our hitherto wakeful Church ? There may be a stillness such as the death-calm of the cemetery, or the country churchyard, where Corruption holds her quiet carnival, and death-worms stealthily feed. There may be just such a sordid and stagnant stillness in the Church, whose silence speaks, and " loudly calls for a resuscitation of discipline," a " reviving again from sleep and death."

" Wednesday, 11th.—I began examining the Society, and not before it was wanted ; for the plague was begun. I found many crying out, ' Faith, faith !' ' Believe, believe !' but making little account of holiness or of good works. In a few days they came to themselves, and had a more thorough understanding of the truth as it is in Jesus." †

We believe that there never was a time in the history of Methodism when so many wealthy Wesleyans were found consecrating themselves and their wealth to the great Giver of all Good. With a

---

* Matt. xxv. 5.   † Wesley's Works, vol. ii., p. 228.

goodly number of these we have, from time to time,
held happy intercourse ; and they are enrolled among
our most esteemed and beloved friends. We have
sojourned in their hospitable homes, and worshipped
at their family altars. We have watched with deep
interest their domestic discipline, the godly training
of their children, their Christian simplicity and self-
denial amid abounding wealth, their large-hearted
benevolence, their condescension to the poor, their
compassion to the sick and suffering, their courteous
conduct towards all with whom they come into contact, their ceaseless activity in all that concerns the
interests of Christ's Church. We have seen and
have glorified the grace of God in them. They
adorn the doctrine of Christ, and are among the best
and brightest ornaments of our Church. But the
danger is, that, side by side with these, there should
arise and grow up another and a widely different class,
whose money is their idol ; whose wealth ministers to
" the lust of the flesh, the lust of the eye, and the
pride of life;" who can hardly enter into the kingdom of God; whose counteracting influences may in
the course of time so change the style and spirit of
our Connexional Church, that she shall no longer be
known as the "Old Body," no longer retain the
essential elements and distinctive lineaments of primitive Wesleyan Methodism ; no longer be signalized
by her chaste simplicity and spirituality, her godly

sincerity and glowing zeal ; no longer be a marvel for her Puritanic piety, her periodical revivals, her perennial life and activity, her " Christianity in earnest ;" no longer bear the badge of " a sect everywhere spoken against ;" no longer encircle her brow with the halo of an unearthly glory; no longer be " a proverb of reproach and love,"—because too much moulded in these modern times after a worldly fashion.

Many among her Ministers and laymen see this to be the *danger* of modern Methodism. One of shrewd mind, of wide observation, of honourable position as a layman, of long, loyal, and loving attachment to Methodism in this and in other lands, a short time ago declared to the writer that he sometimes feared lest the great worldliness that was now getting into our Churches should make the old type of Methodism almost or altogether extinct. Two classes may, without care, arise, as in the Church of England, which could not well coalesce, if they could long co-exist, in a Connexion like ours, in which it has been our peculiar privilege, as our meetings of Christian fellowship have proved, for " all " the members of the wide fold of Wesleyan Methodism to " think and speak the same."

But let it be observed, that although this is the *danger* of modern Methodism in this the time of her *material prosperity*,—a danger of *spiritual decline*,—

it by no means follows that this is her inevitable *destiny.* She has, thank God, a resuscitating power, an elastic and vital power, such as Gibbon's pen could not record in the " Decline and Fall " of ancient Rome. She may yet renew her youth as the eagle's ; she may yet arise and shake herself from the dust, and appear, yet more than ever, " fair as the moon, clear as the sun, and terrible as an army with banners."

Let not the jealous fears of her best friends be regarded as a just ground of hope for her sworn foes or her small friends. For this jealousy may be her great preservative from ruin ; this her " godly fear " may be to her as a " guardian angel," watching over her by night and by day, ministering to her in storms and in sunshine, in adversity and affluence, and keeping her, lest at any time she dash her foot against a stone. The solemn admonition, " Be not high-minded, but fear," has been before her eyes from the day of her small and feeble beginning; and it would be strange and sad if, in the time of her wealth, her grandeur, and glory, " blindness " in this respect should happen to her. On the present height of her prosperity she sees her peril ; she can hardly be ignorant of Satan's devices ; she knows that although she be high as the pinnacle of her temples, Satan cannot cast her down ; and lest she should be so beguiled by the subtle tempter, disguised in some bright angelic form, to cast herself down, in order to try the strength of her pinions, the sound of alarm has gone forth, the trumpet has been blown as by the united breath of more than a thousand watchmen, in appeal and warning to more than three hundred thousand people of her coasts; and their listening ears have conveyed the solemn caution to their awakened consciences and hearts.

"To forget that increasing wealth, social influence, mental culture and refinement, involve new dangers and temptations, were to betray strange heedlessness of the solemn lessons of Church history,—strange ignorance of Satan's devices and the deceitfulness of the human heart,—strange deafness to the warnings of Holy Writ, and gross disregard of the fatherly cautions bequeathed to us by the Founder of Methodism. If side by side with, or still in advance of, this progressive taste for architectural ornament and other external aids to worship, there appear a strengthening attachment to, and a stricter attendance on, those social means of grace through which the highest style of Christian experience has been reached and retained, then the tendencies just named could not carry us astray; but if, along with the demand for that which satisfies the eye and ear, and conciliates and charms the taste, there should be found a spreading apathy as to Christian fellowship and social prayer,—that is to say, if, at any time, our church-

structures and our church-services should draw
off from the true, deep fountains of church-life,—
then the distinctive glory of Methodism must soon
depart." *

There are three R's which are used jocosely to
designate the essential elements of the education
patronized by the Government: there are, if we may
so speak, more than three P's marking important
points at which the Methodism of modern times may
properly and profitably aim, and which may be regarded as the watchwords of the Methodism of this
day ; namely, that "*great plainness*" † and power
which signalized *primitive* Methodism in her PREACH-
ING, her PRAYERS, and her PSALMODY, when she
stirred up to their depths the Churches of Christendom, when she shook this country from the frigid
North to the far-off Land's End,—bade fair soon to
"turn the world upside down," and "set the kingdoms on a blaze;"—PASTORAL VISITATION and
"preaching" by all her Ministers "from house to
house;—and that proper PROVISION for the POOR, in
every possible way, which forms an essential part of
"pure religion and undefiled." Let these things be
done by her, and then, amid so much that is shaking
and seducing, she will remain, "faithful among the

---

* Pastoral Address, 1865.

† Grindrod's Compendium, pp. 93, 94.

faithless," unshaken, unterrified, and unseduced; and the God of our fathers will be the God of their children down to the latest generation;

> "While unborn Churches by their care
> Shall rise and flourish large and fair."

> " What constitutes a Church ?
> Not lofty spires, that pierce the distant clouds,
> Nor well-built towers, nor glittering minarets,
> Nor pealing organ, nor the hymning choir,
> Nor spotless alb, nor sacerdotal stole,
> Nor fragrant incense, e'en from golden censers;
> But God's pure Word, dispensed by holy men,
> And holy sacraments with Gospel rites,
> And fervent praise where heart and voice unite,
> And ardent prayer that Heaven delights to hear,
> And Christ's own presence with His faithful saints :—
> These constitute a Church." LYTHAM.

LONDON:

PRINTED BY WILLIAM NICHOLS,

46, HOXTON SQUARE.